THE ESSENTIAL
MEIN KAMPF

ADOLF HITLER

THE ESSENTIAL
MEIN KAMPF

ADOLF HITLER

TRANSLATED FROM THE GERMAN

BY

THOMAS DALTON

NEW YORK, LONDON
CLEMENS & BLAIR, LLC
2019

CLEMENS & BLAIR, LLC

Introduction, selections, and English translation copyright © 2019 by Thomas Dalton, PhD

All rights reserved. No part of this publication may be reproduced, stored in a retrieval system, or transmitted, in any form or by any means, electronic, mechanical, photocopying, recording, or otherwise.

Clemens & Blair, LLC, is a non-profit educational publisher.

Library of Congress Cataloging-in-Publication Data

Hitler, Adolf (1889-1945)
The Essential Mein Kampf

        p.   cm.
Includes bibliographical references.

ISBN 978-1732-3532-68 (pbk.: alk. paper)

Printing number: 9 8 7 6 5 4 3 2 1

Printed in the United States of America on acid-free paper.

THE ESSENTIAL
MEIN KAMPF

DEDICATION

At 12:30 pm, on 9 November 1923, the following men fell in front of the Feldherrnhalle and in the courtyard of the former War Ministry in Munich, with loyal faith in the resurrection of their people:

Alfarth, Felix; *merchant*; b. 5 July 1901
Bauriedl, Andreas; *hatter*; b. 4 May 1879
Casella, Theodor; *bank clerk*; b. 8 August 1900
Ehrlich, Wilhelm; *bank clerk*; b. 19 August 1894
Faust, Martin; *bank clerk*; b. 27 January 1901
Hechenberger, Anton; *locksmith*; b. 28 September 1902
Körner, Oskar; *businessman*; b. 4 January 1875
Kuhn, Karl; *headwaiter*; b. 26 July 1897
Laforce, Karl; *engineering student*; b. 28 October 1904
Neubauer, Kurt; *valet*; b. 27 March 1899
Pape, Claus von; *businessman*; b. 16 August 1904
Pfordten, Theodor von der; *court councilor*; b. 14 May 1873
Rickmers, Johann; *retired captain*; b. 7 May 1881
Scheubner-Richter, Max Erwin von; *doctor of engineering*; b. 9 January 1884
Stransky, Lorenz von; *engineer*; b. 14 March 1889
Wolf, Wilhelm; *businessman*; b. 19 October 1898

The so-called national authorities refused these dead heroes a common grave.
Therefore, for the common memory, I dedicate to them the first volume of this work. As martyrs to the cause, may they shine forever, as a permanent inspiration to the followers of our movement.

Adolf Hitler
Landsberg am Lech
16 October 1924

CONTENTS

Introduction by Thomas Dalton   15

From
VOLUME ONE

(1)   **CHAPTER 1: IN MY PARENTS' HOUSE** (full)   39
        The Young Ringleader
        'Choice' of Profession
        Never a Civil Servant…
        …But Rather an Artist
        The Young Nationalist
        The German *Ostmark*
        The Struggle for Germanism
        Lessons from History
        Devotion to Wagner
        The Death of my Parents

(2)   **CHAPTER 2: YEARS OF STUDY AND SUFFERING IN VIENNA**
       (excerpts)   55
        Skill as an Architect
        Formation of a Worldview
        Architect and Watercolor Painter
        The Art of Reading
        The Key to Social Democracy
        The Jewish Question
        The So-Called World Press
        Criticism of Kaiser Wilhelm II
        Transformation into an Anti-Semite
        The Jew as Leader of Social Democracy
        Jewish Dialectics
        Study of the Foundations of Marxism
        Marxism as Destroyer of Culture

(3)   **CHAPTER 3: GENERAL POLITICAL REFLECTIONS FROM MY TIME IN VIENNA** (excerpts)   77
        Parliamentarianism
        Lack of Responsibility
        The Destruction of the Idea of Leadership
        The Exclusion of the Individual Leader
        'Public Opinion'
        The Majority Principle
        The Destruction of Character

        Jewish Democracy
        Anti-Semitism on a Religious Basis
        Growing Aversion to the Habsburg State
        The School of my Life

(4)   **CHAPTER 4: MUNICH** (excerpts)   99
        The Four Paths of German Policy
        Acquisition of New Land
        With England, Against Russia
        State and Economy
        The Moment of Decay

(5)   **CHAPTER 5: THE WORLD WAR** (excerpts)   117
        The German War for Freedom
        Enlistment in a Bavarian Regiment
        Baptism by Fire
        From Young Volunteer to Old Soldier
        Artificial Dampening of Enthusiasm
        Misrecognizing Marxism
        The Use of Naked Force
        Attack of a Worldview

(6)   **CHAPTER 7: THE REVOLUTION** (full)   131
        The First Enemy Leaflets
        Wounded
        Boasting of Cowardice
        Slackers
        Hatred of Prussia
        The Army's New Hope
        The Allies are Beaten Down
        "Germany Facing Revolution!"
        Last Wreaths of Immortal Laurel
        Growing Moral Decay
        Poisoned by Mustard Gas
        'Republic'
        All Sacrifice in Vain
        Decision to Enter Politics

(7)   **CHAPTERS 8 and 9: BEGINNING OF MY POLITICAL ACTIVITY and THE "GERMAN WORKERS' PARTY"** (excerpts)   149
        The Fight against International Finance Capital
        The 'Educational Officer'
        The "German Workers' Party"
        The 'Committee Meeting'
        A Final Decision

8)   **CHAPTER 10: CAUSES OF THE COLLAPSE** (excerpts)   161
            Moral Disarmament of a Dangerous Accuser
            Toxins and Symptoms
            The Rule of Money
            Jewish Press Tactics
            Syphilis
            The Sin against Blood and Race
            The Task of Combating Syphilis
            Sound Mind only in Sound Body
            The Fight against Spiritual Poisoning
            Modern Masses of Humanity

(9)   **CHAPTER 11: NATION AND RACE** (full)   177
            The Result of Racial Mixing
            Man and Idea
            Race and Culture
            The Aryan as Founder of Culture
            Effects of Blood-Mixing
            Service to the Community
            Purest Idealism, Deepest Knowledge
            Aryan and Jew
            Consequence of Jewish Egoism
            Sham Culture of the Jews
            The Jew, a Parasite
            Jewish 'Religious Community'
            Jewish Religious Doctrine
            The 'Elders of Zion'
            The Way of Jewry
            Standing of the Factory Worker
            Jewish Tactics
            The Core of the Marxist Worldview
            Organization of Marxist World-Doctrine
            Palestine as Organizational Center
            Dictatorship of the Proletariat
            From National Jews to Racial Jews
            Bastardized People
            Failure to Recognize the Inner Enemy

(10)   **CHAPTER 12: FIRST PERIOD OF DEVELOPMENT OF THE NSDAP** (excerpts)   221
            Nationalization of the Masses
            Education for Struggle
            Education for Respect of the Person
            The First Meeting
            Second Meeting

'Intellectual Weapons,' 'Silent Workers'
First Great Mass Meeting
Drafting the Program
A Movement on the March

From
VOLUME TWO

(11) **CHAPTER 1: WORLDVIEW AND PARTY** (excerpts)   243
Marxism and Democratic Principles
Worldview Against Worldview

(12) **CHAPTER 2: THE STATE** (excerpts)   247
The State is Not an End in Itself
Consequences of our Racial Division
Dangers of Racial Mixing
The Folkish State and Racial Hygiene

(13) **CHAPTER 5: WORLDVIEW AND ORGANIZATION** (excerpts) 259
Worldview and Organization
Struggle and Criticism

(14) **CHAPTER 6: STRUGGLE IN EARLY TIMES** (excerpts)   263
Fight against Poisonous Propaganda
Against the Tide
Politics of the Wide View
Enlightenment about the Peace Treaties

(15) **CHAPTER 7: CONFLICT WITH THE RED FRONT** (excerpts) 269
Old and New Black-Red-Gold
The National Socialist Flag
First Meeting in the Circus
An Attempted Disruption

(16) **CHAPTERS 9, 10, and 11: THE REVOLUTION, FEDERALISM, and BUILDING THE MOVEMENT** (excerpts)   283
The Resulting Disorganization
Jewish Incitement Activity
Denominational Discord
Reorganization of the Movement
Responsibility of the Leader
Building the Movement

(17) **CHAPTER 13: GERMAN POST-WAR ALLIANCE POLICY**
(excerpts) 299
   Present European Power Relations: England and Germany
   England's War Aim Not Achieved
   Political Goals of France and England
   Alliance Possibilities for Germany
   Is Germany Capable of Alliance Today?
   Divergence Between British and Jewish Interests
   Jewish World Incitement Against Germany
   Pandering to France
   Concentration on One Enemy
   Reckoning with the Traitors
   Fascist Italy and Jewry
   England and Jewry
   Japan and Jewry
   Our Fight Against the World-Enemy

(18) **CHAPTER 14: GERMANY'S POLICY IN EASTERN EUROPE**
(excerpts) 317
   Significance of the State's Area
   French and German Colonial Policy
   The Historical Mission of National Socialism
   Resumption of Eastern Policy
   German Alliance with Russia?
   Germany and Russia Before the War
   The German-English-Italian Alliance
   Conditions for Eastern Policy

(19) **CHAPTER 15: THE RIGHT TO EMERGENCY DEFENSE**
(excerpts) 329
   Cowardly Submission Brings No Mercy
   Seven Years to 1813—Seven Years to Locarno
   What Should Have Been Done After the Ruhr Occupation?
   Failure to Reckon with Marxism
   November 1923

(20) **CONCLUSION** 341

Appendix: The 25 Points of the National Socialist Program 343

Bibliography 347

Index 349

THE ESSENTIAL
MEIN KAMPF

THE ESSENTIAL MEIN KAMPF: AN INTRODUCTION

THOMAS DALTON

Mein Kampf is the autobiography and articulated worldview of one of the most consequential and visionary leaders in world history. It is also one of the most maligned and least understood texts of the 20th century. There have been so many obfuscations, deceptions, and outright falsehoods circulated about this work, that one scarcely knows where to begin. Nonetheless, the time has come to set the story straight.

That Adolf Hitler would even have undertaken such a work is most fortunate. Being neither a formal academic nor a natural writer, and being fully preoccupied with pragmatic matters of party-building, he may never have begun such a major task—were it not for the luxury of year-long jail term. In one of the many ironies of Hitler's life, it took just such an adverse event to prompt him to dictate his party's early history and his own life story. This would become volume one of his two-part, 700-page magnum opus. It would have a dramatic effect on world history, and initiate a chain of events that has yet to fully play out. In this sense, *Mein Kampf* is as relevant today as when it was first written.

Perhaps the place to begin is with the rationale for the book. Why did Hitler write it at all? Clearly it was not a requirement; many major politicians in history have come and gone without leaving a personal written record. Even his time in prison could have been spent communicating with party leaders, building support, soliciting allies, and so on. But he chose to spend much of his stay documenting the origins and growth of his new movement. And for this we can be grateful.

The work at hand seems to have served at least four purposes for its author. First, it is autobiographical. This aspect consumes much of volume one. For those curious about the first 35 years of Hitler's life, this is invaluable. It gives an accurate and relevant account of his upbringing, his education, and the early development of his worldview. Like any autobiography, it provides an irreplaceable first-hand description of a life. But as well, it offers the usual temptation to cast events in a flattering light, to downplay shortcomings, or to bypass inconvenient episodes. On this count, Hitler fares well; he provides an honest and open life story, devoid of known fabrications, obvious errors, or significant omissions. This book is essential for understanding his thinking and attitude on social, economic, and political matters that are of central concern.

Second, *Mein Kampf* is a kind of history lesson of Europe around the turn of the 20th century. Hitler was a proximate observer—and often first-hand witness—to many of the major events of the time. He served in the trenches of World War One for more than four years, which was virtually the entire duration of the war. Serving on the 'losing' side, he naturally gives a different interpretation of events than is commonly portrayed by historians of the victorious nations. But this fact should be welcomed by any impartial observer, and in itself makes the book worth reading. With rare exception—such as Jünger's *Storm of Steel*—no other contemporary non-fiction German source of this time is readily available in English. For those interested in the Great War and its immediate aftermath, this book is irreplaceable.

In its third aspect, the book serves to document the origins and basic features of Hitler's worldview. This, unsurprisingly, is the most distorted part of the book, in standard Western accounts. Here we find the insights and trigger events that led a young man without formal higher education, to develop a strikingly visionary, expansive, and forward-looking ideology. Hitler's primary concern, as we read, was the future and well-being of the German people—*all* Germans, regardless of the political unit in which they lived. The German people, or *Volk*, were, he believed, a single ethnicity with unique and singular self-interests. They were—indisputably—responsible for many of the greatest achievements in Western history.

INTRODUCTION

They were among the leading lights in music, literature, architecture, science, and technology. They were great warriors, and great nation-builders. They were, in large part, the driving force behind Western civilization itself. All this is true and undeniable, and Hitler is justly proud of his heritage. Equally is he outraged at the indignities suffered by this great people in then-recent decades—culminating in the disastrous humiliation of WWI and the Treaty of Versailles. He seeks, above all, to remedy these injustices and restore greatness to the German people. To do this, he needs to identify both their primary opponents and the defective political ideologies and structures that bind them. Then he undertakes to outline a new socio-political system that can carry them forward to a higher and rightful destiny. He accomplishes all this, and more.

Finally, in its fourth aspect, *Mein Kampf* is a kind of blueprint for action. It describes the evolution and aims of National Socialism and the NSDAP, or Nazi Party, in compelling detail. Hitler naturally wants his new movement to succeed in assuming power in Germany and in a future German Reich. But this is no theoretical analysis. Hitler is nothing if not pragmatic. He has concrete goals and precise means of achieving them. He has a deep disdain for the *geistigen Waffen*, the intellectual weapons, of the impotent intelligentsia. He demands results, and success. By all accounts, he achieved both.

Importantly, his analysis is, in large part, independent of context. It pertains not only to Germans, or only to the circumstances of the mid-1920s. His is a broadly universal approach based on the conditions of the modern world, and on timeless aspects of human nature. As such, Hitler's analysis of action is relevant and useful for people today—for all those who might strive for greatness in body and spirit.

Origins and Context

A few basic facts of Hitler's life are in order, to establish the context of the work. Born on 20 April 1889 in present-day Austria, he grew up as a citizen of the multi-ethnic state known as the Austro-Hungarian Empire. This diverse amalgamation was formed in 1867, with the union of the Austrian and Hungarian monarchies; thus does Hitler refer to the state as the "Double Monarchy." Throughout its 50-year history, it was always a loose conjunction of many ethnicities, and never a truly unified state. The ethnic Germans in it were a minority, and had to struggle to promote their own interests. This fact caused Hitler no end of distress; he explicitly felt more attachment to the broader German *Volk* than to the multi-ethnic state into which he was born.

As a youth, his interests tended toward the arts, painting, and history. This led to conflict with his obstinate father, who envisioned a safe, comfortable, bureaucratic career for his son. But his father's death on 3 January 1903, when Adolf was 13, allowed the young man to determine his own future. Two years later he moved to Vienna, scraping by with manual labor jobs to survive. In late 1907, his mother died. At the age of 18, he then applied to enter the Viennese arts academy in painting, but was diverted to architecture. He worked and studied for two more years, eventually becoming skilled enough to work fulltime as a draftsman and painter of watercolors.

All the while, he studied the mass of humanity around him. He read the various writings and publications of the political parties. He observed the workings of the press. He watched how unions functioned. He sat in on Parliament. He followed events in neighboring Germany. And he became intrigued by the comings and goings of one particular Viennese minority: the Jews.

Gradually he became convinced that the two dominant threats to German well-being were Marxism—a Jewish form of communism—and the international capitalist Jews. The problems were compounded by the fundamentally inept workings of a representative democracy that tried to serve diverse ethnicities. In the end, the fine and noble concept of democracy became nothing other than a "Jewish democracy," working for the best interests of Jews instead of Austrians or Germans.

Upon turning 23 in 1912, Hitler went to Munich. It was his first extended contact with German culture, and he found it invigorating. He lived there for two years, until the outbreak of WWI in July 1914. Thrilled at the opportunity to defend the German homeland, he enlisted, serving on the Western front in Belgium. After more than 2 years of service, he was lightly wounded in October 1916 and sent back to Germany, spending some time in a reserve battalion in Munich. Appalled at both the role of

INTRODUCTION

Jews there and the negative public attitude, he returned to the front in March 1917.

By this time, the war had been dragging on for some two and a half years, effectively becoming a stalemate. Even the looming entrance of the Americans into the war—President Wilson would call for war the next month, and US troops would soon follow—would have little near-term effect. But there was reason for optimism on the German side by late 1917, as Hitler explains. The Central Powers (primarily Germany and Austria-Hungary) had inflicted a decisive defeat on Italy in the Battle of Caporetto, and the Russians had pulled out of the war after the Bolshevik revolution, thus freeing up German troops for the Western front. Hitler recalls that he and his compatriots "looked forward with confidence" to the spring of 1918, when they anticipated final victory.

November Revolution, and a New Movement

But things would turn out differently. German dissatisfaction with the prolonged war effort was being fanned by Jewish activists calling for mass demonstrations, strikes, and even revolution against the Kaiser. In late January 1918 there was a large munitions strike. Various workers' actions and riots followed for months afterward. The Western front held, but Germany was weakening internally.

In mid-October of 1918, the German front near Ypres, Belgium was hit with mustard gas. Hitler's eyes were badly affected, and he was sent to a military hospital in Pasewalk, north of Berlin. In late October, a minor naval revolt in Kiel began to spread to the wider population. Two major Jewish-led parties, the Social Democrats (SPD) and the Independent Social Democratic Party (USPD), agitated for the Kaiser to abdicate—which he did, on November 9. Jewish activists in Berlin and Munich then declared independent "soviet" states; for a detailed discussion of these events, see Dalton (2014). Germany formally capitulated on November 11. After the dust had settled, a new 'Weimar' government was formed, one that was notably sympathetic to Jewish interests.

Hearing about the revolution from his hospital bed, Hitler was devastated. All the effort and sacrifices made at the front had proven worthless. Jewish agitators in the homeland had succeeded in whipping up local dissatisfaction to the point that the Kaiser was driven from power. The revolutionaries then assumed power and immediately surrendered to the enemy. This was the infamous "stab in the back" that would haunt German nationalists for years to come. And it was the triggering event that caused Hitler to enter politics.

In September 1919, working for the government, he was assigned to follow and report on a little-known group called the *Deutsche Arbeiterpartei*, or German Workers' Party (DAP). He ended up joining the group, and quickly assumed a leadership role. By early 1920, Hitler's speeches were drawing hundreds or even thousands of people. On February 24, he announced that the party would henceforth be known as the National Socialist German Workers' Party, or NSDAP—'Nazi,' in the parlance of its detractors.

The new movement grew rapidly. Hitler formalized his leadership in July 1921. A series of stormy and occasionally violent public events occurred in the following months. In November 1922, ideological compatriot Mussolini took power in Italy, which served to bolster both National Socialist efforts domestically and their international reputation. It was on November 21 that the *New York Times* printed its first major article on Hitler: "New Popular Idol Rises in Bavaria." Calling the Nazis "violently anti-Semitic" and "reactionary" but "well disciplined," the NYT viewed them as "potentially dangerous, though not for the immediate future." Indeed—it would not be for another 10 years that they would assume power in Germany.

Soon thereafter, other events would favor the National Socialists. France occupied the Ruhr valley in January 1923, claiming a violation of Versailles; this was taken as a grave insult to German sovereignty. It was also at this time that the infamous German hyperinflation took hold, wiping out the savings of ordinary Germans and forcing them to haul around bushels of cash for even the smallest purchases. By the end of the year, Germany was in a full-blown financial crisis. This led Hitler and the NSDAP leadership to plan for a revolutionary takeover of Munich on 9 November 1923. This attempted 'putsch,' or coup, would fail. In a brief shoot-out, 16 Nazis and four policemen were killed. Hitler and the other leaders were arrested within days, put on trial in February 1924, and sentenced to light prison terms.

INTRODUCTION

In all, Hitler spent some 13 months in confinement, obtaining release in December of that year. It was during this time that he dictated what would become volume one of his new book. He reportedly wanted to call it "Four and a Half Years of Struggle against Lies, Stupidity, and Cowardice." The publisher adroitly suggested a shorter title: "My Struggle," or *Mein Kampf*. It would initially be published in July of 1925. Hitler then began a second, shorter volume to complete his program. This appeared in December of 1926. The next year, the two volumes were slightly revised and combined into one work. This 1927 'second edition' of *Mein Kampf*, published when Hitler was 38 years old, is the version used in the present translation.

This edition contains detailed excerpts from both volumes of *Mein Kampf*, focusing on the material of most interest, relevance, and importance to present-day readers. Of the original 27 chapters in both volumes, excerpts from 22 are included—three of which are reproduced in full (chapters 1, 7, and 11 of volume one). In all this represents about one half of the full, two-volume set. The excluded material includes lengthy digressions on German history, minor political movements of the time, the role of propaganda, details on the nature of the ideal state, various local personalities, the story of the SA, and the role of trade unions. Interested readers are of course invited to read the full original text, published as Hitler (2018).

In short, what follows is the best of the best—the most interesting and most relevant portions of *Mein Kampf* without the lengthy digressions and side-tracks. It makes for some extremely compelling reading.

Some Contentious Topics

It goes without saying that this book is controversial. In fact, it may well be named as the single most controversial book in history. As such, the typical person is more or less guaranteed to get a slanted and biased account of it, if he knows much about it at all. And this is the first point of note: few people, even the so-called experts, really know what's in this book. Even highly educated people can tell you almost nothing about it. They will recognize the title and author, of course, and perhaps know roughly when it was written—but little more. The book has been functionally censored in the West for decades. And when academics or journalists are compelled to address it, it is always in slanderous and defamatory terms. This is the clearest demonstration that something important is happening in this text—something that most would rather leave unknown.

Of Hitler's many controversial statements and topics, four subjects warrant a brief mention here: National Socialism, race theory, religion, and the Jews.

Of the many simplistic and overused hyperboles in the modern lexicon, the use of 'Nazi' surely ranks among the worst. It's a crude and almost comical synonym for evil, hateful, cruel, tyrannical, and so on. This is consistent with the general demonization of everything Hitler. 'Nazi' is, of course, an abbreviation for National Socialist (*Nationalsozialist*). It was prompted by an earlier term, 'Sozi,' which was short for *Sozialdemokrat*, referring to the Social Democrat party that had been in existence since the mid-1800s. Hitler and colleagues rarely used 'Nazi,' generally viewing it as derogatory—although Goebbels did write an essay and short book titled *The Nazi-Sozi*.

As an ideology, National Socialism is utterly misunderstood. In fact, surprisingly, many people around the world today implicitly endorse some form of it. Take socialism. Most European countries, and many others globally, are some form of socialist. Socialism—loosely defined as government control and oversight of at least certain key portions of the economic sector—stands in contrast to free market capitalism, in which for-profit corporations control such things. Suffice it to say that socialism is a respected political and economic system around the globe.

Nationalism places high priority on the well-being of the nation-state and its traditional residents. It is inward-looking, rather than outward. It tends toward economic independence and autonomy rather than globalization and inter-connectedness. It typically supports and strengthens the dominant ethnicity and culture, and devalues that of minorities. This, too, is hardly controversial; there are strong nationalist movements in many countries around the world today.

Now, it's true that Hitler's form of national socialism went further than these basic concepts. It explicitly targeted Marxists, Jews, and global capitalists as enemies of the German people. It also sought to replace

INTRODUCTION

representative democracy with a more efficient and accountable centralized governance. Hitler had rational arguments for all these issues, as he explains in his book.

In fact, the formal declaration of the National Socialist system—as stated in Hitler's "25 points" (shown in the Appendix)—is remarkably progressive and, dare we say, tame. They call for equal rights (points 2 and 9). They give citizens the right to select the laws and governmental structure (6). They abolish war-profiteering (12). They call for corporate profit-sharing with employees (14). They support retirement pensions, a strong middle class, free higher education, public health, maternity welfare, and religious freedom, including explicit support for "a positive Christianity" (15, 16, 20, 21, 24, respectively).

On the downside, only a relative few points appear threatening or aggressive. They grant citizenship only to ethnic Germans, explicitly denying it to Jews (4). They block further immigration, and compel recent immigrants to leave (8). They seek to prohibit all financial speculation in land (17). They call for a death penalty against "traitors, usurers, and profiteers" (18). They demand that the German-language press be controlled only by ethnic Germans—without restricting press in other languages (23). And they call for "a strong central authority in the state" (25).

As anti-Semitic as Hitler was, it is surprising how lightly the Jews get off. They are banned from citizenship, and therefore from any role in government or the press. Recent (since August 1914) Jewish immigrants, like all immigrants, must leave. And the National Socialist view of religious freedom "fights against the Jewish materialist spirit" (24). But no threats to imprison or kill Jews. Longtime Jewish residents can stay in the country. No confiscation of wealth, with the stated exceptions. And certainly nothing that sounds like a looming 'Holocaust.'

In sum, Hitler's 'Nazism' is essentially the product of German nationalism and progressive socialism, combined with a mild form of anti-Semitism. Hardly the embodiment of evil.

THE ESSENTIAL MEIN KAMPF

Racial Theory

Mein Kampf contains numerous references to 'blood' (*Blut*) and 'race' (*Rasse*). This is always portrayed in the worst possible terms, as some kind of demonic, hate-filled, blind racism. But we must first realize that such talk was commonplace in the early 20th century; Hitler's terminology, though odd-sounding today, was actually quite conventional at the time. Not being a scientist, and few having much understanding of genetics at the time, it's understandable that he would employ such widely-used terms.

Therefore, a literal interpretation of such words is misleading. In modern terminology, Hitler's 'race' is better viewed as 'ethnicity.' He was more an *ethnicist* than a racist. His call for justice for the "German race" is really on behalf of *ethnic* Germans—the *Volk*. Thus understood, his view is much less threatening than commonly portrayed. Yes, he viewed ethnic Germans as superior. Yes, he wanted the best for his people. Yes, he was not much interested in the welfare of minorities or other nationalities. This is hardly a sin. Many people around the world today fight for precisely such things, for their own ethnicities. And they are right to do so.

Even today, it's reasonable and appropriate to discuss issues of race. It is a relevant term in biological taxonomy, indicating the highest-level sub-grouping within the species Homo sapiens. By some accounts, there are three races: White/Caucasian, Black/Negroid, and Mongoloid/Asian. Within each race, we have the various ethnicities—of which there are some 5,000 worldwide. By this measure, Hitler cared little about race. He made a few dismissive comments about Blacks, but nothing that wasn't standard at the time. He actually admired certain people of the Asian race, especially the Japanese. But his primary concern was among the various white ethnicities. He sought a position of strength and influence for ethnic Germans; he sought alliances with ethnic Britons; and he sought to oppose ethnic Jews. He was an ethnicist, not a racist.

Then there is Hitler's infamous talk of 'Aryan.' It's clear that Hitler views the Aryan as the highest human type, the greatest ethnicity, mover and creator of civilization. Notably, he never defines Aryan. Rather, we learn only what the Aryan is *not*: he is not Black, not Oriental, and certainly not Jewish. The Jew is the anti-Aryan, his dark and corrupting counterpart.

INTRODUCTION

The Aryan builds, the Jew destroys. The Aryan produces, the Jew consumes. The Aryan is idealistic, the Jew materialistic. In the end, the Aryan is distinguished not by his superior intelligence, nor his great creativity, but mainly by his altruism: the Aryan is a self-sacrificing person, more willing than any others to work on behalf of society. Thus he builds civilization and culture, and spreads it to the world. Non-Aryans, to the extent that they have a culture, get it from the Aryans, even as they customize it to their own needs. But the original source and sustainer is the self-sacrificing Aryan.

The word 'Aryan' has an interesting origin, and it has nothing to do with Germans. It comes from the Sanskrit *arya*, meaning 'noble.' It originally referred to the people and language that moved into India from the north, around 1500 BC. In the Indian caste system, the Aryans became the Brahmans—the highest and noblest caste. It was they who cultivated the Sanskrit language, and ultimately developed Indian culture. And a final point of interest: Those immigrants from the north came from the region that is known today as the Iranian plateau. In fact, the word 'Iran' derives directly from 'Aryan'; the Iranians were the original Aryans.

Not being a scholar of ancient history, and having no Internet at hand, Hitler knew little of all this. He simply picked up on prior German and European usage. In fact, talk of Aryans as a superior race predated Hitler by several decades. It was a main theme of Frenchman Arthur de Gobineau's book *Essay on the Inequality of the Human Races*, of 1855. It was prominent in Briton-turned-German author Houston Chamberlain's book *Foundations of the Nineteenth Century*, published in 1899. In fact the term had widespread usage among intellectuals and academics from the early 1900s on. By the time Hitler cited the term, it was old hat.

On Religion

Among other calumnies, Hitler is often portrayed as a godless atheist, a devil worshipper, the antichrist, or some kind of maniacal pagan. In fact he was none of these.

Rather, Hitler was broadly supportive of Christianity. He called it "the Religion of Love," and referred to Jesus, indirectly, as its "sublime founder" (vol 1, chap 8). He argued that the masses are not and cannot be philosophical; their ethics must come from traditional religious sources. And he believed in separation of church and state: "political parties have no right to meddle in religious questions" (vol 1, chap 10).

His view on God is quite intriguing. Frequently he refers to a kind of cosmic deity or divine power, but in a variety of unconventional terms. We find many references, for example, to *Schicksal*—fate or destiny. We read of the "Goddess of Destiny" (*Schicksalgöttin*). Elsewhere he writes of "Providence" (*Vorsehung*), "Doom" or "Fate" (*Verhängnis*), and "the Lord" (*Herrn*). Then again we find reference to "Chance" (*Zufall*) and "the eternal Creator" (*ewigen Schöpfer*). Volume one closes with a reference to "the Goddess of Inexorable Vengeance" (*die Göttin der unerbittlichen Rache*). These are not mere metaphors. It seems to be a kind of recognition of higher powers in the cosmos, but not those of traditional religions.

In the end, Hitler was most appalled by crude materialism: the quest for money and material power. This view has no concept of idealism, no notion of spirituality, no vision of higher powers in the universe. Materialism was the essence of both Marxism and capitalism—and both were embodied in the Jew. That's why these things are the mortal enemy of anyone seeking higher aims in life.

Hitler himself was no fan of religious dogma, but seems to have envisioned a future that moved toward a new kind of spirituality, one aligned with the workings of nature. We may perhaps best view him as a 'spiritual but not religious' sort of person—a view that is notably widespread today.

On the Jews

If nothing else, Hitler is inevitably depicted as a confessed anti-Semite and Jew-hater. We should be clear: this is absolutely true. There are many lies spread about Hitler, but this is not one of them. The key is understanding why he held this view.

In chapter 2 of volume one, he describes in striking detail his gradual discovery of the role and effect of Jews in society. He recalls that, as a youth, he had known only one Jewish boy, but had no particular feelings toward him one way or the other. He hadn't even heard them discussed much until his mid-teens, and then only in a vaguely negative political

INTRODUCTION

context. When he moved to Vienna at age 15, he encountered a city of 2 million that was 10 percent Jewish. At first, he barely noticed them. When he did, he viewed them as representatives of a rather strange religion, but since he was generally tolerant of religious diversity, he gave them little thought. He was put off by the "anti-Semitic" press. As he says, "on grounds of human tolerance, I opposed the idea that [the Jew] should be attacked because he had a different faith."

But then Hitler began to pay attention to the mainstream press. They were informative and liberal, but yet often flamboyant and garish. They seemed anxious to curry favor with the corrupt monarchy. And they were uniformly critical of the German Kaiser and his people. He noticed that some of the anti-Semitic papers were actually more skeptical of Viennese authority, and more open-minded regarding the Germans. At the same time, he realized that the Jews were more numerous than he previously believed. In fact, certain districts of Vienna were 50 percent Jewish, or more. And they all seemed to endorse a strange ideology: Zionism.

Furthermore, they were visually and physically repellent. Their black caftans and braided hair locks looked comical. They had their own odd concept of 'cleanliness': "That they were not water-lovers was obvious upon first glance." They smelled bad: "The odor of those people in caftans often made me sick to my stomach." This was topped off by "the unkempt clothes and the generally ignoble appearance." All in all, a sorry sight.

Worst of all, hidden away inside, was their "moral rot." Jews seemed to be involved in all manner of shady, unethical, and illegal activities. Hitler began to study the situation in more detail. "The fact was that 90 percent of all the filthy literature, artistic trash, and theatrical idiocy had to be charged to the account of a people who formed scarcely one percent of the nation. This fact could not be denied." Pornography, lewd art and theater, prostitution, human trafficking...all could be tied to the Jews.

The famed mainstream Viennese press, Hitler discovered, was almost completely a Jewish enterprise. Jewish writers repeatedly praised Jewish actors, authors, and businessmen. People, events, and policies favorable to Jews were lauded, and those that were disadvantageous were condemned. Even the dominant political party, the Social Democrats, was found to be led by Jews. Upon this realization, says Hitler, "the scales fell from my eyes." The whole pattern came together: a Jewish press supporting a Jewish political system, even as other Jews profited from the moral corruption of the people. Profit and power at all cost; lies and deceit without compunction; and an utter lack of concern for fairness, democracy, human welfare, or even human decency. "I gradually came to hate them," he said.

Considered globally, the situation was even worse. Marxism—the product of a Jew, Karl Marx—was promulgated by Jews in Europe and around the world. It sought to dominate and control both human and natural realms. It sought to level all social differences, thereby subverting the natural order in which the truly best people rightly flourish. In essence, it was a teaching and a means by which Jews could ruthlessly assume control of entire nations. Once that happened, millions of natives would die. The 1917 Bolshevik Revolution in Russia was proof enough.

In other parts of Europe, the dominant ideology was capitalism. Here, money ruled. Here, the bankers and corporate moguls dictated even to kings. Markets must be opened, international trade promoted, and loans used to extract wealth from the masses. And when these titans of capital were investigated, they were found to be, more often than not, Jews.

For Hitler, these realizations were devastating. The recognition of the insidious role of the Jews was "the greatest inner revolution that I had yet experienced." Indeed: "From being a soft-hearted cosmopolitan, I became an out-and-out anti-Semite." No hidden views here.

Hitler's conversion to anti-Semitism was remarkable. In contrast to the common view, it was neither arbitrary nor irrational. He was not a born Jew-hater. It was a step-by-step process, taken over a long period of time, and based on actual data and observations about the real world. His was a *rational* anti-Semitism. Any person of dignity and self-respect, anyone with a concern for human life, anyone committed to the integrity of the natural world, will of necessity be an anti-Semite. In their ruthless pursuit of their own self-interest, Jews become the enemy of all mankind. Anyone not recognizing this fact—and acting accordingly—is a fool.

The modern person today winces at such talk. "A monster!" we say. "Hate speech!" "The devil!" And yet, these are not rational responses. The modern man is conditioned to say such things. We must be objective here. Hitler was not inventing facts. His observations were largely true, even if he had no access to formal data or statistics. Jews did dominate in Vienna,

INTRODUCTION

and even more so in Germany. Consider the following numbers, cited by Sarah Gordon (1984: 8-15):

> The reader may be surprised to learn that Jews were never a large percentage of the total German population; at no time did they exceed 1.09 percent of the population during the years 1871 to 1933... [In spite of this, Jews] were overrepresented in business, commerce, and public and private service... Within the fields of business and commerce, Jews... represented 25 percent of all individuals employed in retail business and handled 25 percent of total sales...; they owned 41 percent of iron and scrap iron firms and 57 percent of other metal businesses.... Jews were [also] prominent in private banking under both Jewish and non-Jewish ownership or control. They were especially visible in private banking in Berlin, which in 1923 had 150 private (versus state) Jewish banks, as opposed to only 11 private non-Jewish banks....

This trend held true in the academic and cultural spheres as well: "Jews were overrepresented among university professors and students between 1870 and 1933.... [A]lmost 19 percent of the instructors in Germany were of Jewish origin.... Jews were also highly active in the theater, the arts, film, and journalism. For example, in 1931, 50 percent of the 234 theater directors in Germany were Jewish, and in Berlin the number was 80 percent..." Hitler was not imaging things.

Furthermore, Jews did in fact curry favor with the monarchy when it was in their interest, but they were quick to revolt if that could yield a greater gain. Jewish Marxists had succeeded in Russia, and were prominent in the November Revolution in Germany, making them responsible, in part, for Germany's defeat in WWI. Jews were eager to profit by any means possible: war, corruption, immorality, exploitation, deception. And they were, for the most part, fanatical Zionists: committed to creating a Jewish state in Palestine, and willing to do whatever it took to achieve this.

The facts are what they are. We can pretend they don't exist, but then we only deceive ourselves. Worse: we surrender our future to ruthless Jews, who are only too happy to manipulate and exploit. A nation's failure to appreciate the profound importance of 'the Jewish Question' can only lead to its downfall.

THE ESSENTIAL MEIN KAMPF

What to do? For Hitler, there was only one logical conclusion: Drive them out. This meant pushing them out of society, out of the economy, and restoring control of the media and government to non-Jews. It meant creating a *Judenrein*, or Jew-free, society, one that was free from internal and external manipulation by Jewish interests. This, in fact, was Hitler's conclusion years before he began *Mein Kampf*. In late 1919, as he was just becoming acquainted with the DAP party, he wrote a letter to one of his officers regarding how to respond to the Jewish question. This striking early letter concludes as follows:

> Rational anti-Semitism...must lead to a systematic and legal struggle against, and eradication of, the privileges the Jews enjoy over the other foreigners living among us (Alien Laws). Its final objective, however, must be the total removal of all Jews (*die Entfernung der Juden überhaupt*) from our midst. Both objectives can only be achieved by a government of national strength, never by a government of national impotence. (in Maser 1974: 215)

His view did not change in *Mein Kampf*, nor evidently anytime later in his life. His solution was always the same: drive them out. Total removal. Ruthlessly if necessary, but out they must go.

Here is one striking point, however: With one minor exception, Hitler never called for killing the Jews. Though his terminology shifted over time, his words always referred to some form of removal. Jews should be "deported," "expelled," "rooted out." Their role and their power in the German Reich must be "destroyed" or "liquidated." But explicit words like 'killing,' 'shooting,' 'murder,' 'gassing,' virtually never appear in his speeches, writings, or even private conversations. Even the hostile commentator Ian Kershaw had to admit as much, at least regarding the public addresses: "An explicit call to murder [Jews] can be found in no...speech" (1998: 650). Kershaw fails to inform the reader, though, that the same holds for Hitler's writings and conversations.

The one exception is at the very end of *Mein Kampf*. There were about 600,000 Jews in Germany at the start of WWI, a war that ended in the deaths of over 2 million Germans. Hitler argues that killing "12 or 15 thousand

INTRODUCTION

Hebrew corrupters" at the start of the war, by the same poison gas that fell on the German troops in the battlefield, would have spared a million lives and led to German victory. Not all the Jews, or even most of them; just one or two percent would have sufficed, to subvert their pernicious aims. But this seems to be his last such reference, in any documented writing or speech. In a sense, this exception proves the rule: If Hitler had wanted to speak of killing the Jews, he surely would have. Since we find no such talk after 1925—even during the war—we must assume that he in fact never intended their deaths. Thus, we find no talk of mass murder, extermination camps, genocide, or anything like this in *Mein Kampf*. Hitler's opponents search in vain for signs of an impending 'Holocaust.' The reader is invited to do the same. It is simply not there—much to the chagrin of his critics.

From all this, it should be clear that Hitler had only one real enemy in the Jews. He was not some all-purpose hater of humanity. He disliked the French, respected the British and Americans, and sympathized with the Russians, but didn't hate them. Even the lesser races were never a target of contempt, but rather, if anything, pity. Today we are under the impression that, in 1940, the entire world quivered at the thought of a Nazi takeover. But this was never more than trumped-up propaganda.

In short, *unless you were a Jew, you had nothing to fear*. Whites had nothing to fear—unless they allowed themselves to be ruled by Jewish Marxists or Jewish capitalists. Hispanics, Blacks, and Orientals, though of lower status, had nothing to fear. France and England had nothing to fear—until *they* declared war on Germany. America never had anything to fear—until Roosevelt and his Jewish advisors made the unwise decision to harass Germany and Japan into conflict. It was always and only the Jews who were his enemy.

From the Jewish perspective, of course, this is the ultimate evil: a man who seeks to destroy Jewish power, confiscate their obscene wealth, and create a Jew-free society. Should he succeed, and should his new society flourish, it would mean catastrophe for Jews worldwide. People everywhere would see the pernicious result of Jewish control. People everywhere might also attempt to regain their own self-determination, drive out their own Jews, and create their own flourishing society. And that would be the end of Jewish power globally. For the Jews, this is a nightmare scenario. Thus they use all their might to oppose it.

This is why *Mein Kampf* is so dangerous.

THE ESSENTIAL MEIN KAMPF

Hitler's Legacy

Hitler had a great and noble vision for his German people. He desperately wanted them to assume their rightful place in the world, to be a global power, and to set an example for all those who aspired to something better than a crude material existence. By contrast, the social vision of virtually every other recent world leader pales to insignificance. The ideals of Bush, Blair, Cameron, Sarkozy, Hollande, Macron, Merkel, Obama, Trump... these are bad jokes, at best. But this is what we must expect, given their obeisance to Jewish interests.

Hitler had concrete goals in mind for his nation, and concrete plans to get there. He faced three fundamental challenges: (1) to restore the economy, (2) to achieve security and independence by becoming a world power, and (3) to create an idealistic, uplifting, and sustainable German society. He put his plan into action as soon as he came to power in 1933. And it worked. It worked so well that a beleaguered, beaten-down, hyper-inflated, emasculated German nation rose up to become a world power with astonishing speed. Consider: After just three years, Hitler's Germany had conquered inflation, driven down unemployment, and put industry back to work—all in the midst of a global depression. After six years, it was a world power. After eight years, his nation was so powerful that it took the combined effort of virtually the rest of the world to defeat it.

The first two aspects of his plan were attained. But the rest of the world, driven by Jewish hatred, jealousy, and spite, could not bear this, and so they sought to crush him and his German nation—which they did. The real tragedy of Hitler's story is that he never had time to tackle his third great challenge: to create a flourishing German society. Sadly, we will never know the long-term consequences of National Socialism, or whether a truly great society could have been constructed.

But what about the Holocaust? What about the death camps and gas chambers? Isn't this the terrible, inevitable outcome of Hitler's warped vision?

Here we have perhaps the greatest deception of all. In order to show the world the horrible outcome of a potent anti-Semitism, a tale of monumental human disaster had to be constructed. Once constructed, it then had to be promoted and sustained. The undeniable and tragic death

INTRODUCTION

of several hundred thousand Jews—which included many deaths by old age, disease, injury, suicide, and in combat situations—would have to become "6 million." Tough talk against Jews, aimed at driving them out of Germany, would have to become "euphemisms for mass murder." Rooms designed to disinfest clothing and bedding against disease-carrying lice would have to become "homicidal gas chambers." Hundreds of thousands of Jewish bodies would have to be burned down to ash, and then made to completely vanish. Transit camps constructed to move Jews out of the Reich—Treblinka, Belzec, Sobibor—would have to become "extermination camps" designed for mass-murder; and with diesel engine exhaust, no less. And a forced labor camp in which thousands of Jews died from typhus— Auschwitz—would have to become "the greatest death camp of all time."

Clearly there is much more to be said here. For those interested readers, sources such as Dalton (2015, 2016) or Rudolf (2011) are recommended. Suffice to say that the Holocaust, as commonly portrayed, is an unsubstantiated, unwarranted, and unjustified exaggeration of epic proportions. Nearly every aspect of the story crumbles as soon as it is put to the test. The alleged horror of the Holocaust becomes, in the end, a story of the dismantling and expulsion of one particular minority community that held disproportionate power in a nation that did not want them, and that bore disproportionate guilt for that nation's misfortunes. That they themselves should have suffered as a result is unsurprising.

Reading *Mein Kampf*

Two final things should be kept in mind, by any contemporary reader of this book. First, the obvious point: *the writer did not know the future*. It is very difficult for us, knowing history, to imagine these words being written by a 38-year-old leader of a minor political party who could not have known what was to come. Hitler had visions, ideas, expectations— which turned out to be stunningly accurate. His powers of perception and foresight were astonishing. And yet for him, at the time, they were just thoughts of a possible future. He believed that his NSDAP party would grow to dominate Germany—and it did. He believed that he could restore greatness to a shattered nation—and he did. Conflict with Russia, France, and England; tackling the 'Jewish Question'; a reinvigorated cultural and spiritual life—all these came about, more or less as he anticipated. And the engine behind these events was just as he envisioned: sheer force of will, by a single man.

Did he foresee a world united against him? The loss of some 4 million German lives? His own premature death? Apparently not. But surely he must have known that such things were possible. In a world of perpetual struggle, no victories are guaranteed. Success is always ephemeral. Striving for greatness entails great risk. And yet the alternative is worse—to sink into a miasmatic existence, a placid and tepid peace, in which the global capitalists or communists invade the body politic and drain it of all higher and nobler aims.

Mein Kampf is a remarkable anticipation of things to come. Hitler's vision and worldview were realized more quickly than even he could have thought possible. This is tangible proof of the power of ideas to remake the world, when accompanied by a sense of greatness and higher purpose. Such things are utterly lacking in the world today, and thus they seem strange, odd, and even frightening to us. We forget that, for much of our history, they were the very means by which nations and cultures thrived.

The second point is this: The parallels to the present day are striking. Jewish domination of German society in the 1920s mirrors that of the United States, England, France, and Canada today. The tactics of AIPAC, the role of the Jewish Lobby, the sad state of media and entertainment industries, cowardice in corporate leadership, widespread moral decay, environmental degradation, manipulations of global capitalists and stock-market traders—all these have their counterparts in pre-Nazi Germany.

Hitler surely would have been appalled at the world of today. In America, he would find Jewish leadership in all major media organizations and film studios; Jewish money decisive in all national political races; and an American Supreme Court with three Jews, out of nine justices. Germany today wilts under the so-called leadership of the *Judenknecht* Merkel, who allows that once-great nation to be flooded with a mass of foreign ethnicities, even as she pays monumental Holocaust reparations to the Israeli state. And most all European nations readily sign up to fight Israel's wars in the Middle East and around the world. Malaysian leader Mahathir Mohamad was surely correct when he said, "Today Jews rule the world by proxy; they get others to fight and die for them." Again, just as Hitler had

INTRODUCTION

predicted—the demise of National Socialism would mean the triumph of a Jewish-inspired worldview.

It seems hopeless. And yet, to a young Adolf Hitler in 1920's Germany, things also seemed hopeless. But he knew that, with a bold vision and true force of will, that things could change—and quickly. Thus has it always been so. The future is fixed only to those who cannot envision something better, something higher, something greater. Even in the worst of times, true visionaries have always emerged. It has happened in the past, and it will happen again.

Mein Kampf is one man's assessment of history and vision for the future. It is blunt; it is harsh; it is unapologetic. It does not comply with contemporary standards of politeness, objectivity, and political correctness. It sounds offensive to sensitive modern ears. But the book is undeniably important. It is more consequential than perhaps any other political work in history. It deserves to be read, in a clear and unbiased translation. And each reader will then be free to determine its ultimate value and meaning for themselves.

FROM
VOLUME ONE

– 1 –

IN MY PARENTS' HOUSE

I consider it most fortunate today that destiny selected Braunau-on-the-Inn to be my birthplace.[1] This little town lies on the border between two German states—the union of which seems, at least to us of the younger generation, a task to which we should dedicate our lives and pursue with every possible means!

German-Austria must return to the great German Motherland. And not for mere economic reasons. No, no. Even if the union were a matter of economic indifference, and even if it were to be economically disadvantageous, it still must take place. The same blood should be in the same Reich.[2] The German people have no right to engage in colonialism until they have brought all their sons together in one state. Only when the territory of the Reich embraces all Germans and then finds itself unable to assure them a livelihood, only then will the moral right arise to acquire foreign territory. The plow will then become the sword, and the tears of war will produce our daily bread for generations to come.

And so this little border town appeared to me as the symbol of a great mission. But in another way too, it points to a lesson that is applicable today. More than 100 years ago, this insignificant place was the scene of a tragic calamity that affected the whole German nation. It will be remembered forever, at least throughout German history. At the time of our Fatherland's deepest humiliation, Johannes Palm—Nuremberger, bookseller, uncompromising nationalist, and enemy of the French—was

---

[1] Braunau, Austria lies about 25 km north of Salzburg, and about 50 km east of Munich. It has a present-day population of some 16,000. The river Inn is the border with Germany.

[2] 'Reich' may be translated variously as 'empire,' 'kingdom,' or 'realm.' Throughout the present text, it will often appear as 'empire' but in general will be left untranslated.

put to death here because he had the misfortune to have loved Germany so passionately.³ He stubbornly refused to reveal the names of his colleagues, or rather the leaders who were chiefly responsible for the affair. The same happened with Leo Schlageter.⁴ The former, like the latter, was denounced to the French by a government agent. An Augsburg police chief won this unenviable fame on that occasion, and set the example that was later to be copied by neo-German officials of Herr Severing's regime.⁵

It was in this little town on the Inn—gilded by the memory of a German martyr, a town that was Bavarian by blood but under Austrian rule—that my parents lived, towards the end of the last century. My father was a civil servant who fulfilled his duties very conscientiously. My mother looked after the household and lovingly devoted herself to the care of her children.

I don't remember much from that period because, after a few years, my father had to leave that beloved border town. He took up a new post farther down the Inn, at Passau, hence in Germany itself.

In those days it was typical for an Austrian civil servant to be transferred periodically from one post to another. Soon my father was transferred to Linz, and there he retired to live on his pension. But this didn't mean that the old gentleman would now 'rest.' As the son of a poor cottager, and while still young, he grew restless and left home. When he was barely 13 years old, he slipped on his small backpack and set forth from his native woodland parish. Despite the pleas of villagers who could speak from experience, he went to Vienna to learn a trade. This was in the 1850s.

It was a difficult time, that of deciding to leave home and face the unknown, with three gulden in his pocket. By the time the boy of 13 became a youth of 17, he had passed his apprenticeship examination as a craftsman, but was not content. Quite the contrary. The long period of hardship, constant want, and misery strengthened his resolve to give up working at a trade and strive for 'something higher.' As a boy it had seemed to him that the position of the parish priest in his home village was the

---

³ Palm was executed in 1806 by Napoleon's forces for publishing a pamphlet in defense of Germany.

⁴ Schlageter actively opposed the French occupation of the Ruhr; he was shot in 1923.

⁵ Carl Severing was German Minister of Interior during the Weimar regime. He held office from 1928 to 1930.

—1—

highest in the scale of attainment; but now that the big city had enlarged his outlook, he looked upon the state official as the highest of all. With the tenacity of one whom misery and suffering had already made 'old' while still young, the 17-year-old stuck to his new project. He became a civil servant. He was about 23 years old, I think, when he achieved his life's dream. Thus he was able to fulfill the promise he had made as a poor boy, to not return to his native village until he was a success.

He achieved his goal. But back in the village, there was no one who remembered him as a little boy, and the village itself had become strange to him.

Finally, when he was 56 years old, he retired. But he couldn't bear to be idle for even a single day. On the outskirts of the small market town of Lambach, in Upper Austria, he bought a farm and tilled it himself. Thus, at the end of a long and hard-working career, he came back to the life that his father had led.

THE YOUNG RINGLEADER (section 1.1)

It was at this time that I first began to have ideals of my own. I spent a good deal of time playing out in the open, on the long road from school, and mixing up with some of the roughest boys, which caused my mother many anxious moments. This made me something quite the opposite of a stay-at-home. I gave scarcely any serious thought to the question of choosing a vocation in life; but I certainly had no interest in the kind of career that my father had followed.

I think that an inborn talent for speaking now began to develop in me, during the more or less strenuous arguments with my friends. I became a youthful ringleader, one who learned quickly at school but was rather difficult to manage. In my free time, I practiced singing in the choir of the monastery church at Lambach. I was well-situated to be emotionally impressed again and again by the magnificent splendor of the church ceremonies. It was natural for me to look upon the Abbot as representing the highest human ideal worth striving for, just as the humble village priest had appeared to my father in his day.

For awhile at least, that was this case. But my father didn't appreciate my oratorical gifts as beneficial for a career, and so he naturally couldn't understand my youthful ideas. This internal conflict made him feel somewhat concerned.

As it happened, my short-lived yearnings soon gave way to hopes that were better suited to my temperament. Browsing through my father's books, I happened to come across some publications that dealt with military subjects. One of these was a popular history of the Franco-German War of 1870–71. It consisted of two volumes of an illustrated periodical dating from those years. These became my favorite reading. Soon that great and heroic conflict began to dominate my thinking. And from that time on, I became more and more enthusiastic about everything that was at all connected with war or military affairs.

But this story had a special significance for me on other grounds, too. For the first time, and as yet in only quite a vague way, I began to think: Is there a difference—and if so, what is it—between the Germans who fought that war and the other Germans? Why didn't Austria also take part in it? Why didn't my father and all the others fight in that struggle?

Are we not the same as other Germans?

Do we not all belong together? That was the first time that this problem began to agitate my brain. And from the conclusions that I reached, I was forced to accept the fact—though with a secret envy—that not all Germans had the good luck to belong to Bismarck's Reich.

This was something that I couldn't understand.

'CHOICE' OF PROFESSION (section 1.2)

It was decided that I should study.

Considering my whole personality, and especially my temperament, my father decided that the classical subjects studied at the Gymnasium were not suited to my natural talents. He thought that the *Realschule* would suit me better. My obvious talent for drawing confirmed this for him; in his opinion, drawing was a neglected subject in the Austrian Gymnasium. Another likely factor was the memory of his own hard road, and this contributed to him looking upon classical studies as unpractical; accordingly, he set little value on them. At the back of his mind, he believed that his son should also become a government official. Indeed, he had decided on that career for me.

— 1 —

Due to the difficulties through which he had to struggle in his own case, he overestimated what he had achieved. His success was exclusively the result of his own indefatigable effort and energy. The characteristic pride of the self-made man led him to the idea that his son should follow the same calling—and if possible, to rise even higher. Moreover, this idea was strengthened by the consideration that the results of his own life's work put him in a position to aid his son's advancement in the same career.

It was simply inconceivable to him that I might reject that which had meant everything in life to him. My father's decision was simple, definite, and clear. In his eyes, it was something to be taken for granted. A man of such a nature, who had become domineering by reason of his own hard struggles, could not think of allowing inexperienced and irresponsible young men to choose their own careers.

To act in such a way, where the future of his own son was concerned, would have been a grave and reprehensible weakness in the exercise of parental authority and responsibility; it was something utterly incompatible with his characteristic sense of duty.

And yet things had to turn out differently.

NEVER A CIVIL SERVANT... (section 1.3)

For the first time in my life—I was then 11 years old—I felt myself forced into open opposition. No matter how hard and determined my father might be about putting his own plans and opinions into action, I was no less obstinate in rejecting an idea that didn't appeal to me at all.

I wouldn't become a civil servant.

Neither persuasion nor 'serious' warnings could break down that opposition. I would not, on any account, become a State official. All the attempts that my father made to arouse in me a love for that profession, by envisioning his own career for me, had only the opposite effect. It nauseated me to think that one day I might be chained to an office desk, and that I couldn't control my own time but would be forced to spend the whole of my life filling out forms.

One can imagine what kind of thoughts such a prospect aroused in the mind of a young man who was by no means 'good' in the usual sense of that term!

THE ESSENTIAL MEIN KAMPF

The ridiculously easy school tasks that we were given made it possible for me to spend far more time outdoors than at home. Today—when my political opponents pry into my life with diligent scrutiny, as far back as the days of my boyhood, so as to finally be able to prove what dirty tricks this 'Hitler' was used to in his youth—I thank heaven that I can look back to those happy days and find the memory helpful. The fields and the woods were then the battlefields on which all disputes were decided.

Even attendance at the *Realschule* could not alter my way of spending my time.

...BUT RATHER AN ARTIST (section 1.4)

But now I had another battle to fight.

As long as my father's plan to make me a state functionary contradicted my own inclinations only in theory, the conflict was bearable. I could be discreet about expressing my personal views and thus avoid constantly recurring arguments. My own resolution not to become a government official was sufficient for the time being to put my mind completely at rest. I resolutely held on to that conviction. But the situation became more difficult once I had a positive plan of my own, one that I presented to my father as an alternative. This happened when I was 12 years old.

How it happened, I cannot exactly say now. But one day it became clear to me that I would be a painter—I mean an artist. It was a fact that I had an aptitude for drawing. It was even one of the reasons why my father had sent me to the *Realschule*. But he had never thought of having that talent developed in such a way that I could become a professional painter. Quite the contrary. When, as a result of my renewed refusal to adopt his preferred plan, my father asked me for the first time what I myself really wished to be, my resolve expressed itself almost automatically. For a moment my father was speechless.

"A painter? An artist?"

He wondered whether I was sane. He thought that he might not have heard me right, or misunderstood me. But when I explained my ideas to him, and he saw how seriously I took them, he opposed it with all the determination of his nature. His decision was very fundamental; any consideration of my own natural abilities was out of the question.

—1—

"An artist, no, not as long as I live, never." But seeing as I had inherited much of my father's obstinacy—besides having other qualities of my own—my reply was equally forceful. Except that it stated something quite the contrary.

At that point, our struggle became a stalemate. Father would not abandon his 'Never,' and I became all the more firm in my 'Nevertheless.'

Naturally, the consequences were unpleasant. The old gentleman was bitterly annoyed; and indeed so was I, although I really loved him. My father forbade me to entertain any hopes of taking up the art of painting as a profession. I went a step further and declared that I would not study anything else. With such declarations, the situation became ever more strained, so that the old man irrevocably decided to assert his parental authority at all costs. That led me to adopt an attitude of circumspect silence, but I put my threat into action. I thought that once it became clear to my father that I was making no progress at the *Realschule*, he would be forced to allow me to follow my dream—for better or worse.

THE YOUNG NATIONALIST (section 1.5)

I don't know whether I calculated rightly or not. My failure to make progress in school was obvious. I studied just the subjects that appealed to me, especially those that I thought I might need later as a painter. What didn't appear to have any importance, or what didn't otherwise appeal to me, I completely sabotaged. My school reports of that time were always in the extremes of good or bad, according to the subject. In one column my evaluation read 'very good' or 'excellent.' In another it read 'average' or even 'below average.' By far my best subjects were geography and, even more so, general history. These were my two favorite subjects, and I led the class in them.

When I look back over so many years and try to judge the results of that experience, I find two very significant facts standing out clearly:

First, I became a nationalist.

Second, I learned to understand and grasp the true meaning of history.

THE ESSENTIAL MEIN KAMPF

THE GERMAN OSTMARK (section 1.6)

The old Austria was a multi-national state.

The Germans of the Reich didn't realize that if the Austrian Germans had not been of the best blood, they could never have given their characteristic stamp to an empire of 52 million—such that the erroneous idea arose that Austria was a German state. This error led to dire consequences. But all the same, it was a magnificent testimony to the character of the 10 million Germans in the *Ostmark*.[6] Only very few of the Germans in the Reich itself had an idea of the bitter struggle that those Eastern Germans had to carry on daily for the preservation of their German language, schools, and character.

Only today—when a tragic fate has torn several millions of our kinsfolk away from the Reich and forced them to live under foreign rule, dreaming of that common fatherland towards which all their yearnings are directed, and struggling to maintain the right to use their mother tongue—only now have the wider circles come to realize what it means to fight for one's people. Today perhaps there are some who can assess the greatness of that German spirit that animated the Reich's old *Ostmark*. It enabled those people, left entirely on their own, to defend the Reich against the East for several centuries. They also were able to secure the boundaries of the German language through a guerilla war of attrition, at a time when the Reich was more interested in colonies than in protecting its own flesh and blood at its very doorstep.

THE STRUGGLE FOR GERMANISM (section 1.7)

In this battle over the language of old Austria, there were, as in every such struggle, three groups: the fighters, the slackers, and the traitors.

The sifting process began at school. And it is worth noting that the language-war was waged in perhaps its bitterest form in school; this was the nursery where the seeds had to be watered that were to spring up and form the coming generation. The tactical objective of the fight was to win over the child, and it was to the child that the first rallying cry was addressed:

---

[6] 'Ostmark' was the German nationalist designation for German-Austria, that is, the German part of the Austro-Hungarian Empire.

—1—

"German boy, don't forget that you are a German," and "Remember, little girl, that one day you must become a German mother!"

Those who know something of the youthful spirit can understand how the young will always lend a glad ear to such a rallying cry. The young people led the struggle through many forms, fighting in their own way and with their own weapons.

They refused to sing non-German songs. The greater the efforts made to win them away from their German allegiance, the more they exalted the glory of their German heroes. They went hungry so that they might spare their pennies to help the war chest of their elders. They were incredibly aware of the significance of what the non-German teachers said, and they contradicted them in unison. They wore the forbidden emblems of their own kinsfolk and were happily penalized or even beaten for doing so. On a small scale, they were mirrors of loyalty from which the elders might learn a lesson.

And thus it was that, at a comparatively early age, I took part in the nationalist struggles of old Austria. When meetings were held for the *Südmark* and the School League, we wore cornflowers and black-red-gold colors to express our loyalty. We greeted each other with "*Heil*," and instead of the Austrian anthem we sang *Deutschland über Alles*, despite warnings and penalties. Thus the youth were politically educated at a time when the citizens of the so-called national State knew little of their own nationality except the language.

I, of course, didn't belong to the slackers. Within a short time I had become an ardent 'German Nationalist,' which had a different meaning from our present party concept.

I rapidly moved in the nationalist direction. By the time I was 15 years old, I had come to understand the distinction between dynastic 'patriotism' and 'nationalism' based on the concept of *Volk*, or people—my inclination being entirely in favor of the latter.

LESSONS FROM HISTORY (section 1.8)

Such a preference may not perhaps be clearly intelligible to those who have never taken the trouble to study the internal conditions that prevailed under the Habsburg Monarchy.[7] Among historical studies, universal history was the subject almost exclusively taught in the Austrian schools; there was very little of specific Austrian history. The fate of this state was closely bound up with the existence and development of Germany as a whole—such that a division of history into German history and Austrian history would be practically inconceivable. And indeed it was only when the German people came to be divided into two states that this division of German history began to take place.

The insignia of former imperial glory, which are still preserved in Vienna, appear to cast a magic spell. They guarantee an eternal bond between these two peoples.

When the Habsburg State crumbled to pieces,[8] the Austrian Germans instinctively raised an outcry for union with their German fatherland. That was the voice of a unanimous yearning in the hearts of the whole people for a return to the never-forgotten home of their fathers. But such a general yearning could not be explained except by attributing its cause to the historical training through which the individual Austrian Germans had passed. Therein lay a spring that never dried up. Especially in times of distraction and forgetfulness, its quiet voice was a reminder of the past—bidding the people to look out beyond mere momentary prosperity to a new future.

The teaching of universal history in the so-called high schools is still very unsatisfactory. Few teachers realize that the purpose of teaching history is not the memorizing of certain dates and facts that the student is not interested in knowing: the exact date of a battle, or the birthday of some marshal or other. And the student isn't at all—or only incidentally—interested in knowing when the crown of his fathers was placed on the brow of some monarch. These are certainly not looked upon as important matters.

To study history means to search for and discover the forces that are the causes of those results that appear to us as historical events.

---

[7] The Habsburg Monarchy refers to the family dynasty that ruled in central Europe for 400 years. It began in 1519 with Charles V, and ended in 1918 with Charles I. The Habsburgs were the ruling power in the Austro-Hungarian Empire. The Monarchy was, of course, finished by the time Hitler wrote these words in 1924.

[8] In 1918.

— 1 —

The art of reading and studying consists in this: Remember the essentials and forget what is inessential.

Probably my whole future life was determined by the fact that I had a history professor who understood, as few others understand, how to make this viewpoint prevail in the classroom. This teacher was Dr. Leopold Pötsch, of the *Realschule* at Linz.[9] He was the ideal personification of the qualities necessary for a teacher of history in the sense I mentioned above. An elderly gentleman with a decisive manner but a kindly heart, he was a very compelling speaker and was able to inspire us with his own enthusiasm.

Even today I cannot recall without emotion that venerable personality whose enthusiastic exposition of history so often made us entirely forget the present. He allowed us to be transported into the past, as if by magic. He penetrated through the dim mist of thousands of years and transformed the historical memory of the dead past into a living reality. When we listened to him, we became afire with enthusiasm; sometimes we were even moved to tears.

It was still more fortunate that this professor was able not only to illustrate the past by examples from the present, but from the past he was also able to draw a lesson for the present. He understood better than anyone else the everyday problems that were then stirring in our minds. He used the national fervor that we felt in our own small way as an instrument of our education, in that he often appealed to our national sense of honor. In that way he maintained order and held our attention much more easily than he could have done by any other means.

It was because of him that history became my favorite subject.

As a natural consequence, but without my teacher's deliberate intention, I then and there became a young revolutionary.

After all, who could have studied German history under such a teacher and not become an enemy of that state whose rulers exercised such a disastrous influence on the destinies of the German nation?

And how could one remain a faithful subject of the House of Habsburg, whose past history and present conduct proved it to be always ready to betray the interests of the German people, for the sake of trivial personal interests?

---

[9] Pötsch (1853-1942) taught Hitler from ages 12 through 15.

THE ESSENTIAL MEIN KAMPF

Did we not realize, even as youngsters, that this Austrian State did not, and could not, have any love for us Germans?

That which history taught us about the policy of the House of Habsburg was confirmed by our experiences. In north and south, the poison of foreign races was eating into the body of our people. Even Vienna was steadily becoming more and more a non-German city. The 'Imperial House' favored the Czechs on every possible occasion. Indeed, it was divine retribution that caused Germanism's most deadly enemy in Austria, the Archduke Franz Ferdinand, to fall by the very bullets that he himself had helped to cast. Working from above, he was the chief patron of the movement to make Austria a Slav state.

The burdens laid on the shoulders of the German people were monstrous, and the sacrifices of blood and treasure that they had to make were incredibly heavy. Yet anyone who was not blind must have seen that it was all in vain. What affected us most bitterly was the awareness of the fact that this whole system was morally shielded by the alliance with Germany, whereby the slow rooting-out of Germanism from the old Austrian Monarchy seemed in some way to be more or less sanctioned by Germany herself. Habsburg hypocrisy, which outwardly tried to make the people believe that Austria was still a German State, increased the feeling of hatred against the Imperial House. At the same time, it aroused a spirit of rebellion and contempt.

But in the German Reich itself, its rulers understood nothing of what all this meant. As if struck blind, they stood beside a corpse; in the very symptoms of decomposition, they believed that they saw signs of a renewed vitality.

In that unhappy alliance between the young German Reich and the illusory Austrian State lay the germ of the [First] World War, and also of the final collapse.

In the course of this book, I will go to the root of the problem. Suffice it to say here that in the very early years of my youth, I came to certain conclusions that I have never abandoned. Indeed, I became more profoundly convinced of them as the years passed. They were:

That the dissolution of Austria is a preliminary condition for the defense of Germany; further, that national feeling is by no means identical with dynastic patriotism; finally, and above all, that the House of Habsburg was destined to bring misfortune to the German nation.

—1—

As a logical consequence of these convictions, there arose in me a feeling of intense love for my German-Austrian home, and a profound hatred of the Austrian State.

The kind of historical thinking that I developed through my study of history at school never left me afterwards. World history became more and more an inexhaustible source for the understanding of contemporary historical events—in other words, politics. Therefore I will not 'learn' politics, but rather let politics teach me.

A precocious 'revolutionary' in politics, I was no less a precocious revolutionary in art.

DEVOTION TO WAGNER (section 1.9)

At that time, the provincial capital of Upper Austria had a theater that was, relatively speaking, not bad. Almost everything played there. When I was 12 years old, I saw *William Tell* performed. That was my first theater experience. Some months later I saw *Lohengrin*, the first opera I had ever heard. I was fascinated at once. My youthful enthusiasm for the Bayreuth Master [Wagner] knew no bounds. Again and again I was drawn to hear his operas; and today I consider it a great stroke of luck that these modest productions in the little provincial city made it possible for me to appreciate it more intensely later on.

But all this helped to reinforce my profound distaste for the career that my father had chosen for me. This dislike became especially strong after I outgrew my adolescence—a process that was, in my case, especially painful. I became more and more convinced that I'd never be happy as a state official. And now that the *Realschule* had acknowledged my aptitude for drawing, my own resolution became all the stronger.

Thereafter, neither pleas nor threats could change things.

I wanted to become a painter, and no power in the world could force me to become a civil servant.

Oddly though, as I grew older, I became more and more interested in architecture.

At the time, I considered this a natural development of my talent for painting, and I inwardly rejoiced at this expansion of my artistic interests.

I didn't suspect that things would turn out differently.

THE ESSENTIAL MEIN KAMPF

THE DEATH OF MY PARENTS (section 1.10)

The question of my career was decided much sooner than I could have expected.

When I was 13, I suddenly lost my father. He was still in robust health when a stroke of apoplexy painlessly ended his earthly wanderings, and left us all deeply bereaved. His deepest wish was to be able to help his son advance in a career and thus to save me from the harsh ordeal that he himself had experienced. It appeared to him that he had failed. And yet, though he himself was not conscious of it, he had sown the seeds of a future that neither of us foresaw at that time.

At first, nothing changed outwardly.

My mother felt it her duty to continue my education in accordance with my father's wishes. This meant that she would have me study for the civil service. For my own part, I was more determined than ever to not undertake this career. The school curriculum and teaching methods were so far removed from my ideals that I became profoundly indifferent.

Illness suddenly came to my assistance. Within a few weeks, it decided my future, putting an end to the long-standing family conflict. My lungs became so seriously affected that the doctor strongly advised my mother not to allow me to take up a career that would require working in an office. He ordered me to stop attending the *Realschule* for at least a year. What I had secretly desired for such a long time, and had persistently fought for, now became a reality almost at one stroke.

Concerned about my illness, my mother agreed that I would leave the *Realschule* and attend the Academy.

Those were happy days, and they seemed to me almost as a dream; but they were bound to remain only a dream. Two years later, my mother's death put a brutal end to all my wonderful plans.

She succumbed to a long and painful illness, one that, from the very beginning, permitted little hope of recovery. Though expected, her death came as a terrible blow to me. I respected my father, but I loved my mother.

Poverty and hard reality forced me to decide quickly. The meager family resources had been almost entirely used up by my mother's severe illness. The allowance which came to me as an orphan was not enough for the bare necessities of life. Somehow or other, I would have to earn my own bread.

—1—

With my clothes and linen in hand, and with an indomitable resolution in my heart, I left for Vienna. I hoped to forestall fate, as my father had done 50 years before. I was determined to become 'something'—but certainly not a civil servant.

— 2 —
YEARS OF STUDY AND SUFFERING IN VIENNA

When my mother died, my fate had already been decided, at least in one respect.

During the last months of her illness, I went to Vienna to take the entrance examination for the Academy of Fine Arts. Armed with a pile of drawings, I was sure that I would pass the examination quite easily. At the *Realschule*, I was by far the best student in the drawing class, and since that time I made exceptional progress in the practice of drawing. I was therefore quite pleased with myself, and was proud and happy at the prospect of what I considered to be a sure success.

But there was one misgiving. It seemed to me that I was better qualified for drawing than for painting, especially in the various branches of architectural drawing. At the same time, my interest in architecture was constantly growing. And I advanced more quickly in this direction after my first visit to Vienna, which lasted two weeks; I was not yet 16 years old.

I went to the Court Museum to study the paintings in the art gallery there; but the building itself captured almost all my interest, and from early morning until late at night I spent all my time visiting the various public buildings. And it was always the buildings themselves that were the main attraction for me. I stood for hours in wonderment at the Opera and the Parliament. The whole Ring Strasse had a magic effect upon me, as if it were a scene from the *Thousand-and-one-Nights*.

SKILL AS AN ARCHITECT (section 2.1)

And now here I was, for the second time in this beautiful city, impatiently waiting to hear the result of the entrance exam but confident of success. I was so convinced that, when the news came that I had failed, it struck me like a bolt from the blue. Yet that's what happened. I went to see the Rector and asked him why they refused to accept me as a student in the general School of Painting, which was part of the Academy. He said that my sketches unquestionably showed that painting was not what I was suited for, but rather that they gave clear indications of my aptitude for architectural design. Therefore the place for me was the School of Architecture, which also formed part of the Academy. At first it was impossible to understand this, seeing that I had never been to an architectural school and had never received any instruction in architectural design.

I was quite dejected when I left Hansen Palace, on Schillerplatz. I felt at odds with myself for the first time in my young life. Those words came like a lightning flash, one that revealed a longstanding conflict within myself. But until this point, I couldn't give a clear account of it.

Within a few days, I myself also realized that I would become an architect.

But of course, the path was very difficult. I now bitterly regretted my former conduct in neglecting and despising certain subjects at the *Realschule*. Before taking up courses at the School of Architecture, it was necessary to attend the Technical Building School. But this in turn required a graduation certificate from high school. And I simply didn't have this. The fulfillment of my artistic dream seemed impossible.

After my mother's death, I came to Vienna for the third time. This visit was destined to last several years. Having been there before, I quickly recovered my old calm and determination. My former self-assurance came back, and I fixed my eyes steadily on the goal. I would be an architect. Obstacles are placed in our path in life, not to defeat us but to be surmounted. And I was fully determined to surmount these obstacles, constantly holding the picture of my father in my mind—he who raised himself up by his own efforts to the position of a civil servant, even though he was the poor son of a village shoemaker. I had a better start, and my odds of success were better. At that time, my lot in life seemed to me a harsh one; but today I see in it the wise workings of Providence. The Goddess of Fate took me in her arms and often threatened to smash me; but my will grew stronger as the obstacles increased, and in the end, my will was triumphant.

—2—

I'm thankful for that period of my life because it hardened me and enabled me to be as tough as I am now. And even more so, because I appreciate the fact that I was thereby saved from an empty life of ease, and that a mother's darling was taken from her tender arms and handed over to Adversity as a new mother. Though I fought against it as too hard a fate, I'm grateful that I was thrust into a world of misery and poverty, and thus came to know the people for whom I was later to fight.

FORMATION OF A WORLDVIEW (section 2.2)

It was during this time that my eyes were opened to two dangers, the names of which I had scarcely known before. I had no idea whatsoever of their terrible significance for the existence of the German people. These two dangers were *Marxism* and *Jewry*.

For many people, the name of Vienna signifies innocent pleasure, a festive place for happy people. For me, unfortunately, it's a living memory of the saddest period in my life.

Even today, the mention of that city arouses in me only gloomy thoughts. Five years of poverty in that Phaecian town.[1] Five years in which I had to earn my daily bread—first as a casual laborer and then as a painter of little trifles. And a meager morsel it was indeed, insufficient to calm my constant hunger. That hunger was my faithful guardian, one that never left me and took part in everything I did. Every book that I bought meant renewed hunger, and every visit to the opera meant the intrusion of that inhospitable companion in the days to follow. I was always struggling with my unsympathetic friend. Even so, it was during that time that I learned more than ever before. Apart from my architectural studies and rare visits to the opera—for which I had to go hungry—I had no other pleasure in life except my books.

I read a great deal then, and I thought deeply about what I read. All my free time after work was devoted exclusively to study. Thus within a few years, I was able to acquire a stock of knowledge that I find useful even to this day.

But even more than that:

---

[1] A reference to Homer's *Odyssey* (Book VI). Phaeacia, or Scheria, was an island of legendary happiness, where residents preferred the pursuit of pleasure to hard work.

During those years, a view of life and a definite worldview took shape in my mind. These became the granite foundation of my conduct at that time. Since then, I have extended that foundation only very little, and I have changed nothing in it.

On the contrary.

I am firmly convinced today that, generally speaking, it is in youth that men lay the essential groundwork of their creative thought, wherever that creative thought exists. I distinguish between the wisdom of age—which can only arise from the greater profundity and foresight that are based on the experiences of a long life—and the creative genius of youth. The latter blossoms out in thought and ideas with inexhaustible fertility, without being immediately useful, because of their very exuberance. These ideas furnish the building materials and plans for the future. And it is from them that age takes the stones and constructs the building—unless the so-called wisdom of age smothers the creative genius of youth. ...

ARCHITECT AND WATERCOLOR PAINTER (section 2.11)

As soon as my interest in social questions was awakened, I began to study them in a fundamental way. A new and previously unknown world was thus revealed to me.

In the years 1909-10, I had so improved my position that I no longer had to earn my daily bread as a manual laborer. I was now working independently as a draftsman and painter in watercolors. This career was a poor one indeed, at least as far as earnings were concerned. I barely had enough to meet the necessities of life. Yet it was interesting for me, in light of the profession that I aspired to.

Moreover, when I came home in the evenings, I was now no longer dead-tired as before, when I was unable to glance at a book without falling asleep almost immediately. My present work was therefore aligned with my future profession. Furthermore, I was master of my own time, and could distribute my working-hours better now than before.

I painted to make a living, and I studied for pleasure.

Thus I was able to acquire theoretical knowledge of the social problem, something that was a necessary complement to what I was learning

— 2 —

through daily experience. I studied all the books I could find that dealt with this question, and I thought deeply about what I read.

I believe that those around me considered me an eccentric person.

Apart from my interest in the social question, I naturally devoted myself with enthusiasm to the study of architecture. Along side music, I considered it queen of the arts. It was pleasure, not work, to study it. I could read or draw until late at night without ever getting tired. And I became more and more confident that my dream of a brilliant future would become true, even though I might have to wait years to achieve it. I was firmly convinced that one day I would make a name for myself as an architect.

The fact that, along side my professional studies, I took the greatest interest in everything political did not seem to be especially important. On the contrary—I looked upon this practical interest in politics as the obvious duty of every thinking man. Those who have no understanding of the political world around them have no right to criticize or complain.

I therefore continued to read and study politics extensively.

THE ART OF READING (section 2.12)

Reading, however, had a different meaning for me than it has for the average run of our so-called 'intellectuals.'

I know people who read endlessly, book after book, from cover to cover, and yet I would not call them 'well-read.' Of course they 'know' an immense amount; but their brain seems incapable of sifting and organizing the information they have acquired. They don't have the ability to distinguish between what is useful and what is useless. They may retain the former in their minds and, if possible, skip over the latter while reading it—and if that's not possible, they will throw it overboard as useless ballast.

Reading is not an end in itself, but a means to an end. Its chief purpose is to help towards filling in the framework that comprises each person's talents and abilities. Thus each one acquires for himself the tools and materials needed for the fulfillment of his life's work—regardless whether this is the elementary task of earning one's daily bread or a calling that responds to higher human aspirations. Such is the first purpose of reading. And the second purpose is to provide an overall worldview.

THE ESSENTIAL MEIN KAMPF

In both cases, however, the information acquired through reading must not be stored up in the memory, corresponding to the successive chapters of the book. Rather, each little piece of knowledge thus gained must be treated as if it were a stone to be inserted into a mosaic, so that it finds its proper place among all the other elements that form a general worldview in the reader's mind. Otherwise only a confused jumble of chaotic notions will result from all this reading. That jumble is not merely useless, but it also tends to make the unfortunate possessor of it conceited. He seriously thinks himself to be well-educated, and that he understands something of life. He believes that he has acquired knowledge, whereas the truth is that every increase in such 'knowledge' draws him further away from real life—until he finally ends up either in some sanitorium or in parliament.

Such a person never succeeds in making practical use of his knowledge when the moment calls for it. His mental equipment is not organized to meet the demands of everyday life. His knowledge is stored in his brain as a literal transcript of the books he has read, and in the order in which he has read them. And if fate should one day call upon him to use his book-knowledge, it will have to give him the title and page number—otherwise he will never be able to recall the needed information. But if the page is not mentioned at the critical moment, the bright boy will find himself in a state of hopeless embarrassment. Highly agitated, he searches for comparable cases, and it is almost certain that he will finally deliver the wrong prescription.

If that's an incorrect description, then how can we explain the political achievements of our parliamentary heroes, who hold the highest positions in government? Otherwise we would have to attribute their actions to malice and chicanery, rather than to pathology.

On the other hand, one who has cultivated the art of reading will instantly perceive, in a book or journal or pamphlet, what should be remembered—either because it meets one's needs or it has value in general. What he thus learns is incorporated into his mental picture of a problem or a thing, further correcting or enlarging it, so that it becomes more exact and precise. If some practical problem suddenly demands examination or a solution, memory will immediately select the appropriate information from the mass that has been acquired through years of reading. Memory will also place this information at the service of one's powers of judgment, so as to get a new and clearer view of the problem in question, or to produce a definitive solution.

Only thus can reading have any meaning or purpose.

For example, a speaker who does not have at hand the sources of information that are necessary to a proper treatment of his subject is unable to defend his opinions against an opponent, even though those opinions may be perfectly solid and true. In every discussion, his memory will abandon him. He cannot summon up arguments to support his statements, or to refute his opponent. As long as the speaker only has to defend himself, the situation is not serious; but the evil comes when fate places such a know-it-all—who in reality knows nothing—in charge of a State.

From my earliest youth, I tried to read books in the right way, and I was fortunate to have good memory and intelligence to assist me. From that point of view, my time in Vienna was particularly useful and profitable. My experiences of everyday life there were a constant stimulus to study the most varied problems in new ways. Inasmuch as I was in a position to put theory to the test of reality—and reality to the test of theory—I was protected from the danger of pedantic theorizing on the one hand and, on the other, from being too impressed by superficial aspects of reality.

The experience of everyday life at that time forced me to make a fundamental theoretical study of the two most important questions—apart from the social question.

It is impossible to say when I might have begun to make a thorough study of the doctrine and characteristics of Marxism, were it not for the fact that I ran head-first into the problem! ...

THE KEY TO SOCIAL DEMOCRACY (section 2.19)

What I knew of Social Democracy[2] in my youth was precious little—and for the most part, wrong. ... The more I became acquainted with the external forms of Social Democracy, the greater was my desire to understand the inner nature of its doctrines.

---

[2] Formally called the Social Democratic Workers' Party of Austria (*Sozialdemokratische Arbeiterpartei Österreichs*), or SDAPÖ. The party was founded in 1889 by a Jewish doctor, Victor Adler (1852-1918). From the beginning, it was allied to Marxism.

THE ESSENTIAL MEIN KAMPF

Official party literature was not very useful. On economic questions, its statements were false and its proofs unsound. In treating of political aims, its attitude was insincere. Furthermore, its modern methods of chicanery in the presentation of its arguments were profoundly repugnant to me. Its flamboyant sentences, its obscure and incomprehensible phrases, pretended to contain great thoughts, but they were devoid of thought, and meaningless. One would have to be a decadent urban Bohemian in order to be comfortable in that maze of aberrant reasoning, so that he might discover an 'inner experience' amid this dung-heap of literary Dadaism. They were obviously counting on the proverbial humility of certain of our people, who believe that incomprehensibility equals wisdom.

In confronting the theoretical falsity and absurdity of that doctrine with the reality of the phenomenon, I gradually acquired a clear picture of its aims.

At such times, I was overcome by dark forebodings and fear of something evil. I saw before me a teaching inspired by egoism and hatred, mathematically calculated to win a victory—but the triumph of which would be a mortal blow to humanity.

Meanwhile, I discovered the relationship between this destructive teaching and the specific character of a people who, up to that time, were almost completely unknown to me.

THE JEWISH QUESTION (section 2.20)

Knowledge of the Jews is the only key whereby one may understand the inner nature, and therefore the real aims, of Social Democracy.

The man who comes to know this race succeeds in removing a veil from his eyes, one that shows the aims and meaning of this party in a false light. And then, out of the fog and mist of socialist phrases, rises the grinning figure of Marxism.

It is difficult, if not impossible, for me to now say when the word 'Jew' first began to raise any particular thought in my mind. I don't remember even having heard the word at home during my father's lifetime. If it were mentioned in a derogatory sense, I think the old man would just have considered those who used it to be culturally backward. In his career, he

— 2 —

became more or less a cosmopolitan, with strong views on nationalism, which had its effect on me as well.

In school, too, I found no reason to change the picture of things I had formed at home.

At the *Realschule*, I knew one Jewish boy. We were all on guard in our relations with him; his reticence and certain of his actions warned us to be discreet. Beyond that, my schoolmates and I had no particular opinions about him.

It was not until I was 14 or 15 years old that I frequently ran up against the word 'Jew,' partly in connection with political controversies. These references aroused a mild distaste in me, and an uncomfortable feeling always came over me when I had to listen to religious disputes.

But at that time, I had no other feelings about the Jewish Question.

There were very few Jews in Linz. Over the centuries, the Jews who lived there had become Europeanized in external appearance, and were so much like other people that I even looked upon them as Germans. The reason why I didn't then perceive the absurdity of such an illusion was that I saw no other distinguishing feature but the strange religion. I believed that they were persecuted on account of their faith, and my aversion at hearing such remarks nearly grew into a feeling of abhorrence.

I hadn't the slightest idea that there could be such a thing as a systematic anti-Semitism.

Then I came to Vienna.

Preoccupied by the mass of impressions I received from the architectural surroundings, and depressed by my own troubles, I did not at first distinguish the different social strata of that huge city. Although Vienna then had about 200,000 Jews among its population of 2 million, I didn't notice them.[3] During my first few weeks there, my eyes and my mind were unable to cope with the onrush of new ideas and values. Not until I gradually became accustomed to my surroundings, and the confused picture began to grow clearer, did I gain a more discriminating view of my new world. It was then that I came upon the Jewish Question.

I won't say that the manner of my initial acquaintance with it was particularly unpleasant. I saw in the Jew only a man of a different religion.

---

[3] Jewish population in Vienna was just 6,000 in 1860, but increased rapidly in the latter half of the 19th century: 40,200 in 1870; 118,000 in 1890; and 147,000 in 1900. By 1922, it was over 200,000.

THE ESSENTIAL MEIN KAMPF

Therefore, on grounds of human tolerance, I opposed the idea that he should be attacked because he had a different faith. And so I considered the anti-Semitic press in Vienna to be unworthy of the cultural traditions of a great people. The memory of certain events that happened in the Middle Ages came to mind, and I felt that they should not be repeated.[4] Generally speaking, these anti-Semitic newspapers did not have a good reputation—though at the time, I didn't understand why—and so I regarded them more as the products of jealousy and envy rather than the expression of a sincere, though perhaps mistaken, outlook.

THE SO-CALLED WORLD PRESS (section 2.21)

My own opinions were confirmed by what I considered to be the infinitely more dignified manner in which the big papers replied to those attacks—or even better, simply ignored them.

I diligently read the so-called 'world press'—*Neue Freie Presse, Wiener Tagblatt*, etc.[5]—and I was astonished by the abundance of information they gave their readers, and the impartial way that they presented particular problems. I appreciated their dignified tone. But sometimes the flamboyant style was unconvincing, and I didn't like it. Even so, I attributed all this to the overpowering influence of the whole metropolis.

Since I considered Vienna at that time as just such a world metropolis, I thought this fact sufficient to excuse these shortcomings of the press.

But I was frequently disgusted by the undignified manner in which this press curried favor with the Court. Scarcely a move took place at the Hofburg that was not presented to the reader in glorified colors. It was a foolish practice, one that—especially when it had to do with 'The Wisest

---

[4] Jews were expelled from several European countries in the Middle Ages, including England (1290), France (1306), Spain (1492), and Italy (1593). They were initially expelled from Vienna in 1420. A second expulsion occurred in 1669, under Leopold I. The 1782 'Edict of Tolerance' permitted Jews to return to Austria and granted them limited civil rights.

[5] The *Neue Freie Presse* was co-founded by a Jewish journalist, Max Friedländer, in 1864. Among its correspondents were notorious Zionists Max Nordau and Theodor Herzl. During Hitler's day, the paper was run by the Jewish businessman Moriz Benedikt. The *Wiener Tagblatt* was run by a Jewish industrialist, Rudolf Sieghart.

Monarch of all Time'—reminded me of the mating dance of the mountain cock.

The whole thing seemed artificial.

In my eyes, it was a stain on the ideal of liberal democracy.

To curry favor at the Court like this, and in such an indecent manner, was unworthy of the nation.

This was the first shadow to darken my appreciation of the 'great' Vienna press.

CRITICISM OF KAISER WILHELM II (section 2.22)

While in Vienna, I continued to follow all the events that were taking place in Germany with an ardent zeal—regardless if they were political or cultural questions. I had a feeling of pride and admiration when I contrasted the rise of the young Reich with the decline of the Austrian state. But even though the Reich's overall foreign policy was pleasing, the internal political situation was not always so good.

I didn't approve of the struggle against Wilhelm II.[6] I regarded him not only as the German Emperor but, above all, as the creator of the German Navy. The fact that the Kaiser was prohibited from speaking in the Reichstag made me very angry, because the prohibition came from those with no authority to do so. At a single sitting, those same parliamentary imbeciles cackled together more than did the whole dynasty of emperors—even including the weakest—in the course of centuries.

I was outraged that, in a nation where any half-wit could claim for himself the right to criticize others as a 'legislator' in the Reichstag, the bearer of the imperial crown was himself subject to reprimand by the most miserable assembly of drivellers that has ever existed.

I was even more disgusted at the way this same Viennese press pandered to the every rickety horse in the Court, and then flew into wild ecstasies of joy if he wagged his tail in response. At the same time, these very newspapers displayed anxiety at anything to do with the German Emperor—all the while trying to hide their enmity. But to me, it was poorly cloaked. Of course, they denied any intention of meddling in Germany's internal affairs—God forbid.

---

[6] Kaiser Wilhelm II (1859-1942) ruled Germany as its last emperor from 1888 to 1918. He was effectively forced to abdicate at the close of WWI.

They pretended that, by touching these wounds in a friendly way, they were both fulfilling the duties of the mutual alliance between the two countries and were also meeting their journalistic obligations. Having thus excused themselves, they then poked their finger ruthlessly into the wound.

That sort of thing made my blood boil.

I then began to be increasingly on guard when reading the great Viennese press.

TRANSFORMATION INTO AN ANTI-SEMITE (section 2.23)

I had to acknowledge, however, that on such subjects, one of the anti-Semitic papers—the *Deutsche Volksblatt*—acted more decently.

One thing that got on my nerves was the disgusting manner in which the big newspapers cultivated admiration for France. One really had to feel ashamed of being a German when confronted by those saccharine hymns of praise for 'the great cultural nation.' This wretched Francophilia more than once made me throw away one of those 'world newspapers.' On such occasions, I often turned to the *Volksblatt*, which was much smaller in size but which treated such subjects more decently. I disagreed with its sharp anti-Semitic tone; but I found, again and again, that its arguments gave me grounds for serious thought.

Anyhow, it was as a result of such readings that I came to know the man and the movement that determined Vienna's fate. These were Dr. Karl Lueger and the Christian Socialist Movement.[7]

When I arrived in Vienna, I was opposed to both.

I viewed both the man and the movement as 'reactionary.'

But even an elementary sense of justice forced me to change my opinion when I had the opportunity to know the man and his work. Slowly, as I developed a stronger basis for judgment, that opinion grew into outspoken admiration. Today, more than ever, I hold this man Lueger as the preeminent type of German mayor.

So many of my basic principles were overthrown by this change in my attitude towards the Christian-Socialist movement!

---

[7] Karl Lueger (1844-1910) was the popular mayor of Vienna from 1897 to his death in 1910. He was also co-founder, in 1891, of the Christian Socialist Party of Austria. From 1920 onward, Christian Socialism was the dominant party in Austria. Upon the *Anschluss* with Germany in 1938, the party was dissolved.

— 2 —

My ideas about anti-Semitism also changed in the course of time, and this was my most difficult transformation.

It cost me a great internal struggle, and it was only after a long battle between reason and sentiment that the former emerged victorious. Two years later, sentiment rallied to the side of reason and became its faithful guardian and advisor.

At the time of this bitter struggle between calm reason and my spiritual sentiments, the lessons that I learned on the Vienna streets proved to be invaluable. A time came when I no longer passed blindly along the streets of the mighty city; now my eyes were open to both buildings and human beings.

Once, while passing through the inner city, I suddenly encountered an apparition in a long caftan and wearing black hair-locks.

My first thought was: Is this a Jew?

They certainly didn't have this appearance in Linz. I watched the man stealthily and cautiously; but the longer I gazed at the strange face and examined it feature by feature, the more that my first question became a new question:

Is this a German?

As was always my habit in such cases, I turned to books for help in removing my doubts. For the first time in my life, I bought some anti-Semitic pamphlets for a few cents. But unfortunately they all began by assuming that the reader had at least some degree of knowledge about the Jewish question, or was at least familiar with it. Moreover, the tone of most of these pamphlets made me skeptical once again, both because they were partly superficial and because their 'proofs' were incredibly unscientific.

For weeks, and even months, I returned to my old way of thinking.

The subject appeared so enormous, and the accusations so far-reaching, that I was afraid of dealing with it unfairly; and so I again became anxious and uncertain.

Yet I could no longer doubt that this was not a question of Germans who happened to be of a different religion, but rather one of an entirely different people. As soon as I began to investigate the matter and observe the Jews, Vienna then appeared to me in a different light. Wherever I went, I saw Jews.[8] And the more I saw of them, the more strikingly and clearly

---

[8] By the 1920s, Jews were roughly 10 percent of the Viennese population—

they stood out as a different people from the other citizens. Especially the inner city and the districts north of the Danube, swarmed with a people who, even in outer appearance, had no similarity to the Germans.

Whatever doubts I may still have had at that point were finally removed by the activities of a certain section of the Jews themselves.

There was a great movement among them, well-represented in Vienna, and which strongly confirmed the national character of Jewry: this was *Zionism*.[9]

From outward appearances, it seemed as if only part of the Jews championed this movement, while the great majority disapproved of or even repudiated it. But a close examination showed that those appearances were deliberately misleading. They emerged from a fog of theories that were produced for reasons of expediency, if not outright deception. The so-called liberal Jews did not reject the Zionists as if non-Jews, but only as brother Jews with an impractical or even dangerous way of promoting Jewry.

There was no real conflict in their inner nature.

This fictitious conflict between the Zionists and the liberal Jews soon disgusted me; it was thoroughly false, and in direct contradiction to the moral dignity and immaculate character on which that people had always prided itself.

Cleanliness, whether moral or otherwise, has its own peculiar meaning for these people. That they were not water-lovers was obvious upon first glance, and unfortunately, often also when not looking at them at all. The odor of those people in caftans often made me sick to my stomach.[10] Beyond that, there were the unkempt clothes and the generally ignoble appearance.

---

though in certain districts, they exceeded 50 percent.

[9] Zionism may be defined as the movement to establish a Jewish homeland in Palestine. It was founded in 1899, and rapidly grew during the first few decades of the 20th century.

[10] There is a long history of negative commentary on 'the Jewish stench,' dating back to the Roman poet Martial (ca. 100 AD). Among the more recent commentators was Arthur Schopenhauer, who issued a number of biting remarks on the "*foetor Judaicus*."

— 2 —

All these details were certainly not attractive. But the truly revolting feature was that, beneath their unclean exterior, one suddenly perceived the moral rot of this 'chosen people.'[11]

What soon gave me cause for serious thought, with a slowly rising insight, were the activities of the Jews in certain fields of life.

Was there any shady undertaking, any form of nastiness—especially in cultural life—in which at least one Jew did not participate?[12]

On putting the probing knife carefully to that kind of abscess, one immediately discovers, like a maggot in a rotting corpse, often blinded by the dazzling light: a little Jew.

In my eyes, the charge against Jewry became a grave one the moment I discovered their activities in the press, art, literature, and the theater. All protests to the contrary were now essentially futile. One needed only to look at the posters announcing the monstrous productions of the cinema and theater, and study the names of the authors who were so highly praised there, in order to become permanently unwavering.

Here was a pestilence, a *moral* pestilence, with which the public was being infected—one worse than the Black Death. And in what mighty doses this poison was manufactured and distributed! Naturally, the lower the moral and intellectual level of such artists, the more inexhaustible their fecundity. Sometimes it happened that these fellows, acting like a sewage pump, would spew their filth directly in the face of humanity. We must recall that there is no limit to the number of such people. One must realize that, for every Goethe, nature may bring into existence 10,000 despoilers, who act as germ-carriers of the worst sort, poisoning human souls.

---

[11] "For you are a people holy to the LORD your God. The LORD your God has chosen you to be a people for his own possession, out of all the peoples that are on the face of the earth" (Deut 7:6). The idea of a people being "chosen" by God was a religious innovation of Judaism; no other religion was so self-centered. It naturally prompted Jews to think of themselves as special, different, and better than others. And it led directly to the idea that the Jews harbored "a hatred of all mankind"—a view noted by Hecateus, Tacitus, and many other observers over the centuries. See Dalton (2011) for an elaboration.

[12] Jews have long been prominent in ethically dubious industries, including usury, slavery, war-profiteering, alcohol, drugs, gambling, and pornography. For details, see Davis (2012), Nation of Islam (1991), Gertzman (1999), Darkmoon (2014), and Joyce (2015).

THE ESSENTIAL MEIN KAMPF

It was a terrible thought—and yet it couldn't be avoided, that most of the Jews seemed particularly destined by nature to play this shameful role.

Is this why they can be called 'the chosen people'?

I then began to carefully investigate the names of all the fabricators of these filthy cultural products. As a result, I became even more disgusted with the Jews than I was previously. Even if my feelings might resist a thousand times, reason now had to draw its own conclusions.

The fact was that 90 percent of all the filthy literature, artistic trash, and theatrical idiocy had to be charged to the account of a people who formed scarcely one percent of the nation. This fact could not be denied. It was there, and had to be admitted.

Then I began to examine my beloved 'world press' from a different point of view.

The deeper I probed, the lesser grew my respect for that press that I formerly admired. Its style became even more repellent, and I was forced to reject its ideas as entirely shallow and superficial. The claim that it impartially presented facts and ideas was more lie than truth. And the writers were—Jews.

Thousands of details that I scarcely noticed before now came to deserve new attention. I began to grasp and understand things differently than I had before.

I now saw the liberal press in a different light. Its dignified tone in replying to its opponents' attacks, and its dead silence on other issues, now became clear to me as part of a cunning and despicable way of deceiving the reader. Its brilliant theatrical criticisms always praised the Jewish authors, whereas its negative criticism was reserved exclusively for the Germans. The gentle pinpricks against Wilhelm II showed the persistency of its policy, as did its systematic praise of French culture and civilization. The subject matter of the short story was trashy and often indecent. The entire language of this press had the accent of a foreign people. The general tone was so openly derogatory to the Germans that it must have been intentional.

In whose interest was this?

Was all this merely an accident?

My doubts gradually increased.

— 2 —

THE JEW AS LEADER OF SOCIAL DEMOCRACY (section. 2.24)

Then something happened that accelerated my insight. I began to see the deeper meaning of a whole series of events that were taking place. All these were inspired by a general concept of ethics and morals that were openly practiced by a majority of the Jews—one that had practical applications.

Here again, life on the streets taught me what evil really is.

The relationship of the Jews to prostitution and, even more, to human trafficking, could be studied here better than in any other West European city—with the possible exception of certain ports in southern France. Walking at night along the streets of the Leopoldstadt, at almost every turn, whether one wished it or not, one witnessed certain happenings that were unknown to most Germans—at least, until the war made it possible, or rather inevitable, to see such things on the Eastern front.

A cold shiver ran down my spine when I first realized that it was the cold-blooded, shameless, and calculating Jew who skillfully directed this revolting exploitation of the scum of the big city.

Then I became enraged.

I no longer hesitated about bringing up the Jewish question. No; now I sought it. As I learned to track down the Jew in many different spheres of cultural and artistic life—and in various manifestations of life everywhere—I suddenly found him where I least expected to.

I now realized that the Jews were the leaders of Social Democracy. With that revelation, the scales fell from my eyes. My long inner struggle was at an end.

In my relations with my fellow workers, I was often astonished at how easily and often they changed their opinions on the same questions—sometimes within a few days, and sometimes even within a few hours. I found it difficult to understand how men who were reasonable as individuals suddenly lost this ability as soon as they acted as a mass. This phenomenon often tempted me to despair. I argued with them for hours, and when I succeeded in bringing them to what I considered a reasonable way of thinking, I celebrated my success. But the next day, I found that it was all in vain. It was disgusting to have to begin all over again. Like an eternal pendulum, they would swing back to their absurd opinions.

THE ESSENTIAL MEIN KAMPF

All this was understandable. They were dissatisfied with their lot and cursed the fate that hit them so hard. They hated their employers, whom they looked upon as the heartless administrators of their cruel destiny. They often used abusive language against public officials, whom they accused of being completely unsympathetic to the situation of working people. They conducted public protests against the cost of living, and paraded through the streets in defense of their claims.

All this, at least, could be reasonably explained. But impossible to explain was the boundless hatred against their fellow citizen—how they disparaged their own nation, mocked its greatness, reviled its history, and dragged the names of its most illustrious men through the gutter.

This hostility towards their own kind, their own native land and home, was as irrational as it was incomprehensible. It was deeply unnatural.

One could temporarily cure this malady, but only for a few days or some weeks. But upon later meeting those were converted, one found that they were the same as before.

That unnatural illness once again possessed them.

I gradually discovered that the Social Democratic press was predominantly controlled by Jews. But I didn't attach special importance to this circumstance because the same state of affairs existed in the other newspapers. But there was one striking fact: not a single newspaper connected to the Jews could be called 'national'—as I understood the term.

I swallowed my disgust and tried to read this type of Marxist press; but in doing so, my revulsion increased all the more. I then set about learning something of the people who wrote and published this mischievous stuff.

From the publisher on down, they were all Jews.

I grabbed all the Social Democratic pamphlets I could find, and checked the names of their authors: Jews. I noted the names of all the leaders; most of them were also members of 'the chosen people.' It didn't matter if they were representatives in the Reichsrat or trade union secretaries, organizational heads or street agitators. Everywhere it was always the same sinister picture. I'll never forget the list of names: Austerlitz, David, Adler, Ellenbogen, and others.[13]

---

[13] Friedrich Austerlitz (1862-1931) was a journalist, editor of the *Arbeiter-Zeitung*, and active SDAPÖ member. Wilhelm Ellenbogen (1863-1951) was a doctor, SDAPÖ activist, and member of the Austrian National Assembly. 'Adler' is

— 2 —

One fact became quite evident to me: that this alien people held in its hands the leadership of the Social Democratic Party, with whose minor representatives I had been disputing for months. I was happy to finally know for certain that the Jew is not a German.

Only then did I truly understand who the evil seducers of our people were.

A single year of my sojourn in Vienna sufficed to convince me that no worker is so rooted in his preconceptions that he will not surrender them to better and clearer arguments and explanations. Gradually I became an expert in Marxist doctrine. I used this knowledge as an instrument to drive home my own firm convictions.

Success was almost always on my side.

JEWISH DIALECTICS (section 2.25)

The great masses can be rescued, but only by sacrificing much time and patience.

But a Jew can never be parted from his opinions.

It was simple enough, at that time, to try to show them the absurdity of their teaching. Within my small circle, I talked to them until my throat ached and my voice grew hoarse. I believed that I could finally convince them of the danger inherent in Marxist foolishness. But I only achieved the contrary result. It seemed that the more they understood the destructiveness of Social-Democratic doctrine and its consequences, the more firmly they clung to it.

The more I debated with them, the more familiar I became with their argumentative tactics. At the outset they counted upon the stupidity of

ambiguous; it may refer to Victor Adler, founder of SDAPÖ; or his brother Max Adler (1873-1937), the noted Marxist; or Victor's son Friedrich Adler (1879-1960), secretary-general of SDAPÖ and member of the Austrian National Council (this latter Adler became well-known for assassinating a leading Austrian politician, Karl von Stürgkh, in 1916). The reference to 'David' is ambiguous and unknown.

Hitler might have mentioned other Jewish names as well: Helene Bauer, Otto Braun, Heinrich Braun, Julius Braunthal, Hugo Breitner, Robert Danneberg, Julius Deutsch, Gustav Eckstein, Rudolf Hilferding, Sigmund Kaff, Benno Karpeles, Oskar Pollak, Therese Schlesinger, Friedrich Stampfer, and Julius Tandler. All these individuals were "Social Democratic leaders with Jewish backgrounds" (Maderthaner and Silverman 2009: 79).

their opponents; but when they got so tied up that they couldn't find a way out, they played the trick of acting as innocent simpletons. Should that fail, in spite of their tricks of logic, they acted as if they couldn't understand the counter arguments, and jumped away to another topic of discussion. They stated truisms and platitudes; and if you accepted these, they applied them to other matters of an essentially different nature. If you pointed this out, they escaped again and avoided any precise statement. Whenever one tried to get a firm grip on one of these apostles, one's hand grasped only a jelly-like slime—that slipped through the fingers, and then recombined into a solid mass a moment later.

But if you really struck a blow on one of these adversaries and, due to the audience present, he had to concede the point, a surprise was in store for you the following day. The Jew would be utterly oblivious to what had happened the day before. He would start once again by repeating his former absurdities, as if nothing had happened. If you became indignant and reminded him of yesterday's defeat, he feigned astonishment, and couldn't remember a thing—except that on the day before, he was proven correct.

Sometimes I was simply dumbfounded.

I don't know what amazed me more: the agility of their speech or their art of lying.

I gradually came to hate them.

Yet all this had its good side. The more I came to know the individual leaders of Social Democracy, or at least the propagandists, the more my love for my own people grew. Considering the diabolical craftiness of these seducers, who could blame their unfortunate victims? How hard it was, even for me, to get the best of this race of dialectical liars! How futile it was to try to win over such people with argument, seeing how their mouths distorted the truth—disowning the very words they had just used, and then, a moment later, taking credit for them!

No. The more I came to know the Jew, the easier it was to excuse the workers.

In my opinion, the greatest guilt lay not with the workers but rather with those who didn't find it worthwhile to sympathize with their own people. They should have given the hard-working son of the national family what he was owed, and at the same time placed his seducer and corrupter up against the wall.

— 2 —

STUDY OF THE FOUNDATIONS OF MARXISM (section 2.26)

Urged by my own daily experiences, I now began to investigate more thoroughly the sources of Marxist doctrine. Its effects were well-known to me in detail. As a result of careful observation, its daily progress became obvious. And one needed only a little imagination in order to be able to predict the consequences that must result. The only question now was: Did the founders foresee the effects of their work in the form that they appeared, or were they themselves the victims of an error?

To my mind, both alternatives were possible.

If the latter case, it was the duty of every thinking person to oppose this sinister movement, hoping to avoid the worst results. But if the former were true, then it must be admitted that the original authors of this plague of nations must have been devils incarnate. For only in the brain of a monster, and not that of a man, could such a plan take shape—one whose workings must finally bring about the collapse of human civilization and the devastation of the world.

Such being the case, the only alternative left was to fight. This fight must employ all the weapons that the human spirit, intellect, and will can muster—leaving it to fate to decide who shall prevail.

And so I began to make myself familiar with the authors of this doctrine, in order to study the principles of the movement. The fact that I attained my objective faster than anticipated was due to the deeper insight that I had acquired into the Jewish Question—my prior knowledge having been rather superficial. This newly acquired knowledge, by itself, enabled me to make a practical comparison between the real content and the theoretical pretentiousness of the doctrine laid down by the apostolic founders of Social Democracy; I now understood the language of the Jewish people. I realized that they use language for the purpose of disguising or veiling their thought, so that their real aim cannot be discovered by what they say, but rather only by reading between the lines.

This insight was, for me, the greatest inner revolution that I had yet experienced.

From being a soft-hearted cosmopolitan, I became an out-and-out anti-Semite.

THE ESSENTIAL MEIN KAMPF

MARXISM AS DESTROYER OF CULTURE (section 2.27)

Only on one further occasion—and that for the last time—did oppressing thoughts arise that caused me some moments of profound anguish.

As I critically reviewed the historical activities of the Jewish people, I became anxious. I asked myself if, for some inscrutable reasons beyond mortal comprehension, destiny might not have irrevocably decreed that final victory must go to this little nation?

Is it possible that this people, which has lived only for the earth, was promised the earth as compensation?

Do we have an objective right to struggle for our own self-preservation, or is it merely a subjective thing?

Fate answered the question for me, insofar as it led me to make a detached and exhaustive inquiry into Marxist doctrine, and into the activities of the Jewish people in connection with it.

The Jewish doctrine of Marxism rejects the aristocratic principle of nature, substituting for it the eternal privilege of force and energy, numerical mass and dead weight. Thus it denies the individual value of the human personality, and impugns the idea that nationhood and race have primary significance. In doing so, it takes away the very foundations of human existence and culture.

If this doctrine were ever accepted as the foundation of the universe, it would lead to the disappearance of all conceivable order. Adopting such a law would provoke chaos in the structure of the greatest organism that we know—and the inhabitants of this earth would vanish.

If the Jew, with the aid of his Marxist creed, were to triumph over the people of this world, his crown will be the funeral wreath of mankind. And this planet will once again follow its orbit through space devoid of humanity, just as it did millions of years ago.

Eternal Nature inevitably avenges those who violate her commands.

Hence today I believe that I am acting in accordance with the will of the Almighty Creator: In defending myself against the Jew, I am fighting for the work of the Lord.

— 3 —
GENERAL POLITICAL REFLECTIONS FROM MY TIME IN VIENNA

PARLIAMENTARIANISM (section 3.8)

Among the institutions that most clearly showed unmistakable signs of decay, even to the weak-sighted Philistine, was that which, of all the institutions of state, should have been the most firmly founded—I mean the Parliament, or *Reichsrat* as it was called in Austria.

The pattern for this corporate body was obviously that which existed in England, the land of classic 'democracy.' The whole of that blissful organization was bodily transferred, unchanged, to Vienna.

An Austrian counterpart to the British two-chamber system was established: a Chamber of Deputies and a House of Lords. The 'houses' themselves, considered as buildings, were somewhat different. When Barry built his palaces on the shore of the Thames, he could look to the history of the British Empire for his inspiration.[1] In that history he found sufficient material to fill and decorate the 1,200 niches, brackets, and pillars of his magnificent edifice. The House of Lords and the House of Commons became temples dedicated to the glory of the nation.

This was when the first difficulty came for Vienna. When Hansen, the Danish architect,[2] completed the last gable of the marble palace, he turned to the ancient classical world for subjects to fill out his decorative plan.

---

[1] Charles Barry (1795-1860) designed and rebuilt the Houses of Parliament in the mid-1800s.

[2] Theophil Hansen (1813-1891).

THE ESSENTIAL MEIN KAMPF

This theatrical shrine of 'Western democracy' was adorned with the statues and portraits of Greek and Roman statesmen and philosophers. As if in symbolic irony, the horses of the *quadriga* atop the two Houses are pulling apart in all four directions. There could be no better symbol for the kind of activity going on within the walls of that very building.

The 'nationalities' were opposed to any kind of glorification of Austrian history in the decoration of this building; they insisted that it would constitute an offence to them. Much the same happened in Germany, where Wallot's Reichstag building was dedicated to the Germans only under the thunder of cannons in the World War—and then only in an inscription.

I was not yet 20 when I first entered the Palace on the *Franzensring* to watch and listen in the Chamber of Deputies. That first experience aroused in me a profound feeling of repugnance.

I always hated the Parliament, but not as an institution in itself. On the contrary, as one who cherished ideals of political freedom, I couldn't even imagine any other form of government. In light of my attitude towards the House of Habsburg, I would then have thought it a crime against liberty and reason to consider any kind of dictatorship as a possible form of government.

I had a certain admiration for the British Parliament, and this contributed to the formation of my opinion. This feeling came almost unconsciously, much of it while reading the newspapers when I was young. I couldn't discard that admiration in an instant. The dignified way in which the British House of Commons fulfilled its function impressed me greatly, thanks largely to the glowing terms used by the Austrian press. Could there could be any nobler form of government than self-government by the people?

But these considerations furnished the very basis of my hostility to the Austrian Parliament. The way it was represented here seemed unworthy of its great example. The following thoughts also influenced my attitude:

The fate of the Germans in the Austrian State depended on their position in the *Reichsrat*. Prior to the introduction of universal suffrage by secret ballot, the Germans had a majority in the *Reichsrat*—though not a very substantial one. This was a cause for concern because the Social-Democratic faction of the German majority was unreliable regarding national questions. In matters of critical concern to the Germans, the Social-Democrats always took an anti-German stand because they were afraid of losing support among the other national groups. Even before universal suffrage, the Social-Democratic Party could no longer be considered a German Party. Universal suffrage put an end even to the purely numerical dominance of the German element. The way was now clear for the further de-Germanization of the state.

My nationalist instinct of self-preservation made it impossible for me to welcome a system in which the German element was not really represented as such, but always betrayed by the Social-Democratic faction. Yet all these defects, and many others, could not be attributed to the parliamentary system as such, but rather to the Austrian State in particular. I still believed that if the German majority could be restored in the representative body, there would be no occasion to oppose such a system—as long as the old Austrian State continued to exist.

Such was my general attitude at the time when I first entered those sacred and contentious halls. For me, they were sacred only because of the radiant beauty of that majestic building. A Greek wonder on German soil.

But I soon became enraged by the hideous spectacle that met my eyes!

Several hundred representatives were there to discuss a problem of great economic importance, and each one had the right to have his say.

That experience of a single day was enough to supply me with food for thought during several weeks afterwards.

The intellectual level of the debate was quite low. Sometimes the debaters didn't make themselves intelligible at all. Several of those present didn't speak German, but only their Slav vernaculars or dialects. Thus I had the opportunity of hearing with my own ears what I had previously known only by reading the newspapers. A turbulent mass of people, all gesticulating and screaming at one another, with a pathetic old man shaking his bell and making frantic efforts to call the House to order by friendly appeals, exhortations, and grave warnings.[3]

---

[3] Interestingly, Mark Twain made a similar observation just a decade before. In the non-fiction essay "Stirring times in Austria" (1898), he lampoons the chaotic and sorry state of the Austrian parliament. Notably, he remarks on how all sides found the Jews to blame for their problems: "In all cases the Jew had to roast, no matter which side he was on" (p. 540). A follow-up essay, "Concerning the Jews" (1899), is also relevant for the discussion at hand.

THE ESSENTIAL MEIN KAMPF

I had to laugh.

I paid a second visit several weeks later. It was an entirely different picture—almost unrecognizable. The hall was nearly empty. They were sleeping in the other rooms below. Only a few deputies were in their places, yawning in each other's faces. One was 'speaking.' A deputy speaker was in the chair. He looked around with obvious boredom.

Then I began to reflect seriously on the whole thing. I went to the Parliament whenever I had any time to spare, and silently but attentively watched the spectacle. I listened to the debates, as far as they could be understood. And I studied the more or less intelligent features of those elected representatives of the various nationalities that composed that motley state. Gradually I formed my own ideas about what I saw.

A year of such quiet observation was sufficient to transform or completely eliminate my former convictions regarding the character of this institution. I no longer opposed merely the perverted form that the principle of parliamentary representation had assumed in Austria; no. It became impossible for me to accept the system in itself. Up to that time, I had believed that the disastrous deficiencies of the Austrian Parliament were due to the lack of a German majority. But now I recognized that the very essence and form of the institution itself was wrong.

A number of questions arose in my mind.

I studied the democratic principle of majority rule more closely. And I scrutinized no less carefully the intellectual and moral worth of the gentlemen who, as the chosen representatives of the nation, were entrusted with the task of making this institution function.

Thus I came to know both the institution itself and those in it.

And thus I formed a clear and vivid picture of a typical example of that most dignified phenomenon of our time: the parliamentarian. The picture of him that I then formed became deeply engraved on my mind, and I have never altered its essential character.

Once again, these object-lessons taken from real life saved me from getting firmly entangled by a theory that, at first glance, seems so alluring to many people—though that theory itself is a symptom of human decadence.

Western democracy, as practised today, is the forerunner of Marxism. In fact, the latter would be inconceivable without the former. Democracy is the breeding ground in which the bacilli of the Marxist world-pest can grow and spread. By the introduction of parliamentarianism, democracy produced an 'abomination of filth and fire'[4]—the creative fire of which, however, seems to have died out.

I'm very grateful to Fate that I noticed this problem when I was still in Vienna; if I had been in Germany at that time, I might easily have found only a superficial solution. If I had been in Berlin when I first discovered what an illogical institution 'parliament' is, I might easily have gone to the other extreme. I might have believed—as many did, and not without apparently good reason—that the salvation of the people and the empire could be secured only by restrengthening imperial authority. Those who believed didn't understand the tendencies of their time, and were blind to the aspirations of the people.

In Austria, this was impossible.

Here it wasn't so easy to fall from one error into another. If the Parliament was worthless, the Habsburgs were worse—or at least no better. The problem wasn't solved by rejecting the parliamentary system. A question immediately arose: What then? To repudiate and abolish the Vienna Parliament would have resulted in leaving all power in the hands of the Habsburgs. For me especially, that idea was unthinkable.

Since this problem was particularly difficult in regard to Austria, I was forced, while still quite young, to go more thoroughly into the essentials of the whole question than I would otherwise have done.

LACK OF RESPONSIBILITY (section 3.9)

The aspect of the situation that was most thought-provoking to me was the manifest lack of any individual responsibility.

The parliament takes an action that may have the most devastating consequences, and yet nobody bears responsibility for it. No one can be called to account. Can we call the government responsible if, in the face of a catastrophe, it simply resigns? Or if the coalition is changed, or even if parliament is dissolved?

Can a fluctuating majority of people ever be truly responsible for anything?

Isn't the idea of responsibility bound to an individual person?

---

[4] A reference to Goethe's *Faust* (part 1, line 5356).

Is it even possible to actually hold the parliamentary leaders accountable for any action that originated in the desires of the mass of representatives, and was carried out under their direction?

Instead of developing constructive ideas and plans, does the true statesman's business really consist in the art of making a whole pack of blockheads understand his projects? Is it really his job to beg and plead so that they will grant him their generous consent?

Is it really an indispensable quality in a statesman that he should possess a gift of persuasion commensurate with his ability to conceive great political measures, and to carry them through into practice?

Does it really prove that a statesman is incompetent if he should fail to win over a majority of votes in an assembly that has been called together as the chance result of an electoral system?

Has there ever been a case where such an assembly has worthily appraised a great political concept *before* that concept was proven a success?

In this world, isn't the creative act of genius always a protest against the inertia of the mass? And what should the statesman do if he doesn't succeed in coaxing the parliamentary mob to give its consent?

Should he buy it?

Or, when confronted with the obstinate stupidity of his fellow citizens, should he then refrain from pushing forward the vital necessities? Should he resign or remain in power?

In such a case, doesn't a man of character find himself face to face with an insoluble contradiction between knowledge and moral integrity—or better, his sense of honesty?

THE DESTRUCTION OF THE IDEA OF LEADERSHIP (section 3.10)

Where can we draw the line between public duty and personal honor?

Shouldn't every genuine leader renounce the idea of degrading himself to the level of a political gangster?

And, on the other hand, doesn't every gangster feel the itch to 'play politics,' seeing that the final responsibility will never rest with him personally but rather with an anonymous, unaccountable mob?

Doesn't our parliamentary principle of majority rule necessarily lead to the destruction of the idea of leadership?

— 3 —

Does anyone honestly believe that human progress originates in the brain of the majority, and not in the brain of the individual personality?

Or may it be presumed that future human civilization can dispense with this as a condition of its existence?

Or rather, doesn't this seem today to be more indispensible than ever?

The parliamentary principle of majority rule rejects the authority of the individual and puts a numerical quota of anonymous heads in its place. In doing so, it contradicts the aristrocratic principle, which is a fundamental law of nature—though it must be admitted that this principle is not reflected in the decadence of our upper 10,000.[5]

The devastating influence of this parliamentary institution might not easily be recognized by those who read the Jewish press, unless the reader has learned how to think independently and examine facts for himself. This institution is primarily responsible for the crowded inrush of mediocre people into the field of politics. Confronted with such a phenomenon, a man who is endowed with real qualities of leadership will be tempted to refrain from taking part in politics; under these circumstances, the situation doesn't call for a man who has a capacity for constructive statesmanship but rather for a man who is capable of bargaining for the favor of the majority. The situation appeals to small minds, and it attracts them accordingly.

The narrower the spirit and knowledge of our leather-handlers, the more accurately can they assess their own situation. They will therefore be all the more inclined to praise a system that doesn't demand creative genius or even high-class talent, but rather the craftiness of an efficient town clerk. Indeed, they value this kind of petty craftiness more than the political genius of a Pericles.[6] Such mediocrity never worries about responsibility. From the beginning, our parliamentarian knows that, whatever be the results of his 'statesmanship,' his end is already written in the stars; one day, he will have to clear out and make room for another equally great spirit.

It's a sign of our decadent times that the number of eminent statesmen grows as the caliber of individual personality dwindles. That caliber will inevitably shrink as the individual politician increasingly depends upon parliamentary majorities. A man of real political ability will refuse to be

---

[5] In other words, of the "1%".

[6] Pericles (ca. 495-429 BC) was one of the great Athenian statesmen.

the lackey of idiotic incompetents and big-mouths. And they in turn, being the representatives of the majority—and hence of stupidity—hate nothing so much as a superior mind.

For such an assembly of wise men, it's always a consolation to be led by a person whose intellectual stature is on par with their own. Thus each one may have the occasional opportunity to shine in debate; and above all, each one feels that he too may rise to the top. If Peter be boss today, then why not Paul tomorrow?

THE EXCLUSION OF THE INDIVIDUAL LEADER (section 3.11)

This invention of democracy is very closely connected with a peculiar phenomenon that has recently become a real disgrace—namely, the cowardice of a large section of our so-called political leaders. Whenever important decisions must be made, they always find themselves fortunate in being able to hide behind the so-called majority!

In observing one of these political manipulators, one notices how he begs the majority for their approval for whatever action he takes. He needs to have accomplices, in order to shift responsibility to other shoulders whenever it is convenient to do so. That's the main reason why this kind of political activity is abhorrent to men of character and courage. At the same time, it attracts inferior types; for a person who is not willing to accept responsibility for his own actions, but is always seeking to hide, is a cowardly scoundrel. Whenever a national leader comes from that low class of politicians, evil consequences will soon follow. No one will then have the courage to take a decisive step. They will submit to abuse and defamation rather than rise up and take a stand. And thus nobody is left who is willing to risk his position and his career, if necessary, in support of a determined line of policy.

One truth must always be kept in mind: the majority can never replace the man. The majority represents not only ignorance but also cowardice. And just as a hundred blockheads don't equal one wise man, so a hundred cowards are incapable of any heroic action.

The lighter the burden of responsibility on each individual leader, the greater will be the number of those who, in spite of their sorry mediocrity, will come to place their immortal energies at the service of the nation. They are so anxious that they find it hard to wait their turn. They stand in

— 3 —

a long line, painfully and sadly counting the number of those ahead of them, and calculating the hours until their turn comes. They watch every change in personnel, and they are grateful for every scandal that thins the ranks ahead of them.

And if someone sticks to his stool too long, they consider this as almost a breach of a holy pact of solidarity. They grow vindictive, and don't rest until that inconsiderate person is finally driven out and forced to hand over his cosy berth back to the public. After that, he will have little chance of getting another opportunity. Usually those creatures who have been forced to give up their posts try to get in line again, unless they are hounded away by the protests of the others.

The result of all this is that, in such a state, the succession of sudden changes in public offices has a very troubling effect in general, one that may easily lead to disaster. It's not only the ignorant and the incompetent person who may fall victim to those parliamentary conditions; the genuine leader may be affected just as much as the others, if not more so, whenever Fate has placed a capable man in a leadership position. If the superior quality of such a leader becomes recognized, it will result in a united front against him—particularly if that leader, though not coming from their ranks, should fall into the habit of intermingling with this exalted society. They want to have only their own types as company, and they will quickly take a hostile attitude towards any man who might show himself superior to them. Their instinct, which is so blind in other ways, is very sharp in this respect.

The inevitable result is that the intellectual level of the ruling class steadily declines. One can easily predict how much the nation and state are bound to suffer from such a condition—provided one doesn't belong to that same class of 'leaders.'

The parliamentary régime in the old Austria was the purest form of this institution.

Though the Austrian prime minister was appointed by the emperor and king, this act of appointment merely gave practical effect to the parliamentary will. The huckstering and bargaining that went on in regard to every ministerial position showed all the typical marks of Western democracy. The results that followed were in keeping with the principles applied. The intervals between the replacement of one person by another gradually became shorter, finally ending up in a veritable chase. With each change, the quality of the 'statesman' in question deteriorated, until finally only the petty type of political gangster remained. In such people, the qualities of statesmanship were measured and valued according to the skill with which they pieced together one coalition after another; in other words, their craftiness in manipulating the pettiest political transactions, which is the only kind of practical activity suited to the aptitudes of these representatives.

In this sphere, Vienna was the school that offered the most impressive examples.

Another feature that engaged my attention even more was the contrast between the talents and knowledge of these representatives of the people on the one hand and, on the other, the nature of the tasks they had to face. Willingly or unwillingly, one couldn't help thinking seriously of the narrow intellectual outlook of these chosen representatives of the various nationalities. And one couldn't avoid contemplating the methods through which these noble figures in our public life were first discovered.

It was worthwhile to make a thorough study of the way in which the real talents of these gentlemen were devoted to the service of their country—in other words, to thoroughly analyze the technical process of their activities.

The more I penetrated into the intimate structure of parliamentary life, and the more I studied the persons and principles of the system in a spirit of ruthless objectivity, the more deplorable it became. Indeed, it's mandatory to be strictly objective in the study of an institution whose sponsors speak of 'objectivity' as the only fair basis of examination and judgment. If one studied these gentlemen and the laws of their sordid existence, the results were surprising.

'PUBLIC OPINION' (section 3.12)

Objectively considered, there is no other principle that turns out to be quite so ill-conceived as parliamentarianism.

Here we may pass over the methods according to which the election of the representatives takes place, as well as the ways that bring them into office and bestow new titles on them. It is quite evident that public wishes are satisfied only to a small degree, by the manner in which an election takes place. Everyone who properly estimates the political intelligence of

— 3 —

the masses can easily see that it is insufficient to independently form a general political outlook, or to select the men who might be competent to carry out their ideas.

Whatever definition we may give of the term 'public opinion,' only a very small part of it originates from personal experience or individual insight. The greater portion results from the manner in which public matters have been presented to the people, through an overwhelmingly impressive and persistent system of 'information.'

In the theologial sphere, religious yearnings slumber in the soul, and the profession of a denominational belief is largely the result of education. So too, the political opinions of the masses are the final result of influences systematically operating on the human soul and intelligence, in light of a method that is applied with unbelievable thoroughness and perseverance.

By far the most effective branch of political education—that which is best expressed by the word 'propaganda'—is conducted by the press. The press is the chief means employed in the process of political 'enlightenment.' It represents a kind of school for adults. This educational activity, however, is not in the hands of the state but in the clutches of powers that are of a very inferior character.

While still a young man in Vienna, I had excellent opportunities for coming to know the men who owned this machine for mass instruction, as well as those who supplied it with ideas. At first I was quite surprised when I realized how little time was necessary for this great evil power within the state to produce a certain belief among the public. In doing so, the genuine will and convictions of the public were often completely misconstrued. It took the press only a few days to transform some ridiculously trivial matter into an issue of national importance—while vital problems were completely ignored or hidden away from public view.

The press succeeded in the magical art of producing names from nowhere within just a few weeks. They made it appear that the great hopes of the masses were bound up with those names. And so they made those names more popular than any man of real ability could ever hope for. All this was done, despite the fact that such names were utterly unknown, even up to a month before the press publicly extolled them.

At the same time, older figures in politics and other spheres of life quickly faded from the public memory, and were forgotten as if they were dead—though they were still vigorous and healthy. Or they were so vilely abused that it looked as if their names would soon stand as permanent symbols of villainy. To understand the really pernicious influence that the press can exercise, one must study this infamous Jewish method whereby honorable and decent people are besmirched with filth, in the lowest form of abuse and slander, from hundreds of directions simultaneously—as if by magic.

These spiritual robbers will grab at anything that might serve their evil ends.

They would poke their noses into the most intimate family affairs, and not rest until they had sniffed out some petty issue that could be used to destroy the victim's reputation. But even if nothing were discovered in the private or public life of the victim, they continued to hurl abuse at him in the belief that some of their charges would stick, even though refuted a thousand times. In most cases, it finally became impossible for the victim to continue his defense because the accuser worked together with so many accomplices that his slanders were repeated interminably.

But these slanderers would never admit that they were acting from motives that were believable or comprehensible to the common run of humanity. God forbid! The scoundrel who defamed his contemporaries in this villainous way would, like an octopus, cover himself with a cloud of respectability and clever phrases about his 'journalistic duty' and other such nonsense. When these pests gathered together in large numbers at meetings and congresses, they would dish out a lot of slimy talk about a special kind of 'honor'—namely, the professional honor of the journalist. Then the assembled species would bow their respects to one another.

This rabble fabricates more than two-thirds of the so-called public opinion, from whose foam the parliamentary Aphrodite eventually arises.[7]

THE MAJORITY PRINCIPLE (section 3.13)

Several volumes would be needed if one were to give an adequate account of all its hollow fallacies. But if we pass over the details and look at the product itself while in operation, I think this alone will suffice to

---

[7] The name 'Aphrodite' means literally 'foam-risen.' In Greek mythology, Aphrodite arose from the foam of the sea.

— 3 —

open the eyes of even the most innocent and naïve person, so that he may recognize the absurdity of this institution by looking at it objectively.

This human aberration is as harmful as it is absurd. In order to see this, the best and easiest method is to compare democratic parliamentarianism with a genuine German democracy.

The remarkable characteristic of the parliamentary form of democracy is the fact that a number of persons, let us say 500—these days, including women also—are elected to parliament and invested with authority to give final judgment on everything. In practice, they alone are the governing body; for although they may appoint a cabinet that outwardly seems to direct state affairs, this cabinet has no real existence of its own. In reality this so-called government can't do anything against the will of the assembly. It can never be called to account for anything, since the right of decision is not vested in the cabinet but in the parliamentary majority. The cabinet always functions only as the executor of the will of the majority. Its political ability can be judged only by how far it succeeds in adapting to the will of the majority, or in persuading the majority to agree to its proposals.

But this means that it must descend from the level of a real governing power to that of a beggar, one who has to beg for the approval of a majority. Indeed, the main job of the cabinet is to secure for itself the favor of the majority then in power or, failing that, to form a new majority that will be more favorably disposed. If it should succeed in either of these efforts, it may go on 'governing' for a little while. If it should fail to win or form a majority, it must resign. Whether its policy per se was right or wrong doesn't matter at all.

For all practical purposes, responsibility is abolished.

The consequences of such a state of affairs can easily be understood from the following simple considerations:

Those 500 deputies who have been elected by the people come from various dissimilar callings in life; they show widely varying degrees of political capacity, with the result that the whole picture is incoherent and deplorable. Surely nobody believes that these elected representatives of the nation are the choice spirits or first-class intellects! No one, I hope, is foolish enough to pretend that hundreds of true statesmen can emerge from papers placed in the ballot box by voters who are just of average intelligence.

THE ESSENTIAL MEIN KAMPF

The absurd notion that men of genius are born out of universal suffrage cannot be too strongly repudiated. In the first place, those times may be really called blessed when *one* genuine statesman appears among a people. Such statesmen don't appear by the hundreds or more. Secondly, the broad masses instinctively display a definite antipathy towards every outstanding genius. There's a better chance of a camel passing through the eye of a needle than of a truly great man being 'discovered' through an election.

Throughout world history, exceptional events have mostly been due to the driving force of an individual personality.

But here, 500 persons of sub-par intellectual qualities pass judgment on the most important problems affecting the nation. They form governments, that in turn learn to win the approval of the illustrious assembly for every legislative step—which means that the policy to be carried out is actually the policy of the 500.

And that's just what it usually looks like.

But let's pass over the intellectual qualities of these representatives and ask what is the nature of the task set before them. If we consider the fact that the problems to be addressed are variable and diverse, we can very well realize how inefficient a governing system must be that entrusts the right of decision to a mass assembly, one in which only very few possess the requisite knowledge and experience to properly deal with the matters. The most important economic measures are submitted to a tribunal in which not more than 10 percent have studied economics. This means that final authority is vested in men who are utterly devoid of any preparatory training that would make them competent to decide on the questions at hand.

The same holds true of every other problem. It's always a majority of ignorant and incompetent people who decide on each measure. The composition of the institution does not change, while the problems to be dealt with come from the most varied spheres of public life. An intelligent judgment would be possible only if different deputies had the authority to deal with different issues. It's out of the question to think that the same people are qualified to decide on transportation questions as well as, say, on questions of foreign policy—unless each is a universal genius. But scarcely more than one true genius appears in a century.

— 3 —

Here we are scarcely ever dealing with real thinkers, but only with dilettantes who are as narrow-minded as they are conceited and arrogant—intellectual prostitutes of the worst kind. That's why these honorable gentlemen show such astonishing levity in debating matters that would demand the most painstaking consideration, even from great minds. Measures of momentous importance for the future existence of the state are discussed in an atmosphere more suited to the card-table. Indeed, the latter would be a much more fitting occupation for these gentlemen than that of deciding the destinies of a race.

Of course, it would be unfair to assume that *every* member in such a parliament was endowed by nature with such a small sense of responsibility.

No, by no means.

THE DESTRUCTION OF CHARACTER (section 3.14)

But this system, by forcing the individual to pass judgment on questions for which he is not competent, gradually debases his moral character. Nobody will have the courage to say, "Gentlemen, I'm afraid we know nothing about what we are talking about. I for one have no competency in the matter at all." (Besides, if such a declaration were made, it wouldn't change matters very much; such outspoken honesty would not be understood. The person who made the declaration would be deemed an honorable ass who shouldn't be allowed to spoil the game.) Those who know human nature know that nobody likes to be considered a fool among his associates; and in certain circles, honesty is taken as a measure of stupidity.

Thus even a man who was originally honest, once he finds himself elected to parliament, may eventually be forced to acquiesce in a line of conduct that is base in itself, and which amounts to a betrayal of the public trust. This destroys every real sense of honor that might occasionally rise up in the conscience of one person or another. Finally, the otherwise upright deputy will succeed in persuading himself that he is by no means the worst of the lot, and that by playing along, he may prevent something worse from happening.

An objection may be raised here. It may be said that, of course, the individual member may not have a knowledge of what's required for addressing this or that question. But in such a case, the party sets up special committees of experts who have more than the required knowledge for dealing with the questions before them.

At first glance, that argument seems sound. But then another question arises: namely, why are 500 persons elected if only a few have the wisdom that is required to deal with the more important problems?

Yes—this is the worm in the apple.

JEWISH DEMOCRACY (section 3.15)

It isn't the aim of our modern democratic parliamentary system to bring together an assembly of intelligent and well-informed men. The aim rather is to bring together a group of non-entities who are dependent on others for their views, and who can be all the more easily led, the narrower their mental outlook. This is the only way that party policy—according to the evil meaning it has today—can be put into effect.

Only in this way is it possible for the wire-puller, who exercises real control, to remain in the dark, so that he personally can never be held accountable. Under such circumstances, none of the decisions taken, no matter how disastrous they may be, can be laid at the foot of the scoundrel who is truly to blame. All responsibility is shifted to the shoulders of the party as a whole.

In practice, no actual responsibility remains. It arises only from personal duty and not from the obligations that rest with a parliamentary assembly of empty talkers.

The parliamentary institution attracts liars and moles, people who shun the light of day. No upright man, who is ready to accept personal responsibility for his acts, will be attracted to such an institution.

That's the reason why this brand of democracy has become a tool in the hand of that race that, because of its inner goals, must shun the open light—as it has always done and always will do. Only the Jew can praise an institution which is as corrupt and false as himself.

By contrast, consider a truly German democracy. Here the leader is freely chosen and is obliged to accept full responsibility for all his actions and omissions. Problems are not put to a majority vote, but they are decided upon by the individual. As a guarantee of responsibility for those decisions, he pledges his worldly belongings, and even his life.

— 3 —

The objection may be raised here that, under such conditions, it would be very difficult to find a man who would be ready to devote himself to so risky a task. There is only one answer to that:

Thank God that our German democracy will prevent the chance careerist, who may be intellectually worthless and a moral slacker, from coming to power in devious ways. The fear of undertaking such far-reaching responsibilities, under German democracy, will scare off the ignorant and the incompetent.

But if it happens that such a person sneaks in, it will be easy enough to ruthlessly identify and challenge him—somewhat as follows: "Be gone, you scoundrel! Don't soil these steps with your feet; these are the steps of the Pantheon of History, and they are not meant for status-seekers but for men of noble character!"

Such were the views I formed after two years of attending the sessions of the Viennese Parliament.

Then I never went back. ...

ANTI-SEMITISM ON A RELIGIOUS BASIS (section 3.27)

The failure of this [Christian-Socialist] party to fulfill its dream of saving Austria from dissolution must be attributed to two main defects in the means they employed, and also the lack of clarity regarding the goal itself.

First: The anti-Semitism of the new movement was based on religious instead of racial principles. The reason for this mistake gave rise to the second error also.

The founders of the Christian-Socialist Party believed that they couldn't base their position on the racial principle if they wished to save Austria, because they felt that a general disintegration of the state might quickly result. In the opinion of the party chiefs, the situation in Vienna demanded that all factors that tended to estrange the nationalities from one another should be carefully avoided, and that all factors making for unity should be encouraged.

At that time, Vienna was so permeated with foreign elements, especially Czechs, that great tolerance was necessary if these elements were to be enlisted in any party that was not anti-German on principle. If Austria was to be saved, those elements were indispensable. And so attempts were made to win the support of the small traders—a great number of whom were Czechs—by combating liberal Manchesterism. And they believed that by adopting this attitude, they had found a slogan against Jewry that would unite all the different nationalities that made up the population of old Austria.

It was obvious, however, that this kind of anti-Semitism didn't upset the Jews very much, simply because it had a purely religious foundation. If worst came to worst, a few drops of baptismal water could always save the Jew and the business at the same time.

On such superficial grounds, it was impossible to deal with the whole problem in a serious and rational way. The result was that many people couldn't understand this kind of anti-Semitism, and therefore refused to join it. The attractive force of the idea was thus restricted exclusively to narrow-minded circles, because the leaders failed to go beyond the mere emotional appeal and didn't ground their position on a truly rational basis. The intellectuals were opposed to such a policy on principle. It looked more and more as if the whole movement was a new attempt to convert the Jews or, on the other hand, as if it merely wished to compete with other movements.

Thus the struggle lost all traces of having been organized for a higher spiritual mission. Indeed, it seemed to some people—and these were by no means the worst ones—to be immoral and reprehensible. The movement failed to awaken a belief that this was a problem of vital importance for the whole of humanity, and that the destiny of the whole non-Jewish world depended on a solution.

Through this half-hearted approach, the anti-Semitism of the Christian-Socialists turned out to be worthless.

It was a sham anti-Semitism—almost worse than none at all. The pretence gave rise to a false sense of security among people, who believed that the enemy had been taken by the ears. But in reality, the people themselves were being led by the nose.

The Jew readily adapted to this form of anti-Semitism. In fact, its continuance was more beneficial to him than its absence would have been.

This led to great sacrifices being made for the sake of that multi-national state; but much greater sacrifices were required by the German element.

One didn't dare to be a 'nationalist,' even in Vienna, lest the ground should fall away from under one's feet. It was hoped that the Habsburg State might be saved by quietly avoiding the nationalist question; but this policy led that state to ruin. The same policy also led to the collapse of Christian Socialism, as this movement lost the only source of energy from which a political party can draw the necessary driving force. It became a party like any other. ...

GROWING AVERSION TO THE HABSBURG STATE (section 3.29)

My inner aversion to the Habsburg State was steadily increasing.

The more I paid special attention to questions of foreign policy, the more my conviction grew that this state would surely bring misfortune on the Germans. I realized more and more that the destiny of the German nation couldn't be decisively influenced from here, but only in the German Reich itself. And this was true not only in regard to general political questions but also—and to an equal degree—regarding the whole sphere of cultural life.

Here too, in all matters affecting national culture and art, the Austrian State showed all the signs of degeneration—or at least, of ceasing to be of any consequence to the German nation. This was especially true of its architecture. The new architecture couldn't produce any great results in Austria because, since the building of the Ring Strasse, architectural activities—at least in Vienna—became insignificant when compared with the progressive plans arising in Germany.

And so I came, more and more, to lead a double life. Reason and reality told me to continue my harsh but beneficial apprenticeship in Austria. But my heart was elsewhere.

A growing sense of discontentment made me depressed, the more that I came to realize the inner hollowness of this state, and the impossibility of saving it from collapse. At the same time, I felt perfectly certain that it would bring nothing but misfortune to the German people.

I was convinced that the Habsburg State would hinder and oppress every German who might show signs of real greatness—while at the same time, it would aid and abet every non-German activity. I was repelled by the conglomeration of heterogeneous races that the capital of the Dual Monarchy showed me: this motley crew of Czechs, Poles, Hungarians, Ruthenians, Serbs, and Croats, etc. And above all, that eternal fungus of humanity—Jews and more Jews.

The giant city seemed to be the incarnation of racial depravity.

The German vernacular of my youth was the local idiom of Lower Bavaria. I never forgot that particular style of speech, and I never learned the Viennese dialect. The longer I lived there, the stronger became my hatred for the mixture of foreign peoples that had begun to erode that ancient ground of German culture.

The idea that this state could maintain its existence much longer was quite laughable.

Austria was then like an ancient mosaic, one in which the cohesive cement had dried up and become old and crumbly. As long as it remains untouched, it may hold together and continue to exist. But the moment some blow is struck, it then breaks up into a thousand fragments. The question was only when the blow would come.

Because my heart was always with the German Reich and not the Austrian monarchy, the hour of Austria's dissolution as a state appeared as only the first step towards the emancipation of the German nation.

THE SCHOOL OF MY LIFE (section 3.30)

All these considerations intensified my desire to go to that country that my heart had been secretly longing for, since the days of my youth.

I hoped someday to make my mark as an architect, and that I could devote my talents to the service of my country on a large or small scale, according to the will of fate.

But finally I wanted to enjoy the happiness of living and working in the land from which the movement that I had always longed for would be launched: namely, the union of my beloved homeland with our common fatherland, the German Reich.

There are many who may not understand how such a yearning can be so strong. But I appeal especially to two groups of people. The first includes all those who are still denied the happiness I have spoken of; and the second embraces those who once enjoyed that happiness but had it cruelly torn from them. I turn to all those who have been torn from their motherland, who have to struggle for the preservation of their sacred language, and who are persecuted and harried because of their loyalty and love for the homeland. To such people I address my words, and I know: they will understand me!

— 3 —

Only he who has experienced in his inner being what it means to be German, and yet denied the right of belonging to his fatherland, can appreciate the profound longing caused by enforced exile. It's an eternal heartache; and there's no place for joy and contentment until the doors of the paternal home are thrown open, and all those of kindred blood find peace and tranquility in their common Reich.

Vienna was and remains the hardest, though most profound, school of my life. I was scarcely more than a boy when I came to live there, and when I left it, I had grown to be a grave and thoughtful man. In Vienna I acquired the foundations of a worldview, and I developed a faculty for analyzing political questions in particular. That worldview and the political ideas then formed have never been abandoned—though they were later expanded upon in certain directions. Only now can I fully appreciate how valuable those years of study were for me.

That's why I have given a detailed account of this period. There, in Vienna, stark reality taught me the truths that now form the fundamental principles of the party that, within the course of five years, has grown from modest beginnings to a great mass movement. I don't know what my attitude towards Jewry, Social Democracy, even more to Marxism in general, to the social problem, etc., would be today, if I hadn't acquired a stock of personal beliefs at such an early age, under the duress of fate—and by my own hard study.

For, although the misfortunes of the Fatherland may have stimulated many thousands to ponder over the inner causes of the collapse, that couldn't lead to such a thorough knowledge and deep insight as a man may develop, who has fought a hard struggle for many years so that he might be the master of his own destiny.

— 4 —

MUNICH

Finally I came to Munich, in the spring of 1912.[1]

The city itself was as familiar to me as if I had lived there for years. This was because my architectural studies had been constantly turning my attention to the metropolis of German art. One must know Munich if one would know Germany, and it's impossible to acquire a knowledge of German art without seeing Munich.

In any case, this period was by far the happiest and most contented time of my life. My earnings were very meager. But after all, I didn't live for the sake of painting; I painted in order to get the bare necessities of life while I continued my studies. I was firmly convinced that I would finally succeed in reaching the goal I set for myself. And this conviction alone was strong enough to enable me to bear the petty hardships of everyday life without worrying too much about them.

Moreover, almost from the very first moment of my sojourn there, I came to love that city more than any other place I had known. A German city! How different from Vienna! It was with a feeling of disgust that I recalled that Babylon of races. I enjoyed the spoken language; the Munich idiom recalled the days of my youth, especially when I spoke with those who had come to Munich from Lower Bavaria. There were a thousand or more things that I truly loved, or came to love, during the course of my stay. But what attracted me most was the marvelous marriage of native folk-energy with the fine artistic spirit of the city—that unique harmony from the Hofbräuhaus to the Odeon, from the Oktoberfest to the Pinakothek, and so on.[2] Today I am more

---

[1] At age 23.

[2] The Hofbräuhaus is a large, state-owned beer hall in central Munich; it was founded in 1589. The Odeon was a concert hall and ballroom, built in 1828. The Pinakothek is the main art museum of Munich, dating originally from 1836.

attached to this city than any other; it will remain inseparably connected to the development of my own career. My feelings of inner happiness and satisfaction with the place can be attributed to the charm of the Residence of the Wittelsbachs;[3] it has attracted probably everyone who is blessed with a feeling for beauty, as well as a calculating mind....

THE FOUR PATHS OF GERMAN POLICY (section 4.2)

[In light of Germany's defective alliance policy] the only questions were the following: What form will the life of the nation take in the near future? And by what means can the necessary foundation and security be guaranteed, within the framework of the general power distribution among the European nations?

A clear analysis of the principles on which the foreign policy of German statecraft were to be based should have led to the following conclusions:

The annual population increase in Germany amounts to almost 900,000 souls. The difficulties of feeding this army of new citizens must grow from year to year, and must finally lead to a catastrophe, unless ways and means are found to forestall the danger of misery and hunger.

There were four ways of avoiding this terrible future calamity:

(1) It was possible to follow the French example and artificially restrict the number of births, thus avoiding an excess of population.

Nature herself—in periods of distress or under bad climatic condition, or if the soil becomes depleted—tends to restrict the increase of population among certain countries and races. And her method is quite as ruthless as it is wise. It doesn't impede the procreative faculty per se; but it does restrict the further existence of the offspring by submitting them to such tests and privations that everything that is less strong, or less healthy, is forced to retreat into the bosom of the unknown. Whatever survives these hardships of existence has been tested and tried a thousand-fold; it is hardened, and rendered fit to continue the process of procreation. Hence the same thorough selection will begin all over again. By thus dealing brutally with the individual, and recalling him the very moment he shows

---

[3] The Wittelsbachs are a famous Bavarian royal family, having ruled in the region since the year 1200.

— 4 —

that he is not fit for the trials of life, nature preserves the strength of the race and the species; she raises it to the highest degree of efficiency.

A *decrease* in numbers therefore implies an *increase* in strength of the individual, and in this way the species is invigorated.

But the case is different when man himself starts to restrict his own numbers. Man is not carved from the same wood as nature; he is 'humane.' He thinks he knows better than the ruthless Queen of Wisdom. He doesn't impede the preservation of lesser individuals, but prevents procreation itself. To the individual, who always sees only himself and not the race, this approach seems more humane and more justified than the opposite way. But unfortunately, the consequences are also the opposite:

By leaving the process of procreation unchecked, and by submitting the individual to the hardest tests in life, nature selects the best from an abundance of individuals; she stamps them as fit to live and carry on the conservation of the species. But man, when he restricts the procreative faculty, obstinately works to keep alive all who have been born. This 'correction' of the Divine Will seems to him to be wise and humane; he rejoices at having trumped nature's card—in one game at least—and thus 'proves' that she is inadequate. The dear little ape of an all-mighty Father is delighted to see that he has succeeded in reducing human numbers. But he would be very upset to hear that his system brings about a degeneration in personal value.

As soon as the procreative faculty is thwarted and the number of births diminished, the natural struggle for existence, which allows only healthy and strong individuals to survive, is replaced by a sheer desire to 'save' feeble and even diseased ones at any cost. And thus the seeds are sown for a human progeny that will become more and more deplorable from one generation to another, as long as nature's will is scorned.

And if that policy is carried out, the final results must be that such a nation will eventually terminate its own existence on this earth. Though man may defy the eternal laws of procreation for a little while, vengeance will sooner or later follow. A stronger race will oust that which has grown weak. The vital urge, in its ultimate form, will break all the absurd chains of this so-called humanitarianism for the individual, and will replace it with the humanity of nature—which destroys what is weak in order to make way for the strong.

THE ESSENTIAL MEIN KAMPF

Any policy that aims at securing the existence of the German nation by restricting the birth-rate, robs that nation of its future.

(2) There is a second solution, one that is frequently proposed and recommended in our own time: internal colonization. It's a suggestion that is well-intended, but is misunderstood by most people. Thus it's the source of an unimaginable amount of harm.

Undoubtedly, the productivity of the soil can be increased somewhat; but only within defined limits, and not indefinitely. By increasing the productive powers of the soil, it will be possible to balance the effect of a surplus birth-rate in Germany for a short period of time, without running any danger of hunger. But we have to face the fact that the general life-demands are rising more quickly than even the birth rate. The need for food and clothing are becoming greater from year to year, and are disproportionate to those of our ancestors of, say, 100 years ago. It would, therefore, be crazy to argue that continuous increase in the productive powers of the soil will supply the needs for an increasing population. No; this is true up to a certain point only, for at least a portion of the increased productivity will be consumed by the growing demands caused by a steady rise in the standard of living.

But even if these demands were restricted to the narrowest range possible, we would still reach a definite limit, one that is conditioned by the inherent nature of the soil itself. No matter how hard we work, we cannot increase agricultural production beyond this limit.

Therefore, though we may postpone the time of distress, it will eventually arrive. First, there will be the recurrence of famine periods from time to time, after bad harvests, etc. The intervals between these famines will become shorter and shorter, the more the population increases. Finally, famine will disappear only in those rare years of plenty, when the granaries are full. And a time will ultimately come when, even in those years of plenty, there won't be enough to go around. Hunger will dog the footsteps of the nation. Nature will then step in once more and select those who are to survive—or else man will help himself by artificially preventing his own increase, with all the fatal consequences for the race and species mentioned above.

It may be objected here that, in one form or another, this future is in store for all mankind, and that the individual nation cannot escape the general fate.

— 4 —

At first glance, this objection seems correct. But we have to take the following into account:

The day will certainly come when the whole of mankind will be forced to restrict the growth of the human species, because there will be no further possibility of adjusting the productivity of the soil to the perpetual increase in population. Nature must then be allowed to use her own methods; or man may possibly take the task of regulation into his own hands and establish the necessary equilibrium, using better means than we have today. But then it will be a problem for all of mankind, whereas now only those races must suffer which no longer have the strength and daring to acquire sufficient soil to meet their needs. As things stand today, there are vast spaces uncultivated spaces all over the surface of the globe. Those spaces are only waiting to be used. And it's quite certain that nature didn't set those territories apart for any one nation or race; such land awaits the people who have the strength to acquire it and the diligence to cultivate it.

Nature knows no political boundaries. She begins by establishing life on this globe, and then watches the free play of forces. Those who show the greatest courage and industry are the children nearest to her heart. They will be granted the sovereign right of existence.

If a nation confines itself to internal colonization while other races are perpetually increasing their territories, that nation will be forced to restrict the growth of its population at a time when the others are increasing theirs. This situation must eventually arrive, and it will arrive sooner if the nation has a small territory. It is unfortunately true that, only too often, the best nations—or rather, the only really cultured nations, who are also the standard-bearers of human progress—have decided, in their blind pacifism, to refrain from the acquisition of new territory, and to be content with 'internal' colonization. But at the same time, inferior nations succeed in grabbing large spaces for colonization all over the globe. This must lead to the following result:

Races that are culturally superior but less ruthless will be forced to restrict their increase, because of insufficient territory to support their population; less civilized races could increase indefinitely, owing to the vast territories at their disposal. In other words: Should that state of affairs continue, then the world will one day be possessed by that portion of mankind that is culturally inferior but more energetic.

THE ESSENTIAL MEIN KAMPF

A time will come, even though in the distant future, when there can be only two alternatives: Either the world will be ruled according to our modern concept of democracy, in which case every decision will be in favor of the numerically larger races. Or the world will be governed by the law of the natural distribution of power—and then those nations will succeed who possess a more brutal will, and not the nations who have practiced self-restriction.

No one can doubt that this world will one day be the scene of dreadful struggles for existence on the part of mankind. In the end, only the instinct of self-preservation will triumph. This so-called humanitarianism—which connotes only a mixture of stupidity, cowardice, and self-conceit—will melt away like snow under a March sun. Man has become great through perpetual struggle. In perpetual peace, he must decline.

For us Germans, the slogan 'internal colonization' is fatal because it encourages the belief that we have discovered a means that is in accordance with our innate pacifism, and that will enable us to work for our livelihood in a half-slumbering existence. If such a teaching were taken seriously by our people, it would mean the end of all effort to acquire our rightful place in the world. If the average German were convinced that he could ensure his life and future this way, it would mean the end of any attempt to take an active and fruitful role in sustaining the vital demands of his country. Should the nation adopt such an attitude, then any really useful foreign policy might be looked upon as dead and buried—together with all hope for the future of the German people.

Once we understand these consequences, we can no longer consider it a mere accident the fact that, among those who propagate this dangerous mentality in our people, the Jew is always first in line. He knows well that his softies are ready to be the grateful victims of every swindle that promises them a gold-brick in the shape of a discovery that will enable them to outwit nature, and thus avoid the hard and inexorable struggle for existence—and finally that they may become lords of the earth, partly by working, partly by doing nothing, depending on how things 'turn out.'

It cannot be too strongly emphasized that any German internal colonization must only serve to relieve social abuses. To carry out such a system, the most important preliminary measure would be to free the soil from the grip of the speculator. But such a system could never suffice to assure the future of the nation without acquiring new territory.

— 4 —

If we adopt a different plan, we will soon arrive not only at the end of our soil, but also at the end of our strength.

In conclusion, the following must be said:

The limitation to a small area of land—inherent in internal colonization, and similar to the effect achieved by restricting procreation—leads to an exceptionally unfavorable military and political situation for the nation.

The size of the national territory is a determining factor in the external security of a nation. The larger the territory that a people has at its disposal, the stronger are its national defenses. Military decisions against people living in a small area are more quickly and easily—and thus more completely and effectively—achieved, than against states that have large territories. Moreover, the size of a national territory is in itself a certain guarantee that an outside power will not hastily invade. In that case, the struggle would be long and exhausting before victory could be gained. The risk of assault would be great, and would not be undertaken without exceptional reasons. Hence the very size of a state furnishes a basis upon which national liberty and independence can be maintained with relative ease. Conversely, a state whose territory is small offers a natural temptation to the invader.

Actually, so-called nationalist circles in the German Reich rejected those first two possibilities of establishing a balance between the increasing population and a fixed national territory. But the reasons given for that rejection were different from those just mentioned: It was mainly on the basis of certain moral sentiments that a restricted birth rate was rejected. Proposals for internal colonization were indignantly refused because it was suspected that such a policy might mean an attack on the big landowners, and that this might be the forerunner of a general assault on the principle of private property. The form of the latter solution [i.e. internal colonization] perhaps justified the concerns of the big landowners.

Overall, the resistance to the broad masses wasn't very clever, and in any case didn't go to the root of the problem.

Only two further ways were left open in which work and bread could be secured for the increasing population.

(3) Either it was possible to consider acquiring new territory, on which the excess of the increasing population could be settled each year; or else

(4) Industry and commerce could be organized for export, and thus support the people by the increased financial surplus.

In other words: Either territorial expansion, or a colonial and commercial policy.

Both ways were considered, examined, recommended, and rejected, from various standpoints—and as a result, the last alternative was finally adopted.

The sounder alternative, however, was undoubtedly the first [i.e. number (3)].

ACQUISITION OF NEW LAND (section 4.3)

The principle of acquiring new territory on which to settle the surplus population has many advantages to recommend it, especially if we look to the future.[4]

In the first place, it's impossible to overestimate the need to maintain a healthy peasant class, as the basis of the national community. Many of our present evils have their origin exclusively in the imbalance between urban and rural populations. A solid group of small- and mid-scale farmers has always been the best protection against social disease. Moreover, this is the only solution that guarantees the daily bread of a nation, within the framework of its domestic national economy.

With this guaranteed, industry and commerce would recede from their present unhealthy position of dominance, and would take their due place in the economy, adjusting the balance between supply and demand. They would no longer constitute the basis of national subsistence, but would be supporting institutions. By fulfilling their proper role—to adjust the balance between national production and consumption—they allow the nation to be more or less free from foreign countries. This ensures the freedom and independence of the nation, especially in times of difficulty.

Such a territorial policy, however, cannot be fulfilled in the Cameroons, but rather exclusively here in Europe. One must calmly and squarely face the truth that it certainly cannot be Divine Will to give 50 times as much land to one nation as to another. In the present case, one mustn't allow existing political borders to distract attention from what should exist on the basis of eternal justice. If this earth has sufficient room

---

[4] What follows is an elaboration of alternative (3), Hitler's preferred choice.

for all, then we should have that share of the land that is absolutely necessary for our existence.

But people will not do this willingly. Then the right of self-preservation comes into effect. And when attempts to settle the difficulty in an amicable way fail, then the fist must take by force. If our ancestors had based their political decisions on pacifist nonsense like our present generation does, we wouldn't possess more than one-third of our present territory. And likely there would be no German nation to worry about its future in Europe. No—we owe the two Ostmarks of the Reich to the natural determination of our forefathers in their struggle for existence.[5] From this same policy arises our present inner strength, something that is based on the greatness of our state and national territory, and which alone has made it possible for us to persist.

And there is still another reason why that solution would have been correct:

Many contemporary European nations are like pyramids standing on their peaks. Their European territory is ridiculously small when compared with the enormous overhead weight of their colonies, foreign trade, etc. One may say: apex in Europe, and the base all over the world—quite different from the USA, which has its base on the American continent and touches the rest of the world only through its apex. This accounts for the incomparable inner strength of the USA and the corresponding weakness of most of the colonial European powers.

England is no proof to the contrary, because a quick glance at the British Empire overlooks the whole Anglo-Saxon world. England cannot be compared with any other state in Europe, since it forms a vast community of language and culture together with the USA.

Therefore the only possibility that Germany had to conduct a sound territorial policy was to acquire new territory in Europe itself. Colonies cannot serve this purpose, since they aren't suited for large-scale European settlement. From the 19th century on, it was no longer possible to peacefully acquire such colonies. Therefore any attempt at such a colonial expansion would have meant an enormous military struggle. Thus it was more practical to undertake that military struggle for new territory in Europe, rather than to wage war for foreign acquisition.

---

[5] The two Ostmarks are German-Austria and East Prussia. This latter is today a region covering parts of Poland, Russia, and Lithuania.

Such a decision naturally demands the nation's undivided attention. A policy like this requires all available energy on the part of everyone concerned, and cannot be carried out by half-measures or hesitatingly. The political leadership of the German Reich should have been exclusively devoted to this goal. No step should have been taken other than one that served as a means to this end. It should have been clear that such a goal could only be reached by war; and this prospect should have been faced with calm and collected determination.

All alliances should have been envisioned and judged only from this standpoint. If new territory were to be acquired in Europe, it should have been mainly at Russia's expense. Once again, the new German Reich should have set out on the same road as was formerly traveled by the Teutonic Knights—this time to acquire soil for the German plow by means of the German sword, and thus provide the nation with its daily bread.

WITH ENGLAND, AGAINST RUSSIA (section 4.4)

Such a policy, however, could have only one possible European ally: England.

Only by alliance with England was it possible to safeguard the rear of the new German crusade. And the justification for undertaking such an expedition was stronger than that of our forefathers. Not one of our pacifists refuses to eat the bread made from grain grown in the East; and yet the first plow here was 'the sword'!

No sacrifice should have been considered too great, in order to win England's friendship. Colonial and naval ambitions should have been abandoned, and attempts to compete against British industries avoided.

Only a clear and definite policy could achieve such a goal. This would involve renunciation of global trade and colonies, renunciation of a German navy, and a concentration of state military power on land forces.

The result would have been a temporary limitation, but for the sake of a great and powerful future.

There was a time when England might have reasoned with us, on such grounds. It would have understood that the problem of a steadily rising population would force Germany to look for a solution either within Europe— with the help of England—or without England, elsewhere in the world.

—4—

This outlook was probably the chief reason why London tried to draw nearer to Germany at the turn of the century. For the first time, an attitude became evident that, in recent years, has displayed itself in a most tragic way. People were unhappy with the thought of having to pull England's chestnuts out of the fire—as if there could ever be an alliance on any basis other than mutual benefit. Such a deal could have been made with England. British diplomats were still wise enough to know that an equivalent must be offered in reply to any such services rendered.

Let's suppose that our German foreign policy was managed astutely enough in 1904 to enable us to take the part that Japan played. We can scarcely measure the beneficial consequences for Germany.

There would have been no 'World War.'

Any bloodshed in 1904 would have been a tenth of that shed from 1914 to 1918.

And what a position Germany would hold in the world today!

SOLUTION TO THE AUSTRIAN ALLIANCE (section 4.5)

In any case, the alliance with Austria was then an absurdity.

This mummified state didn't attach itself to Germany for the purpose of carrying out a war, but rather to maintain a perpetual state of peace—one that was to be exploited for the purpose of slowly but surely rooting out the German element in the Dual Monarchy.

Another reason for the impossible nature of this alliance was that no one could expect such a state to take an active part in defending German national interests, given that it had insufficient strength to end de-Germanization within its own borders. If Germany herself was neither sufficiently motivated nor ruthless to deny that absurd Habsburg State the right to decide the destinies of 10 million Germans, surely it was out of the question to expect the Habsburg State to assist in any great and courageous German undertaking. The attitude of the old Reich towards the Austrian question could have been considered a test of its stamina in the struggle of national destinies.

In any case, the policy of oppression against the German population in Austria should never have been allowed to continue and to strengthen year by year. The value of Austria as an ally could be determined only by preserving the German element there.

But that path was not followed.

Nothing was feared as much as war; and yet they were ultimately forced to confront it, at the most unfavorable moment.

They wanted to flee from destiny, but it held them fast. They dreamt of maintaining world peace, but landed in a world war.

And this was the most significant reason why the above-mentioned third alternative was not even considered. New territory could be gained only in the East; but this meant war, whereas they wanted peace at any cost. Previously, the slogan of German foreign policy was: Preserve the German nation at all costs. Now it was changed to: Maintain world peace at all costs. We know the outcome.

I will return to this point in detail later on....

STATE AND ECONOMY (section 4.12)

The deeper reasons why it was possible to foist upon the people this absurd notion of 'peacefully conquering the world through commerce' lay in the generally sick condition of the whole body of German political thought. This also shows how it was possible to put forth the maintenance of world peace as a national aim.

The triumphant progress of technical science in Germany, and the marvelous development of German industries and commerce, led us to forget that a powerful state was the necessary prerequisite of that success. On the contrary, certain circles went even so far as to promote the theory that the state owed its very existence to these phenomena—that it was, above all, an economic institution and should be structured according to economic interests. Therefore, it was held, the state was dependent on economic structure. This condition of things was praised as the healthiest and most natural arrangement.

But the truth is that the state, in itself, has nothing whatsoever to do with any definite economic conception or development.

It's not a collection of contracting parties within a defined and limited space, for the purpose of serving economic ends. The state is a community of living beings who have kindred physical and spiritual natures. It's organized for the purpose of assuring the preservation of their own kind, and to help towards fulfilling those ends assigned by Providence. Therein,

— 4 —

and therein alone, lay the purpose and meaning of a state. Economic activity is one of the many auxiliary means that are necessary for the attainment of those aims. But economic activity is never the origin or purpose of a state—except where it has been founded on a false and unnatural basis.

And this alone explains why a state per se doesn't necessarily need a certain delimited territory. This becomes necessary only among those people who are ready to carry on the struggle for existence by means of their own work. People who can sneak their way into the human body politic and, like parasites, make others work for them, can form a state without possessing any specific territory. This is chiefly applicable to that parasitic nation which, today more than ever, preys upon the honest portion of mankind: the Jews.

The Jewish State has never been delimited in space. It has been spread all over the world, without any borders whatsoever, and has always been constituted by only one race. That's why the Jews have always formed a State within the State.[6] One of the most ingenious tricks ever devised has been to make this state sail under the flag of 'religion,' thus assuring it of the religious tolerance that Aryans are always ready to grant.[7] But the Mosaic religion is really nothing else than the doctrine of the preservation of the Jewish race. It therefore takes in all spheres of sociological, political, and economic knowledge that have any bearing on this function.

---

[6] This was a long-standing complaint against the Jews, going back at least to the German philosopher Johann Fichte. In 1793, he wrote, "Throughout almost all the countries of Europe there is spreading a mighty hostile state that is at perpetual war with all other states, and in many of them imposes fearful burdens on the citizens: it is the Jews. ... Do you not remember the state within the State? Does the thought not occur to you that if you give to the Jews, who are citizens of a state more solid and more powerful than any of yours, civil rights in your states, they will utterly crush the remainder of your citizens?" (cited in Poliakov 1965: 512).

[7] This is Hitler's first explicit mention of 'Aryan' in *Mein Kampf*. The word itself is ancient, dating back at least to the 6th century BC, when it simply meant 'Iranian.' It was in widespread use in the 1850s, due in part to the work of French theorist Arthur de Gobineau. And it achieved considerable publicity in Germany in the early 1900s, thanks to such writers as Houston S. Chamberlain. Despite common belief, 'Aryan' was not an invention of Hitler or the Nazis. Hitler elaborates extensively on Aryanism in section 9 of the present book.

THE ESSENTIAL MEIN KAMPF

The instinct for the preservation of one's own species is the primary cause that leads to the formation of human communities. Hence the state is a racial organism, and not an economic organization. The difference between the two is so great as to be incomprehensible to our contemporary so-called 'statesmen.' That's why they like to believe that the state may be constituted as an economic structure, whereas the truth is that it has always resulted from a will to preserve the species and the race.

But these qualities always exist and operate through the heroic virtues, and have nothing to do with commercial egoism. The preservation of the species always presupposes that the individual is ready to sacrifice himself. Such is the meaning of the poet's lines:

> *If you do not stake your life,*
> *You will never win life for yourself.*[8]

Individual sacrifice is necessary in order to ensure the preservation of the race. Hence, the most essential condition for the establishment and maintenance of a state is a certain feeling of solidarity, one grounded in an identity of character and species, and in a willingness to defend these at all costs. For a people with their own territory, this results in a development of the heroic virtues. With a parasitic people, it will develop the arts of subterfuge and malignant cruelty—unless these are intrinsic racial characteristics, in which case the varying political forms are only the outward manifestations of these qualities.

At least in the beginning, the formation of a state can only result from a manifestation of the heroic qualities. And the people who fail in the struggle for existence—that is, those who become vassals and are thereby condemned to vanish—are those who do not display the heroic virtues, or who fall victim to the trickery of the parasites. And even in this latter case, the failure is not so much a lack of intelligence but rather of courage and determination—which then tries to conceal itself beneath a cloak of humanitarianism.

The qualities that are employed for the foundation and preservation of a state have therefore little or nothing to do with economics. And this is clearly demonstrated by the fact that the inner strength of a state only

---

[8] From Friedrich Schiller's *Wallenstein* trilogy (1799).

— 4 —

very rarely coincides with its economic prosperity. On the contrary, there are many examples showing that such prosperity indicates the approaching decline of a state. If it were correct to attribute the foundation of human societies to economic forces, then the power of the state would be at its peak during periods of economic prosperity, and not vice versa.

It is particularly difficult to understand how the belief that the state exists by virtue of economic forces could become accepted in a country that has given proof of the opposite, in every phase of its history. The history of Prussia shows, in a particularly clear and distinct way, that it's not material qualities but rather ideal virtues alone that lead to the formation of a state. Only under the protection of those virtues can economic activities be developed; the latter will continue to flourish until a time comes when the creative political capacity declines. Then the economic structure will also break down—a phenomenon that's happening now, in an alarming manner, before our eyes. The material interests of humanity can prosper only in the shadow of heroic virtues. As soon as they become the primary considerations of life, they destroy the basis of their own existence.

Whenever German political power was particularly strong, the economic situation also improved. But whenever economic interests dominated the life of the people, and pushed transcendent ideals into the background, the state collapsed; and economic ruin followed soon thereafter.

If we ask about those forces that are necessary for the creation and preservation of a state, we find them under one single heading: The capacity and readiness of the individual to sacrifice for the common welfare. That this has nothing at all to do with economics can be proved by observing the simple fact that man doesn't sacrifice himself for material interests. In other words, he will die for an ideal, but not for a business.

The marvelous English gift for public psychology was clearly shown in the way they presented their case in the World War. We were fighting for our bread; but the English declared that they were fighting for 'freedom'—and not even their own freedom. No—for the freedom of the small nations. The Germans laughed at this effrontery, and were angered by it. But in doing so, they showed how much political thought had declined among our so-called diplomats in Germany, even before the war. We didn't have the slightest idea of the essence of that force that causes men to freely and willingly face their own death.

As long as the German people, in 1914, continued to believe that they were fighting for ideals, they stood firm. As soon as they were told that they were fighting only for their daily bread, they began to give up the struggle.

Our clever 'statesmen' were astounded at this change of attitude. They never understood that as soon as man is called upon to struggle for purely material causes, he'll avoid death as best he can; clearly, death and the enjoyment of the material rewards are quite incompatible. The frailest woman will become a heroine when the life of her own child is at stake. And only the will to save the species and the hearth—or the state that protects them—has, in all ages, compelled men to face the weapons of their enemies.

The following may be proclaimed as an eternal truth:

A state has never arisen from peaceful economic means, but always from the instinct to maintain the species—whether this instinct manifest itself in the heroic sphere, or in that of cunning craftiness. In the first case, we have the Aryan states, based on the principles of work and culture. In the second case, we have the Jewish parasitic colonies. But as soon as economic interests begin to predominate over the instincts in a people or a state, the situation quickly leads to subjugation and oppression.

THE MOMENT OF DECAY (section 4.13)

The belief that prevailed in Germany before the war—that the world could be opened up and even conquered for Germany through a system of peaceful commerce and a colonial policy—was a typical symptom that indicated the decline of those real qualities whereby states are created and preserved. It also showed the decline of the insight, will power, and practical determination that belong to those qualities. The penalty for this, like a law of nature, was the World War, with its attendant consequences.

To anyone who hadn't thought deeply about the matter, this general attitude of the German people must have seemed an insoluble enigma. After all, Germany itself was a magnificent example of an empire that had been built up purely through a policy of power. Prussia, which was the generative cell of the German Reich, was created by brilliant heroic deeds, and not by financial or commercial operations. And the Reich itself was

— 4 —

but the magnificent compensation for a leadership that conducted a policy of power and military valor.

How then did it happen that the political instincts of this very same German people became so degenerate? It wasn't merely one isolated phenomenon that pointed to this decadence, but morbid symptoms which appeared in alarming numbers all over the body politic, eating into the nation like a gangrenous ulcer. It seemed as if some all-pervading poisonous fluid had been injected, by some mysterious hand, into the bloodstream of this once heroic body—bringing about a creeping paralysis that affected rationality and the basic instinct of self-preservation.

During the years 1912–14, I wondered endlessly about those problems that related to the policy of the Triple Alliance and the economic policy then being pursued by the German Reich.[9] Once again, I came to the conclusion that the only explanation for this enigma lay in the operation of that force that I had already become acquainted with in Vienna, though from a different angle of vision: the Marxist doctrine and worldview, and its organized action throughout the nation.

---

[9] The Triple Alliance was a pact between Germany, Austria-Hungary, and Italy. It was formed in 1882 and survived until the start of WWI.

— 5 —
THE WORLD WAR

During my boisterous youth, nothing dampened my wild spirits so much as the thought that I was born at a time when there would be no more temples of fame, except to honor businessmen and state officials. The historical tempest had subsided, and the future seemed to be given over to 'the peaceful competition of nations'—in other words, to a cozy mutual swindling match without the use of violence. Individual countries became commercial enterprises, grabbing customers and striving for concessions from each other. And it was all accompanied by loud but innocuous shouting.

This trend seemed destined to steadily and permanently progress. It seemed bound to eventually transform the world into a giant department store. In the entryway of this emporium, there would be rows of busts of profiteers and sheepish governmental officials. The salesmen were represented by the English, and the administrative officials by the Germans. The Jews would be sacrificed to the position of ownership—since, as they claim, they make no money and are always being called upon to 'pay out.' Moreover, they have the advantage of being versed in the foreign languages.

I used to ask, Why wasn't I born a hundred years ago? Perhaps around the time of the Wars of Liberation,[1] when a man was still of some value, even though he had no 'business'!

Thus I thought of it as an ill-deserved stroke of bad luck that I had arrived too late on this earth. I was chagrined at the idea that my life would have to run its course along peaceful and orderly lines. As a boy, I was anything but a pacifist, and all attempts to make me so were futile.

---

[1] Also known as the German Campaign of 1813. It liberated the Germans states from French control.

Then came the Boer War, like a flash of lightning.[2] Day after day, I gazed intently at the newspapers, and I devoured the telegrams and communiqués. I was overjoyed at witnessing that heroic struggle, even from so great a distance.

When the Russo-Japanese War came, I was older and better able to judge for myself.[3] For nationalistic reasons, I then took the side of the Japanese in our discussions. I looked upon the defeat of the Russians as a blow to Austrian Slavism.

Many years have passed between that time and my arrival in Munich. I now realized that what I formerly believed to be a morbid decadence was only the lull before the storm. During my Vienna days, the Balkans were already in the grip of that sultry pause that precedes a violent storm. Flashes of lightning occasionally appeared; but they rapidly disappeared in the sinister gloom. Then the Balkan War broke out.[4] The first gusts of the forthcoming tornado then swept across a highly-strung Europe. The intervening calm was an atmosphere of foreboding—so much so that the sense of an impending catastrophe was transformed into a feeling of anticipation. People wished that heaven would give free rein to a fate that could no longer be curbed. Then the first great bolt of lightning struck the earth. The storm broke, and a heavenly thunder intermingled with the roar of the cannons in the World War.

When news reached Munich that the Archduke Franz Ferdinand had been murdered, I was at home all day and didn't get the particulars of how it happened.[5] At first I feared that the shots may have been fired by some German-Austrian students who had become furiously aroused by his pro-Slav activities, and wished to free the Germans from this internal enemy. It was easy to imagine what the result of such a mistake would have been: a new wave of persecution, all 'justified' and 'explained' to the world. But

---

[2] Formally, the "second" Boer War, which ran from 1899 to 1902. In this war, Britain reasserted its control over black South Africans.

[3] The Russo-Japanese War ran from 1904 to 1905, over territory in Manchuria. It ended in Japanese victory.

[4] The Balkan War was a two-phase offensive, over the years 1912 to 1913. The Balkan states defeated the Ottoman Empire, though it regained some ground in the latter phase of the conflict.

[5] On 28 June 1914. This event precipitated World War I.

— 5 —

soon afterwards, I heard the names of the presumed assassins, and also that they were known to be Serbs. I was somewhat dumbfounded by the inscrutable vengeance that destiny had wrought.

The greatest friend of the Slavs fell victim to the bullets of Slavic fanatics.

Anyone observing the relationship between Austria and Serbia during the past few years could have no doubt: a stone had been set rolling, and it couldn't be stopped. ...

THE GERMAN WAR FOR FREEDOM (section 5.2)

For me, these hours came as a deliverance from the distress that had weighed upon me during the days of my youth. I'm not ashamed to admit today that I was carried away by the enthusiasm of the moment. I sank down on my knees and thanked heaven, out of the fullness of my heart, for the good fortune of living at such a time.

The fight for freedom had begun, on an unparalleled scale in world history. From the moment that fate took the helm, a conviction grew among the masses that now it wasn't a question of deciding the destinies of Austria or Serbia, but that the very existence of the German nation itself was at stake.

At last, after many years, the people clearly saw the future. Therefore, almost immediately after the gigantic struggle began, an excessive enthusiasm was replaced by a more earnest and more fitting undertone; the rapture of the popular spirit was not a mere passing frenzy. It was only too necessary that the gravity of the situation be recognized. At that time there was, generally speaking, not the slightest presentiment or conception of how long the war might last. People dreamed of the soldiers being home that winter, and that they would then resume their daily work in peace.

Whatever a man wants is what he hopes for and believes in. The overwhelming majority of the people have long since tired of the perpetual insecurity in public affairs. Hence it was only natural that few anticipated a peaceful conclusion to the Austro-Serbian conflict; they looked forward to a definitive resolution. I, too, was one of these millions.

The moment the news of the assassination reached Munich, two thoughts came into my mind: First, that war was absolutely inevitable; and second, that the Habsburg State would now be forced to honor its alliance. What I had most feared was that one day Germany itself, perhaps as a result of the alliance, would become involved in a conflict not directly caused by Austria. In this case, Austria might not be able to muster the will to fight on behalf of its ally. The Slavic majority in the empire would have immediately begun to undermine any such intentions, and would have always preferred to shatter the entire state rather than to aid its ally. But now this danger was removed. The old state was compelled to fight, whether it wished to or not.

My own attitude towards the conflict was equally simple and clear. I believed that it wasn't a case of Austria fighting to get satisfaction from Serbia, but rather a case of Germany fighting for her own existence—for the life or death of the German nation, for its freedom and for its future. Bismarck's work must now be carried on. Young Germany must show itself worthy of the blood shed by our fathers on so many heroic battlefields, from Weissenburg to Sedan and Paris. And if this struggle should bring us victory, our people will again rank foremost among the great nations. Only then could the German Reich assert itself as the mighty champion of peace, without needing to restrict the daily bread of its children for the sake of maintaining the peace.

As a boy and young man, I often wished for the occasion to prove that my national enthusiasm was no mere empty whim. Cheering sometimes seemed to me to be a kind of sinful indulgence, though I couldn't give any justification for that feeling. After all, who has the right to shout a triumphant word if he hasn't won the right to do so in a place where there is no play-acting, and where the Goddess of Destiny's inexorable hand tests the truth and sincerity of nations and men? Just as millions of others, I felt a proud joy in being permitted to go through this test. I had so often sung *Deutschland über Alles,* and so often roared '*Heil,*' that I now saw it as a kind of belated grace that I was allowed to appear before the Court of Eternal Justice, and to testify to the truth of those feelings.

One thing was clear to me from the very beginning, namely, that in the event of war—which now seemed inevitable—my books would have to be set aside. I also realized that my place would have to be where my inner voice directed me.

I left Austria principally for political reasons. Even more rational, however, was that, now that the war had begun, that I should put into practice the logical consequences of my political opinions! I had no desire to fight for the Habsburg cause, but I was prepared to die at any time for my own people and the Reich to which they belonged.

ENLISTMENT IN A BAVARIAN REGIMENT (section 5.3)

On 3 August 1914, I presented an urgent petition to His Majesty, King Ludwig III, requesting to be allowed to serve in a Bavarian regiment. In those days, the chancellery certainly had its hands full, and I was therefore all the more pleased when I received an answer the next day. I opened the document with trembling hands; and no words could describe the joy that I felt on reading that I was instructed to report to a Bavarian regiment. Within a few days, I was wearing the uniform that I was not to take off again for nearly six years.

For me, as for every German, the most memorable period of my life now began. Face to face with that mighty struggle, everything past fell away into oblivion. I look back on those days with a wistful pride, especially because we are now approaching the tenth anniversary of that memorable event. I think back on those early weeks of war, when kind Fate allowed me to take my place in that heroic struggle among the nations.

As I recall the scene, it seems like only yesterday. I see myself among my young comrades on our first parade drill, exercising, and so on, until at last the day came for us to march off.

Like so many others, I had one worry during those days: that we might not reach the front in time. Again and again, that thought disturbed me; every announcement of a victorious battle left a slight bitter taste—which only increased as news of further victories arrived.

BAPTISM BY FIRE (section 5.4)

At long last, the day came when we left Munich to fulfill our duty. For the first time in my life, I saw the Rhine; we journeyed westwards to stand guard before that historic German river, against its traditional and greedy enemy. As the first soft rays of the morning sun broke through the light mist, showing the Niederwald Statue,[6] the whole transport train broke into strains of *Die Wacht am Rhein*. I felt as though my heart would burst.

---

[6] The Niederwald Statue was begun in 1871 by Kaiser Wilhelm I, to commemorate the unification of Germany. It was dedicated in 1883.

Then followed a damp, cold night in Flanders. We marched in silence throughout the night, and as the morning sun came through the mist, an iron greeting suddenly burst above our heads. Shrapnel exploded in our midst, spluttering in the damp ground. But before the smoke of the explosion disappeared, a wild 'Hurrah' arose from 200 throats, in response to this first greeting of death. Then began the whistling of bullets and the booming of cannons, the shouting and singing of the combatants. With eyes straining feverishly, we pressed forward, quicker and quicker, until we finally came to hand-to-hand combat—there beyond the beet-fields and meadows. Soon the strains of a song reached us from afar. Nearer and nearer, from company to company, it came. And while death began to wreak havoc in our ranks, we passed the song on to those beside us: *Deutschland, Deutschland über Alles, über Alles in der Welt!*

FROM YOUNG VOLUNTEER TO OLD SOLDIER (section 5.5)

After four days in the trenches, we came back. Even our step had changed. Boys of 17 now looked like men.

The volunteers of the List Regiment may not have learned how to fight properly, but they knew how to die like old soldiers.

That was the beginning.

And thus we carried on from year to year. A feeling of horror replaced the romantic fighting spirit. Enthusiasm gradually cooled down, and exuberant spirits were quelled by the fear of ever-present death. A time came for each of us to experience the conflict between the urge to self-preservation and the call of duty. I, too, had to go through that conflict. As death unrelentingly sought its prey everywhere, a vague something rebelled within the body. It tried to pass as common sense; but in reality, it was fear. Fear took on this cloak in order to impose itself on the individual. Yet the more this voice called for caution, and the louder and more persistent its demands, the stronger our resistance became. Finally, the internal struggle was over, and the call of duty was triumphant. By the winter of 1915–16, I had come through that inner struggle. My will had asserted its indisputable mastery.

In the early days, I went into the fight with a cheer and a laugh. Now, however, I was calm and resolute. And that frame of mind endured. Fate could now put me to the final test without my nerves or reason giving way.

— 5 —

The young volunteer had become an old soldier.

This same transformation took place throughout the whole army. Constant fighting had aged, toughened, and hardened it, so that it stood firm and dauntless against every assault.

Only now is it possible to judge that army. After two or three years of continuous fighting, and having been thrown into one battle after another, bravely facing superior numbers and superior armament, suffering hunger and privation, the time had come when one could assess the value of that singular fighting force.

For a thousand years to come, no one will dare to speak of heroism without recalling the German Army of the World War. And then, from the dim past, there will emerge an immortal vision of those solid ranks of steel helmets that never flinched and never faltered. As long as Germans live, they will be proud to remember that these men were the sons of their people.

ARTIFICIAL DAMPENING OF ENTHUSIASM (section 5.6)

I was a soldier then, and didn't really wish to meddle in politics—all the more so because the time was inopportune. I still believe that the humblest stable-boy of those days served his country better than the best of, let's say, our 'parliamentarians.' My hatred for those big-mouths was never greater than in the days when all decent men, who had anything to say, said it point-blank to the enemy's face; or else, failing this, kept their mouths shut and did their duty elsewhere. Yes, I hated all those politicians. And if I had my way, I would have formed them into a labor battalion and given them the opportunity to babble amongst themselves all they liked, without offence or harm to decent people.

In those days, I cared nothing for politics. But I couldn't help forming an opinion on certain manifestations that affected not only the whole nation but also us soldiers in particular.

There were two things that caused me the greatest anxiety at that time, and which I had come to regard as harmful.

First: Shortly after our first series of victories, a certain section of the press already began to throw cold water, drip by drip, on public enthusiasm. At first this wasn't obvious. It was done under the mask of good intentions and solicitude. The public was told that big victory celebrations were somewhat out of place, and weren't worthy expressions of the spirit of a great nation. The fortitude and valor of German soldiers were accepted facts that didn't necessarily call for celebration. Furthermore, foreign opinion would have much to say about such activities. It would react better to a quiet and sober form of celebration rather than to a bunch of wild jubilation. Surely the time had come for us Germans to remember that this war was not our doing, and thus that we should always be willing to contribute our share to a reconciliation of mankind. For this reason, it wouldn't be wise to besmirch the radiant deeds of our army with unbecoming jubilation; the rest of the world would never understand this. Furthermore, nothing is more appreciated than the modesty with which a true hero quietly and unassumingly carries on—and willingly forgets the past. Such was the gist of their warning.

Instead of taking these fellows by their long ears, dragging them to some ditch, and stringing them up on a rope—so that the victorious enthusiasm of the nation would no longer offend the aesthetic sensibilities of these knights of the pen—a general campaign was conducted against what was called 'unseemly' forms of celebration.

No one seemed to have the faintest idea that, once public enthusiasm is damped, nothing can spark it again, when the need arises. It's an intoxication, and must be maintained in that form. Without the power of an enthusiastic spirit, how would it be possible to endure a struggle that made such immense demands on the spiritual qualities of the nation?

I was only too well acquainted with the psychology of the broad masses not to know that, in such cases, a high 'aesthetic' tone cannot fan the fire enough to keep the iron hot. In my eyes, it was even a mistake not to have tried to raise the pitch of public enthusiasm higher still. Therefore I couldn't at all understand why they adopted the opposite policy—that is, of damping the public spirit.

MISRECOGNIZING MARXISM (section 5.7)

The second thing that irritated me was the manner in which Marxism was regarded and accepted. In my eyes, all this proved how little they knew about this plague. It was believed, in all seriousness, that the abolition of party distinctions during the war made Marxism a mild and moderate thing.

— 5 —

But this was no question of party. It was a matter of a doctrine that must lead to the destruction of all humanity. The intention of this doctrine was misunderstood because nothing was said about it in our Jew-ridden universities, and because our arrogant bureaucratic officials didn't think it worthwhile to study a subject that wasn't included in the university curriculum. This mighty revolutionary trend was going right in front of them; but those 'intellectuals' didn't pay any attention. That's why state institutions nearly always lag behind private enterprises. It is to such people, by God, that the maxim applies: 'What the peasant doesn't know, won't bother him.' Here too, a few exceptions only confirm the rule.

In August of 1914, the German worker was looked upon as a Marxist. That was absurd. When those fateful hours dawned, the German worker shook off the poisonous clutches of that plague; otherwise he wouldn't have been so ready and willing to fight. People were stupid enough to imagine that Marxism had now become 'national'—another demonstration of the fact that the authorities never took the trouble to study the essence of Marxist teaching. If they had done so, they never would have made such foolish errors.

Marxism—whose final objective was, is, and will continue to be the destruction of all non-Jewish national states—saw in those days of July 1914 how the German working classes were aroused by a national spirit, and rapidly entered the service of the Fatherland. Within a few days, the deceptive smoke-screen of that infamous national betrayal vanished into thin air, and the gang of Jewish bosses suddenly found themselves alone and deserted. It was as if no vestige remained of the folly and madness that was foisted upon the mass of the German people for 60 years. That was a bad day for the betrayers of the German working class. The moment, however, that the leaders recognized the danger that threatened them, they pulled the magic cap of deceit over their ears, and insolently mimicked the national awakening.

The time had come for taking action against these Jewish poisoners of the people. That was the time to deal with them, regardless of any whining or protestation. At one stroke, in August of 1914, all the empty nonsense about international solidarity was knocked out of the heads of the German working classes. A few weeks later, instead of this stupid talk ringing in their ears, they heard the noise of American-made shrapnel bursting over the heads of the marching columns; there was your 'international brotherhood.' Now that the German worker had rediscovered the road to nationhood, it should have been the duty of any caring government to mercilessly root out the agitators who were misleading the nation.

If the best were dying at the front, the least we could do is to exterminate the vermin.

Instead, His Majesty the Kaiser held out his hand to these old criminals, thus sparing these treacherous murderers of the nation and allowing them to regain their composure.

And so the viper could begin his work again—this time, more carefully than before, but even more destructively. While honest people dreamt of reconciliation, these perjured criminals were organizing a revolution.

THE USE OF NAKED FORCE (section 5.8)

Naturally I was distressed at the half-measures that were adopted at that time; but I never thought it possible that the final consequences could have been so disastrous.

But what should have been done? Throw the ringleaders into jail, prosecute them, and rid the nation of them. Uncompromising military measures should have been adopted to root out this pestilence. Parties should have been abolished, and the Reichstag brought to its senses at the point of the bayonet, if necessary—or better still, immediately dissolved. Just as the Republic today dissolves the parties when it wants to, so in those days there was even more justification for doing so, seeing that the very existence of the nation was at stake!

Of course, this suggestion would give rise to the question: Is it possible to eradicate ideas with the sword? Can a worldview be attacked by means of force?

At that time, I turned these questions over and over again in my mind.

By studying analogous cases in history, particularly those arising from religious circumstances, I came to the following fundamental conclusion:

Ideas and philosophical systems, as well as movements grounded on a definite spiritual foundation, whether true or not, can never be broken by the use of force after a certain stage, except on one condition: namely, that this use of force is in the service of a new creative idea or worldview.

— 5 —

The application of force alone, without moral support based on a spiritual concept, can never bring about the destruction of an idea or halt its propagation—unless one is willing to ruthlessly root out its last remaining defenders, and also to destroy any remaining tradition. Now, in most cases, the result of such action has been to exclude such a state, either temporarily or forever, from the sphere of political significance. But experience has also shown that such a blood sacrifice arouses the better segment of the people. As a matter of fact, every persecution that is unsupported by spiritual motives is morally unjust; it raises opposition among the best elements of the population—to the point that they are driven to champion the very ideas that are unjustly persecuted. With many people, this arises from a sheer feeling of opposition to every attempt at suppressing ideas by brute force.

In this way, the number of convinced followers of the persecuted doctrine grows as the persecution increases. Hence the total destruction of a new doctrine can be accomplished only by a complete rooting-out—which ultimately means the loss of some of the best blood in a nation or state. As a consequence, even though a so-called 'internal' clean-up may occur, it will cause a collapse in the nation's strength. And such a procedure is always condemned to futility from the very start, if the attacked doctrine has spread beyond a small circle.

That's why in this case, as with all other growths, the doctrine can best be destroyed in its earliest stages. As time goes on, its powers of resistance increase—until it approaches old age and then gives way to younger ideas, but in another form and from other motives.

ATTACK OF A WORLDVIEW (section 5.9)

The fact remains that nearly all attempts to root out a doctrine and its organizational manifestations, without having some spiritual basis of attack against it, are doomed to failure. In many cases, in fact, the very opposite was achieved, for the following reasons:

When sheer force is used to combat the spread of a doctrine, then that force must be employed systematically and persistently. In other words, the chances of success in the suppression of a doctrine lie only in the persistent and uniform application of the methods chosen. The moment hesitation is shown, and periods of tolerance alternate with the application of force, the targeted doctrine will not only recover strength, but every successive persecution will bring with it new adherents who have been shocked by the oppressive methods used. The old followers will become more embittered, and their allegiance will thereby be strengthened. Therefore, when force is employed, success is dependent on the consistent manner in which it is used.

This persistence, however, is nothing less than the product of definite spiritual convictions. Every form of force that isn't supported by a spiritual backing will always be indecisive and uncertain. Such a force lacks the stability that can be found only in a worldview that has its devoted champions. Such a force is the expression of individual energies; it therefore is periodically dependent upon the change of persons in charge, and also upon their characters and capacities.

But there is something else to be said:

Every worldview, whether religious or political—and it's sometimes hard to differentiate the two—fights not so much for the negative destruction of the opposing world of ideas as for the positive realization of its own ideas. Its struggle thus lies more in attack rather than in defense. It has the advantage of knowing where its objective lies, and this objective represents the realization of its own ideas.

Inversely, it's difficult to say when the negative aim of the destruction of a hostile doctrine is achieved. For this reason alone, an aggressive worldview is more powerful and decisive in action than one that takes up a merely defensive attitude. If force is used to combat a spiritual power, that force remains a defensive measure, as long as its advocates aren't the standard-bearers and apostles of a new spiritual doctrine.

To sum up, we can establish the following:

That every attempt to combat a worldview by means of force will turn out futile in the end, if the struggle fails to take the form of an offensive for the establishment of an entirely new spiritual attitude. It is only in the struggle between two worldviews that physical force, consistently and ruthlessly applied, will eventually succeed.

This is why the fight against Marxism failed.

This was also the reason why Bismarck's anti-socialist legislation failed, and was bound to fail in the long run, despite everything. It lacked

— 5 —

the basis of a new worldview to serve as the basis for the development and extension of the struggle. To say that the drivel about so-called 'state authority' or 'law and order' was an adequate foundation for the spiritual driving force in a life-or-death struggle is just what one would expect to hear from the 'wise ones' in high official positions.

It was because there were no adequate spiritual motives behind this offensive that Bismarck was compelled to hand over the administration of his socialist legislative measures to the judgment of those who were themselves the product of the Marxist teaching. Thus the Iron Chancellor surrendered the fate of his struggle against Marxism to the goodwill of the bourgeois democracy. He left the goat to take care of the garden.

But this was only the necessary result of the failure to find a fundamentally new anti-Marxist worldview, one with a stormy will to conquer.

And thus the result of the Bismarckian campaign was deplorable.

Were the conditions any different during the World War, or at the beginning of it? Unfortunately, no.

— 6 —
THE REVOLUTION

In 1915, the enemy started his propaganda among our soldiers. From 1916 onwards, it steadily became more intensive, and at the beginning of 1918, it became a virtual flood. One could now judge the effects of this proselytizing movement at every step. Gradually our soldiers began to think just as the enemy wished them to.

On the German side, it was a complete failure.

At that time, the army authorities, under our able and determined commander, were also willing and ready to take up the propaganda fight, but unfortunately they didn't have the necessary means to make it happen. And in any case, it would have been a psychological error if they had done so. To be effective, propaganda had to come from home. Only then would it have been a success among men who, for nearly four years, were performing immortal deeds of heroism and privation for the homeland.

But what were the people at home doing?

Was their failure to act stupidity, or criminal?

In midsummer 1918, after the evacuation of the southern bank of the Marne, the German press adopted a policy that was so woefully inadequate, and even criminally stupid, that a question arose—one that made me more furious every day: Is there no one who will dare to put an end to this spiritual sabotage of our heroic troops?

What happened in France during 1914, when our armies invaded that country in a storm of victory? What happened in Italy when their armies collapsed on the Isonzo front?[1] What happened in France again during the spring of 1918, when German divisions took the main French positions by storm, and heavy long-distance artillery bombarded Paris?

---

[1] The Isonzo River, in present-day Slovenia, was the site of a number of battles between Austria-Hungary and Italy between 1915 and 1917.

How they whipped up the courage of those troops who were retreating, and fanned the fires of national enthusiasm among them! How their propaganda and their ingenious mass-influence reawakened the fighting spirit in that broken front, and hammered into them a firm belief in final victory!

Meanwhile, what were our people doing?

Nothing, or even worse than nothing!

Again and again, I became enraged and indignant as I read the latest papers and realized the nature of the psychological mass-murder they were committing.

More than once, I was tormented by the thought that if Providence had put me in charge of German propaganda, instead of those incompetent and even criminal ignoramuses and scoundrels, the outcome of our battle with fate might have been different.

During those months, I felt for the first time that a malicious Destiny was keeping me on the fighting front and in a position where any random bullet from some nigger might finish me off—while elsewhere I could have done a real service for the Fatherland!

I was then rash enough to believe that I would have been successful.

But I was a nameless soldier, one among 8 million!

And so it was better for me to keep my mouth shut and do my duty as best I could.

THE FIRST ENEMY LEAFLETS (section 7.1)

In the summer of 1915, the first enemy leaflets were dropped on us.

They all told more or less the same story, with some minor variation: Suffering was steadily increasing in Germany. The war would last indefinitely. The prospect of victory for us was becoming fainter by the day. The people at home were longing for peace, but that 'militarism' and the 'Kaiser' would not permit it. The whole world—which knew this very well—wasn't waging war against the German people but only against the man who was exclusively responsible, the Kaiser. And finally, that until this enemy of world-peace was removed, there could be no end to the conflict. When the war was over, the liberal and democratic nations would receive the Germans as colleagues in the league for world peace. This would happen the moment that 'Prussian militarism' was destroyed.

— 6 —

To illustrate and substantiate all these statements, the leaflets often contained 'Letters from Home.' The contents appeared to confirm the enemy's assertions.

Generally speaking, we only laughed at all these efforts. The leaflets were read, sent to base headquarters, and then forgotten—until the wind once again blew a fresh batch into the trenches. These were mostly dropped from airplanes that were specially used for that purpose.

One feature of this propaganda was very striking: namely, in sections where Bavarian troops were stationed, every effort was made to stir up feelings against the Prussians. It assured the soldiers that Prussia and Prussia alone was the guilty party who was responsible for the whole war, and that there was no hostility whatsoever towards the Bavarians. But that there would be no possibility of coming to their assistance as long as they continued to serve Prussian interests and helped to pull the Prussian chestnuts out of the fire.

This persistent propaganda began to have a real effect in 1915. The feelings against Prussia grew quite visibly among the Bavarian troops; but those in authority did nothing to counteract it. This was more than a mere sin of omission. Sooner or later, not only were the Prussians bound to suffer for it, but the whole German nation and consequently the Bavarians as well.

In this direction, enemy propaganda began to achieve undoubted success from 1916 onwards.

In a similar way, letters coming directly from home had long since been exercising their effect. There was now no further need for the enemy to broadcast such letters in leaflet form. And also against this influence from home, nothing was done—except a few supremely stupid 'warnings' uttered by the 'government.' The whole front was drenched in this poison sent by thoughtless women at home. They didn't suspect for a moment that the enemy's chances of final victory were thereby strengthened, or that the sufferings of their own men at the front were thereby being prolonged and rendered more severe. These senseless letters written by German women eventually cost the lives of hundreds of thousands of our men.

THE ESSENTIAL MEIN KAMPF

WOUNDED (section 7.2)

Thus, by 1916, several distressing phenomena had already appeared. The whole front was complaining and grousing, and discontented over many things—often justifiably so. While they were hungry and suffering, and while their relatives at home were in distress, others were feasting and celebrating. Yes—even on the front itself, everything was not as it should have been.

Even in the early stages of the war, the soldiers were sometimes prone to complain; but such criticism was confined to 'internal affairs.' The man who, at one moment, groused and grumbled, ceased a few minutes later, and went about his duty silently, as if all were in order. The same company that was initially discontented now clung to its piece of trench with tooth and nail, as if Germany's fate depended on these few hundred meters of mud holes. The glorious old army was still at its post!

A sudden change soon gave me first-hand experience of the contrast between this old army and the homeland.

At the end of September 1916, my division was sent into the Battle of the Somme. For us this was the first of a series of heavy engagements, and it created an indescribable impression—more like hell than war.

We stood firm through weeks of incessant artillery bombardment—at times ceding a little ground but then taking it back again, and never giving way.

On 7 October 1916, I was wounded

I had the good luck of getting back to the rear, and I was then ordered to be sent by transport to Germany.

Two years had passed since I left home—an almost endless period, in such circumstances. I could hardly imagine what Germans looked like without uniforms. In the field hospital at Hermies, I was startled when I suddenly heard the voice of a German nurse who was talking with one of the wounded men lying near me.

After two years—to first hear such a sound!

The nearer our train approached the German border, the more restless each of us became. En route we recognized all these places through which we passed two years before as young volunteers: Brussels, Louvain, Liège. Finally we recognized the first German homestead, with its familiar high gables and picturesque window-shutters.

— 6 —

The Fatherland!

In October 1914, we burned with stormy enthusiasm as we crossed the border. Now, silence and emotion reigned. Each of us was happy that fate allowed us to again see that which we had defended with our lives. And each was ashamed to let another look into his eye.

It was almost on the anniversary of the day that I left for the front, when I reached the hospital at Beelitz near Berlin.

What a change! From the mud of the Somme battlefields to the spotless white beds in this wonderful building! We hesitated to lie in them. Only gradually did we grow accustomed to this new world again.

But unfortunately this world was also different in another respect.

BOASTING OF COWARDICE (section 7.3)

The spirit of the army at the front was foreign here. For the first time, I encountered something that was unknown at the front: boasting of one's own cowardice. Though we certainly heard complaining and grousing at the front, this was never an incitement to insubordination, and certainly not a glorification of one's fear. No! There, a coward was a coward, and nothing more. And the contempt for him that was aroused in others was quite general, just as the real hero was widely admired. But here in hospital, it was nearly the opposite. Loudmouthed agitators were heaping ridicule on the good soldier, and lauding the spineless coward.

A couple of miserable human specimens set the tone. One of them boasted of having intentionally injured his hand in barbed-wire in order to get sent to hospital. Although his wound was slight, it appeared that he had been here for a long time. He got sent here in the transport train through some sort of a swindle. This poisonous specimen actually had the audacity to parade his cowardice as the result of a higher courage, one that was superior to that of the brave soldier who dies a hero's death. Many listened in silence, others left, but some assented.

Personally I was disgusted at the thought that such a seditious agitator was allowed to remain there. What could be done? The authorities must have known who and what he was; and actually they did know. But still they did nothing.

THE ESSENTIAL MEIN KAMPF

SLACKERS (section 7.4)

As soon as I was able to walk again, I obtained leave to visit Berlin.

Dire misery was everywhere. The metropolis, with its teeming millions, was suffering from hunger. The talk in the soldiers' homes was much like that at the hospital. It seemed that these agitators had deliberately singled out such places, in order to spread their views.

But conditions in Munich were far worse!

After my discharge from hospital, I was sent to a reserve battalion there. I didn't recognize anything. Anger, discontent, complaints—wherever one went! This was partly due to the highly inept manner in which the soldiers who had returned from the front were treated by the non-commissioned officers—they who had never seen a day's active service, and who were thus incapable of creating a decent relationship towards the old soldiers. The old soldiers displayed certain characteristics that had been developed from their time in the trenches. The reserve officers couldn't understand these peculiarities. On the other hand, the officer home from active service was at least in a position to understand them himself. As a result, he received more respect from the men than the home officers.

But apart from all this, the general spirit was miserable. The art of slacking was looked on as almost proof of higher intelligence, and devotion to duty was considered a sign of weakness or bigotry. Government offices were filled with Jews. Almost every clerk was a Jew, and nearly every Jew was a clerk. I was amazed at this multitude of combatants who belonged to the chosen people; and I couldn't help comparing it with their slim numbers at the front.

In the business world, the situation was even worse. Here the Jewish people had actually become 'indispensable.' Like spiders, they were slowly sucking the blood from the pores of the national body. Through the war corporations, they found an instrument whereby all national free trade could be finished off.

Special emphasis was placed on the necessity of unhampered centralization.

Thus as early as 1916-17, practically all production was under the control of Jewish finance.

But against whom was the anger of the people directed?

It was then that I foresaw a looming disaster, one that would inevitably lead to collapse unless actions were taken in time.

— 6 —

HATRED OF PRUSSIA (section 7.5)

While the Jew was busy robbing the nation and tightening the screws of his despotism, incitement against 'the Prussians' increased. And just as at the front, nothing was done to stop this poisonous propaganda. No one seemed capable of understanding that the collapse of Prussia could never bring about the rise of Bavaria. On the contrary, the collapse of the one would necessarily drag the other down into the abyss.

This kind of behavior affected me very deeply. I could see in it only a clever Jewish trick for diverting public attention from themselves to others. While Prussians and Bavarians were squabbling, the Jews were taking away the sustenance of both from under their very noses. While Prussians were being abused in Bavaria, the Jew organized the Revolution, and with one stroke smashed both Prussia and Bavaria.

I couldn't tolerate this execrable squabbling among German peoples, and I longed to be at the front once again. Therefore, not long after arriving in Munich, I reported again for service.

At the beginning of March 1917, I had rejoined my old regiment.

THE ARMY'S NEW HOPE (section 7.6)

Towards the end of 1917, we seemed to have gotten over the worst phases of moral depression at the front. After the Russian collapse, the whole army recovered its courage and hope.[2] All were gradually becoming more and more convinced that the struggle would end in victory. We could sing once again, and the naysayers faded from view. People once again believed in the future of the Fatherland.

The Italian collapse in the autumn of 1917 had a wonderful effect.[3] This victory proved that it was possible to break through another front, besides

---

[2] The Russian Revolution of 1917 consisted of two phases: A worker's revolt in February that overthrew the Czar, and then the Bolshevik revolution in October that put the Jewish revolutionaries in power. Once in power, the Bolsheviks pulled Russia out of the war. This, as Hitler states, freed up German troops for the western front.

[3] The Battle of Caporetto took place from October 24 to November 19, near the present-day town of Kobarid, Slovenia, just across the Italian border. The Italians were routed by the Germans.

the Russian. An inspiring faith became dominant in the minds of millions, and it encouraged them to look forward with confidence to the spring of 1918. The enemy was visibly depressed. During this winter, the front was somewhat quieter than usual. But that was the calm before the storm.

Just when preparations were being made to launch a final offensive and bring this interminable war to an end—while endless columns of transports brought men and munitions to the front, and while the men were being trained for that final onslaught—then it was that the greatest act of treachery in the whole war occurred in Germany.

Germany would not win the war: At the last moment, when victory seemed ready to fly with German banners, a means was arranged for the purpose of striking at the heart of the German spring offensive with one blow from the rear, thus making victory impossible.

A munitions strike was organized.[4]

If this had succeeded, the German front would have collapsed, and the wishes of the *Vorwärts* that victory not take the side of the German banners would have been fulfilled.[5] For lack of munitions, the front would be broken through within a few weeks, the German offensive would be effectively stopped, and the Entente saved. International finance would assume control over Germany, and the internal goal of the Marxist national betrayal would be achieved.

Their objective was the destruction of the national economic system and the establishment of international capitalistic domination in its place. And this goal has really been reached, thanks to the stupidity and credulity of the one side and the bottomless cowardice of the other.

The munitions strike, however, didn't bring the final success that was hoped for: namely, to starve the front of ammunition. It lasted too short a time for any lack of ammunition to bring disaster to the army, as was originally planned. But the moral damage was much more terrible!

In the first place: What was the army fighting for, if the people at home didn't wish for victory? For whom were these enormous sacrifices and privations being made? Should the soldiers fight for victory, while the home front goes on strike against it?

And secondly: What effect did this move have on the enemy?

---

[4] This occurred on 28 January 1918.

[5] *Vorwärts* was the official paper of the Social Democrats.

— 6 —

THE ALLIES ARE BEATEN DOWN (section 7.7)

In the winter of 1917-18, dark clouds hovered in the firmament of the Entente. For nearly four years, many onslaughts were made against the German giant, but they failed to bring him to the ground. He fought them off with the one arm that held the defensive shield, because his other arm had to wield the sword against his other enemies, in the East and the South. But at last these enemies were overcome. Rivers of blood were shed in accomplishing that task. But now the sword was free to join with the shield on the western front. And since the enemy was thus far unable to break the German defense, he himself was now facing attack.

The enemy feared and trembled in the face of a German victory.

In Paris and London, conferences followed one after another, in unending series. Even the enemy propaganda encountered difficulties. It was no longer so easy to demonstrate the hopelessness of a German victory.

The same applied at the front. The insolence of their masters had suddenly subsided. A disturbing truth began to dawn on them. Their opinion of the German soldier had changed. Previously he was a fool destined for defeat. But now he was the destroyer of their Russian ally. The policy of restricting the offensive to the East, which in fact was a necessity, now appeared as a stroke of genius. For three years, these Germans had been battering away at the Russian front without any apparent success. Those fruitless efforts were almost sneered at; it was thought that, in the long run, the Russian giant would triumph through sheer force of numbers, while Germany would be worn out from shedding so much blood. And reality seemed to confirm this hope.

Since the September days of 1914, when for the first time endless columns of Russian war prisoners poured into Germany after the Battle of Tannenberg, it seemed as if the stream would never end. As soon as one army was defeated and routed, another would take its place. The gigantic empire gave the Czar an inexhaustible supply of new soldiers—and the war its new victims. How long could Germany hold out in this race? Wouldn't the day finally come when the Germans would win their last victory, and still the Russian armies would be marching into battle? And then what? In all likelihood, a Russian victory over Germany might be delayed, but it would inevitably come in the long run.

Now all these hopes were at an end. The ally, Russia, who had sacrificed the most blood on the altar of their mutual interests, came to the end of his resources, and lay prostrate before his unrelenting foe. A feeling of terror and dismay came over the Entente soldiers, who had previously been sustained by blind faith. They feared the coming spring. Seeing that they had previously failed to break the Germans when they could concentrate only part of the fighting strength on the western front, how could they count on victory now that the entire power of that amazing heroic state appeared to be gathering for an attack in the west?

The shadow of the events that took place in South Tyrol, the specter of General Cadorna's defeated armies,[6] were reflected in the gloomy faces of the Entente troops in misty Flanders. Faith in victory gave way to fear of defeat to come.

"GERMANY FACING REVOLUTION!" (section 7.8)

Then—on those cold nights, when one almost heard the tread of the German armies advancing to the great assault, and the decision was being awaited in fear and trembling, suddenly a flaming red light was set aglow in Germany, sending its rays into the last shell-hole on the enemy's front. At the very moment when the German divisions were receiving their final orders for the great offensive, a general strike broke out in Germany.

At first the world was dumbfounded. Then the enemy propaganda became active again and pounced on this theme at the eleventh hour. Suddenly a means appeared that could be used to revive the sinking confidence of the Allied soldiers. The probability of victory was now presented as certain, and the anxious foreboding about coming events was transformed into a determined confidence. The regiments awaiting German attack could now be inspired by the conviction that the decisive event in the war was not the boldness of the German attack, but rather the persistence of the defense. Let the Germans have whatever victories they liked; the revolution, and not the victorious army, was at the door of the homeland.

---

[6] Luigi Cadorna (1850-1928) was an Italian general who led his troops into defeat on the Isonzo front.

— 6 —

British, French, and American newspapers began to spread this belief among their readers, while a shrewd propaganda campaign boosted the morale of the troops at the front.

'Germany Facing Revolution! Allied Victory Inevitable!' That was the best medicine to set the staggering *poilu* and Tommy on their feet once again. Our rifles and machine guns could now open fire once again; but instead of creating a panic-stricken retreat, they were met with a determined resistance.

This was the result of the munitions strike. It strengthened the enemy's belief in victory, and it relieved that paralyzing feeling of despair at the front. Consequently, the strike cost the lives of thousands of German soldiers. And the despicable instigators of that dastardly strike were candidates for the highest public offices in revolutionary Germany.

At first it was apparently possible to overcome the repercussion of these events on the German soldiers. But on the enemy's side, they had a lasting effect. The resistance lost all the character of an army fighting for a lost cause, and in its place was a grim determination to struggle through to victory.

Now, according to best judgment, victory would be assured if the western front could hold out against the German attack for only a few months. The Allied parliaments recognized the possibilities of a better future, and voted huge sums of money for on-going propaganda to disrupt Germany.

LAST WREATHS OF IMMORTAL LAUREL (section 7.9)

It was my good luck to fight in the first two offensives, and in the last. These became the most stupendous impressions of my life—stupendous, because now for the last time, the struggle lost its defensive character and became that of an offense, just as it was in 1914. A sigh of relief went up from the German trenches and dug-outs when finally, after three years of endurance in that inferno, the day of retribution arrived. Once again the lusty cheering of victorious battalions was heard, as they hung the last crowns of the immortal laurel on the banners they consecrated to victory. Once again the strains of patriotic songs soared upwards to the heavens above the endless columns of marching troops, and for the last time the Lord smiled on his ungrateful children.

THE ESSENTIAL MEIN KAMPF

In midsummer of 1918, a feeling of sultry oppression hung over the front. At home they were quarrelling. About what? We heard a great deal among various units at the front: that the war was now a hopeless affair; that only fools could think of victory; that it wasn't the people but the capitalists and the monarchy who were interested in carrying on. Such were the ideas that came from home and were discussed at the front.

At first there was only very slight reaction. What did universal suffrage matter to us? Is this why we fought for four years? It was a dastardly piece of robbery thus to steal from the graves of our heroes the ideals for which they had fallen. It wasn't for the slogan, 'Long Live Universal Suffrage' that our troops in Flanders faced certain death, but for the cry *'Deutschland über Alles in der Welt'*—a small but not unimportant difference. And most of those who were shouting for this suffrage were absent when it came to fighting for it. The front was unknown to this political rabble. During those days, only a small fraction of these parliamentarian gentlemen were to be seen where honest Germans gathered.

The old soldiers who had fought at the front had little liking for those new war aims of Messrs. Ebert, Scheidemann, Barth, Liebknecht, and others.[7] We couldn't understand why, all of a sudden, the slackers should grant all executive powers to themselves, without having any regard to the army.

From the very beginning, I had my own definite personal views. I hated the whole gang of miserable party politicians who had betrayed the people. I long ago realized that national interests played only a very small part with this disreputable crew, and that what counted with them was the possibility of filling their own empty pockets. My opinion was that those people thoroughly deserved to be hanged, because they were ready to sacrifice the peace, and allow Germany to be defeated, just to serve their own ends. To consider their wishes would mean to sacrifice the interests of the working classes for the benefit of a gang of thieves. These wishes could only be fulfilled by sacrificing Germany.

---

[7] Friedrich Ebert (1871-1925) was a leader of the German Social Democrats, and the first President of Germany, post-WWI. Philipp Scheidemann (1865-1939) was a post-war Chancellor of Germany in 1919, succeeding Ebert. Emil Barth (1879-1941) was a key figure in the November Revolution of 1918. Karl Liebknecht (1871-1919) was also central to the Revolution; he was killed, along with Jewish socialist Rosa Luxemburg, shortly thereafter. Liebknecht was half-Jewish, the others German.

— 6 —

Such, too, was the opinion still held by the majority of the army. But the reinforcements that came from home were fast becoming worse and worse—so much so that their arrival was a source of weakness rather than of strength. The young recruits in particular were mostly useless. Sometimes it was hard to believe that they were sons of the same nation that sent its youth into the battles for Ypres.

GROWING MORAL DECAY (section 7.10)

In August and September, the symptoms of moral disintegration increased rapidly, although the enemy's offensive was not at all comparable to the terror of our former defensive battles. In contrast, the battles of the Somme and Flanders were much more terrible.

At the end of September, my division occupied, for the third time, those positions that we had once taken by storm as young volunteers.

What a memory!

Here we had received our baptism by fire, in October and November 1914. With a burning love of the homeland in our hearts and a song on our lips, our young regiment went into action as if going to a dance. The dearest blood was given freely here in the belief that it was shed to protect the freedom and independence of the Fatherland.

In July 1917 we set foot for the second time on what we regarded as sacred soil. Our best comrades lay here, some of them little more than boys—the soldiers who had rushed into death, with gleaming eyes, for the one true Fatherland.

The older ones among us, who had been with the regiment from the beginning, were deeply moved as we stood on this sacred spot where we had sworn 'Loyalty and Duty unto Death.'

Three years ago the regiment had taken this position by storm; now it was called upon to defend it in a grueling struggle.

With an artillery bombardment that lasted three weeks, the English prepared for their great offensive in Flanders. There the spirits of the dead seemed to live again. The regiment dug itself into the mud, clung to its shell-holes and craters, neither flinching nor wavering. Our numbers grew steadily smaller, until finally the British launched their attack on 31 July 1917.

We were relieved in the beginning of August.

The regiment had dwindled down to a few companies, who staggered back, mud-crusted, more like ghosts than human beings. Besides a few hundred meters of shell-holes, death was the only reward that the English gained.

Now, in the autumn of 1918, we stood for the third time on the ground we had stormed in 1914. The village of Comines, which formerly had served us as a base, was now within the fighting zone. Although little had changed in the surrounding battlefield, the men became different. They now talked 'politics.' Like everywhere else, the poison from home was having its effect here also. The young recruits succumbed to it completely—they came directly from home.

POISONED BY MUSTARD GAS (section 7.11)

During the night of October 13-14, the British opened an attack with gas on the front, south of Ypres. They used mustard gas, whose effect was unknown to us, at least from personal experience. I would experience it that very night. On a hill south of Wervick, in the evening of October 13, we were subjected for several hours to a heavy bombardment with gas bombs, which continued throughout the night with more or less intensity. About midnight, a number of us were put out of action—some forever. Towards morning, I also began to feel pain. It increased with every quarter of an hour; and at about 7:00 my eyes were scorching as I staggered back and delivered the last dispatch that I would carry in this war.

A few hours later, my eyes were like glowing coals, and all was darkness around me.

I was sent to a hospital at Pasewalk in Pomerania, and it was there that I had to experience—the Revolution!

For a long time, there was something in the air that was indefinable and repulsive. People were saying that something was bound to happen within the next few weeks, although I couldn't imagine what this meant. First I thought of a strike, similar to the one that took place in spring. Unfavorable rumors were constantly coming from the Navy, which was said to be in a state of ferment. But this seemed to be the fanciful creation of a few isolated malcontents. At the hospital, they were all talking about

— 6 —

the end of the war and hoping that this was not far off, but no one counted on anything immediately. I wasn't able to read the newspapers.

In November, the general tension increased.

Then one day, disaster broke upon us suddenly and without warning. Sailors came in trucks and proclaimed the revolution. A few Jewish youth were the 'leaders' in that combat for the 'Liberty, Beauty, and Dignity' of our national being. Not one of them saw active service at the front. By way of a so-called 'hospital for venereal disease,' these three Orientals had been sent back home. Now their red rags were being raised here.[8]

After a few days, I began to feel somewhat better. The burning pain in my eye sockets diminished. Gradually I was able to distinguish the rough outlines of my immediate surroundings. And I allowed myself to hope that I would at least recover my sight sufficiently to be able to take up some profession later on. But it was out of the question that I might ever draw again. In any case, I was on the way to recovery when the monstrous hour arrived.

My first thought was that this outbreak of high treason was only a local affair. I tried to encourage this belief among my comrades. My Bavarian hospital friends were particularly responsive to this. Their mood was anything but 'revolutionary.' I couldn't imagine this madness breaking out in Munich; loyalty to the House of Wittelsbach was, after all, stronger than the will of a few Jews. And so I couldn't help but believe that this was merely a local revolt by the Navy, and that it would be suppressed within the next few days.

'REPUBLIC' (section 7.12)

With the next few days came the most terrible information of my life. The rumors grew more and more persistent. What I had taken as a local

---

[8] It's unclear to which "few" or "three" Jews Hitler is referring. Many Jews were active in the German revolt, as with other revolutions throughout Europe at that time. Prominent among the Jewish leaders of the Social Democrats were Otto Landesberg, Eduard Bernstein, and Rudolf Hilferding. The primary agitator, though, was the Independent Social Democratic Party (USPD), which was dominated by Jews: Kurt Eisner, Rosa Luxemburg, Hugo Haase, Karl Liebknecht (half-Jewish), Leo Jogiches, Karl Radek, Alexander Parvus, Ernst Toller, Gustav Landauer, and Erich Muehsam. For a detailed account of the Jewish role in the Revolution, see Dalton (2013, 2014).

affair was in reality a general revolution. In addition to this, shameful news came from the front. They wanted to capitulate. Was such a thing possible?

On November 10 the local pastor gave a short address at the hospital; now we learned the whole story.

I was in a state of extreme agitation as I listened to the address. The reverend old gentleman seemed to be trembling as he informed us that the House of Hohenzollern would no longer wear the imperial crown. The Fatherland had become a 'Republic,' and we should pray to the Almighty to grant us his blessing in the new order of things and to not abandon our people in the days to come. In delivering his speech, he couldn't do more than briefly express appreciation to the royal house, its services to Pomerania, to Prussia, indeed, to the whole of the German Fatherland, and—here he began to weep. A feeling of profound dismay fell upon the people in that little hall, and I don't think there was a single dry eye in the crowd.

As for myself, I broke down completely when the old gentleman tried to resume his story by informing us that we must now end this long war. The war was lost, he said, and we were at the mercy of the victor. The Fatherland would have to bear heavy burdens in the future. We were to accept the terms of the armistice, and trust in the magnanimity of our former enemies. It was impossible for me to stay and listen any longer. Darkness surrounded me as I staggered and stumbled back to my ward and buried my aching head into the blankets and pillow.

I hadn't cried since the day I stood beside my mother's grave. Whenever fate dealt cruelly with me in my youth, my spirit of determination grew stronger. During all those long years of war, when death claimed many friends and comrades, it would have been almost sinful to have uttered a word of complaint—they died for Germany! And finally, in the last few days of that titanic struggle, when the waves of poison gas enveloped me and began to penetrate my eyes, and the thought of becoming permanently blind unnerved me, my voice of conscience cried out: 'Miserable fellow, will you start howling when there are thousands of others whose lot is a hundred times worse than yours?' And so I accepted my misfortune in silence, realizing that nothing else could be done, and that my personal suffering was nothing compared with the misfortune of the Fatherland.

— 6 —

ALL SACRIFICE IN VAIN (section 7.13)

So all had been in vain. In vain all the sacrifices and privations; in vain the hunger and thirst for endless months; in vain those hours that we stuck to our posts even though mortal fear gripped our souls; and in vain the deaths of two million. Of those hundreds of thousands who set out with hearts full of faith in their Fatherland, and never returned—shouldn't their graves now open, so that the spirits of those heroes splattered with mud and blood may come home and take vengeance on those who had so despicably betrayed the greatest sacrifice that a human being can make for his country? Was it for this that the soldiers died in August and September 1914? For this, that the volunteer regiments followed the old comrades in the autumn of the same year? For this, that those boys of 17 sank into the earth of Flanders? Was this the meaning of the sacrifice that German mothers made for their Fatherland when, with heavy hearts, they said goodbye to their sons who never returned? Has all this been done so that a gang of despicable criminals could lay their hands on the Fatherland?

Was this why the German soldier struggled through sweltering heat and blinding snowstorm, enduring hunger and thirst and cold, fatigued from sleepless nights and endless marches? Was it for this that he lived through an inferno of artillery bombardments, gasping and choking during gas attacks, neither flinching nor faltering, but always thinking of his duty to defend the Fatherland against the enemy?

Certainly these heroes deserved a headstone: "Wanderer, when you come to Germany, tell those at home that we lie here, true to the Fatherland and faithful to our duty."[9]

And at home?

But—was this the only sacrifice that we had to consider? Was the Germany of the past less valuable? Did she not owe a certain duty to her own history? Were we still worthy to partake in the glory of the past? How could we justify this act to future generations?

Despicable and degenerate criminals!

The more I tried to gain some clarity on this monstrous event, the more my head burned with rage and shame. What was the pain in my eyes

---

[9] A variation on a saying by Herodotus, recalling a message inscribed in stone by the Greek defenders of Thermopylae. See *Histories* (7.228).

compared with this tragedy?

The following days were terrible to bear, and the nights worse still. I knew that all was lost. Only fools, liars, or criminals could depend on the mercy of the enemy. During those nights, my hatred grew—hatred for the originators of this crime.

DECISION TO ENTER POLITICS (section 7.14)

In the days that followed, my own fate became clear to me. I had to laugh at the thought of my personal future, which only recently was the cause of so much concern. Was it not ridiculous to build something on such a foundation? Finally, it became clear that the inevitable had happened, something that I had long feared, though I didn't have the heart to believe it.

Kaiser Wilhelm II was the first German Emperor to offer the hand of friendship to the Marxist leaders, not suspecting that they were scoundrels without honor. While they held the imperial hand in theirs, the other hand was already reaching for the dagger.

There is no coming to agreement with the Jews, but rather only the hard 'either-or.'

It was then that I decided to take up politics.

— 7 —
BEGINNING OF MY POLITICAL ACTIVITY and THE "GERMAN WORKERS' PARTY"

At the end of November 1918, I returned to Munich. I went to the replacement battalion of my regiment, which was now in the hands of the 'soldiers' council.' Their whole administration was quite repulsive to me, and so I decided to leave it as soon as possible. With my faithful war-comrade Ernst Schmiedt, I went to Traunstein and remained there until the camp was broken up.

In March 1919 we were back again in Munich.

The situation there was unsustainable; a further extension of the revolution was inevitable. Eisner's death served only to hasten this development, and it finally led to a dictatorship of the councils—or, to put it more correctly, to a Jewish hegemony.[1] This turned out to be transitory, but it was the original aim of those who had instigated the revolution.

At that time, countless plans took shape in my mind. I spent days pondering about what could be done. Unfortunately, every project gave way before the hard fact that I was quite unknown and therefore didn't have even the minimum requirements for effective action. Later on I will explain the reasons why I didn't join any of the existing parties.

As the new revolution of the Councils ran its course in Munich, my activities began to draw the ire of the Central Council. In the early morning of 27 April 1919, I was supposed to have been arrested. But the three fellows who came for me didn't have the courage to face my rifle, and withdrew just as they had arrived.

---

[1] Kurt Eisner (1867-1919) was a leading Jewish revolutionary of Bavaria. He temporarily took power in late 1918, but was killed in February 1919 by German soldiers who had reasserted control over the region.

THE ESSENTIAL MEIN KAMPF

A few days after the liberation of Munich, I was ordered to appear before the inquiry commission that was set up in the 2nd Infantry Regiment for the purpose of watching revolutionary activities.

That was my first more-or-less purely political activity.

A few weeks later I received orders to attend a 'course' that was being given to members of the army. This course was meant to teach certain fundamental civic principles. For me, the advantage of this organization was that it gave me a chance to meet fellow soldiers who were of the same mind, and with whom I could discuss the actual situation. We were all more or less firmly convinced that Germany could not be saved from imminent disaster by those who had participated in the November treachery—which is to say, the Center and the Social Democrats. Also, the so-called Bourgeois National group couldn't repair the damage that had been done, even if they had the best intentions. They lacked a number of prerequisites, without which such a task could never be successful. The years that followed justified the opinions that we held at that time. ...

THE FIGHT AGAINST INTERNATIONAL FINANCE CAPITAL (section 8.5)

When I heard Gottfried Feder's first lecture on 'breaking interest-slavery,' I understood immediately that here was a truth of transcendental importance for the future of the German people.[2] The absolute separation of stock exchange capital from the national economy would make it possible to oppose the internationalization of the German economy without at the same time attacking capital per se. Doing so would jeopardize the foundations of our national independence. I clearly saw what was developing in Germany, and I realized then that the hardest battle we would have to fight would not be against the enemy nations, but against international capital. In Feder's speech I found an effective rallying-cry for our coming struggle.

Here, again, later events proved how correct our impression was. The fools among our bourgeois politicians don't laugh at us now. Even they

---

[2] Feder (1883-1941) was an economist by training, and one of the central founders of the National Socialist party. When Hitler came to power in 1933, Feder joined the government, quickly rising to the level of Reich commissioner. But by 1935 he had withdrawn from politics, preferring a university professorship in Berlin. He stayed there until his death in 1941, at age 58.

now see—insofar as they are not deliberate liars—that international stock-exchange capital was not only the chief instigator for the war, but that now when the fighting has ended, it turns the peace into a hell.

The struggle against international finance capital and loan-capital has become one of the most important points in the program of the German nation's fight for economic independence and freedom.

Regarding the objections raised by so-called practical people, the following answer must suffice: All fears concerning the terrible economic consequences that would follow the abolition of interest-capital slavery are superfluous. In the first place, the economic principles followed thus far have proven nearly fatal to the interests of the German people. This situation recalls similar advice once given by experts in earlier times—such as the Bavarian Medical College, on the question of introducing railroads. None of the fears expressed by that august body of experts were realized. Those who travelled in the coaches of the new 'steam horse' didn't get dizzy. Those who looked on didn't become ill. And the board fences that were erected to conceal the new invention were eventually taken down. Only those board fences that obscured the vision of the so-called 'experts' were preserved for posterity.

In the second place, the following must be noted: Any idea may be a source of danger if it is seen as an end in itself, when really it's only the means to an end. For me and all true National Socialists, there is only one doctrine: People and Fatherland.

We have to fight to safeguard the existence and reproduction of our race and people, the sustenance of our children, the purity of our blood, and the freedom and independence of the Fatherland. Only then may our people fulfill the mission assigned to them by the creator of the universe.

All ideas and ideals, all teaching and all knowledge, must serve these ends. Everything must be examined from this viewpoint and turned to practical uses, or else discarded. Thus a theory can never become a mere dead doctrine, since everything must serve life.

Thus it was that Gottfried Feder's conclusions caused me to make a fundamental study of a question with which I had previously not been very familiar.

I began to study again, and thus it was that I came to truly understand the substance and purpose of the life-work of the Jew Karl Marx. His

Capital became intelligible to me now for the first time.[3] I now exactly understood the Social Democrats' fight against national economics—a fight that was to prepare the ground for the hegemony of a true international and stock exchange capital.

THE 'EDUCATIONAL OFFICER' (section 8.6)

In another direction too, this course of lectures had important consequences for me.

One day I asked to speak. Another participant felt obligated to break a lance for the Jews, and entered into a lengthy defense of them. This aroused my opposition. An overwhelming majority supported my views. The consequence of it all was that, a few days later, I was assigned to a regiment then stationed at Munich, and given a position there as a so-called 'educational officer.'

At that time, the discipline of the troops was rather weak. It was still suffering from the after-effects of the period when the soldiers' councils were in control. Only gradually and carefully was it possible to replace 'voluntary obedience'—a cute name given by Kurt Eisner's pig-sty of a regime—with a spirit of military discipline and subordination. The soldiers had to be taught to think and feel in a national and patriotic way. In these two directions lay my future line of action.

I began my work with the greatest enthusiasm and love. Here I was presented with an opportunity to speak before quite a large audience. I was now able to confirm what I had previously merely felt: I could 'speak.' My voice had become so much better that I could be clearly understood in all parts of the small squadron hall.

No task could have been more pleasing to me than this. Now, before being discharged, I was in a position to render useful service to an institution that was infinitely dear to my heart: the army.

I can now say that my talks were successful. During the course of my lectures, I led hundreds and even thousands of my fellow countrymen back to their people and Fatherland. I 'nationalized' these troops, and in doing so I helped to restore general discipline.

Here again I made the acquaintance of several like-minded comrades, who later came to form the core of the new movement. ...

---

[3] Marx's book *Das Kapital* ('Capital') was initially published in 1867.

—7—

THE "GERMAN WORKERS' PARTY" (section 9.0)

One day I received an order from my superiors to investigate the nature of an apparently political association. It called itself "The German Worker's Party," and was soon to hold a meeting at which Gottfried Feder would speak.[4] I was ordered to attend this meeting and report on the situation.

The curiosity of the army authorities toward political parties can be very well understood. The revolution gave the soldiers the right to take an active part in politics, and it was particularly those with the least experience who made the most of this right. But when the Center and the Social Democratic parties were forced to recognize that the soldiers' sympathies had turned away from the revolutionary parties and towards the national movement and reawakening, they felt obligated to withdraw the right to vote from the army and to forbid it all political activity.

The fact that the Center and Marxism adopted this policy was instructive, because if they hadn't thus curtailed 'civil rights'—as they called the political rights of the soldiers after the revolution—the 'November State' would have been overthrown within a few years, and thus the dishonor and disgrace of the nation wouldn't have been prolonged. At that time, the soldiers were on the verge of ridding the nation of the bloodsuckers and henchmen who served the cause of the Entente within our country. But the fact that the so-called 'national' parties voted enthusiastically for the doctrinaire policy of the November criminals also helped to render the army ineffective as an instrument of national restoration; it thus showed once again where men might be led by the purely doctrinaire ideas accepted by these most gullible people.

The bourgeois middle classes became so senile that they sincerely believed the army could once again become what it had previously been, namely, a stronghold of German power. The Center and Marxism intended only to extract the poisonous fang of nationalism, without which an army must always remain just a police force, and can never be a military organization capable of fighting against the enemy. This truth was amply proved by subsequent events.

Or did our 'national politicians' believe that the development of our army

---

[4] *Deutsche Arbeiterspartei*, or DAP. This would be the forerunner of the National Socialist DAP, or NSDAP. To its detractors, it was the "Nazi" party.

could be other than national? This might have been possible, and could be explained by the fact that, during the war, they weren't soldiers but talkers; in other words, parliamentarians. As such, they didn't have the slightest idea of what was in the hearts of those men who remembered the greatness of their own past, and that they were once the best soldiers in the world.

THE "GERMAN WORKERS' PARTY" [cont.] (section 9.1)

I decided to attend the meeting of this party, which had previously been entirely unknown to me.

When I arrived that evening in the 'guest room' of the former Sternecker Brewery, I found approximately 20 to 25 people present, most of them belonging to the lower classes.

The theme of Feder's lecture was already familiar to me, so I could therefore focus my attention on the organization itself.

The impression was neither good nor bad—a new organization, just like any other. In those days, everyone felt called upon to form a new party whenever he was unhappy with the course of events and lost confidence in the existing parties. Thus it was that new associations sprang up all around, only to disappear just as quickly. Generally speaking, the founders of such associations didn't have the slightest idea of what it means to bring together a number of people for the formation of a party or a movement. Therefore, these associations disappeared because of their utter lack of anything like an adequate grasp of the necessities of the situation.

My opinion of the "German Workers' Party" was no different. I was glad when Feder finally came to a close. I had observed enough and was just about to leave when an open discussion period was announced; I decided to stay. At first this was just more of the same, when suddenly a 'professor' began to speak. He opened by throwing doubt on the accuracy of what Feder had said, and then—after Feder's able reply—the professor suddenly began arguing on what he called 'the basis of facts.' He recommended that the young party take up 'secession' from 'Prussia.' In a most self-assured way, this man kept insisting that German-Austria should join Bavaria, and that the peace would then function much better...and other nonsense. At this point, I felt bound to ask for permission to speak and to tell the learned gentleman what I thought. As a result, and even

— 7 —

before I finished, he slipped out of the hall like a wet poodle. While I spoke, the audience listened with an astonished expression on their faces. When I was just about to say good night to the assembly and leave, a man came after me quickly and introduced himself (I didn't quite catch his name). He placed a little booklet in my hand, which was obviously a political pamphlet, and asked me very urgently to read it.

I was quite pleased; in this way, I could come to know about this association without having to attend its tiresome meetings. Moreover, this apparent workman made a good impression on me.[5] I then left the hall.

At that time, I was living in one of the barracks of the 2nd Infantry Regiment. I had a little room that still bore the unmistakable traces of the revolution. During the day I was mostly out, with the 41st Rifle Regiment, or otherwise attending meetings or lectures held elsewhere. I spent only the night in my room. Since I usually woke up about 5:00 every morning, I got into the habit of amusing myself by watching little mice playing around in my small room. I placed a few pieces of hard bread or crust on the floor and watched the funny little creatures playing around and enjoying themselves with these delicacies. I had suffered so much poverty in my own life that I well knew what hunger was, and I could thus imagine the pleasure of these little creatures.

The next morning, around 5:00 AM, I was fully awake in bed, watching the mice playing and vying with each other. Since I couldn't sleep, I suddenly remembered the booklet that the worker had given me. I began to read. It was a small pamphlet, of which this worker was the author. He described how his mind had thrown off the shackles of Marxist and trade-union phraseology, and that he came back to nationalist ideals. That was the reason why he had entitled his little book: *My Political Awakening*.[6] The pamphlet grabbed my attention the moment I began to read, and I read it with interest to the end. The process described was similar to that which I had experienced in my own case, 12 years earlier. Unconsciously, my own development came again to mind. During that day, my thoughts returned several times to what I had read; but eventually I forgot about it. A week or so later, however, I received a postcard that informed me, to my

---

[5] The worker turned out to be Anton Drexler, one of the original founders of the DAP.

[6] *Mein Politisches Erwachen*, by Anton Drexler (1920; E. Boepple, Munich).

astonishment, that I had been admitted to the DAP. I was asked to reply to this communication and to attend a meeting of the Party Committee the next Wednesday.

This method of 'winning' members amazed me, and I didn't know whether to be angry or laugh. I had no intention of joining any existing party, but wanted to found one of my own. It was presumptuous of them to ask and, for me, completely out of the question.

I was about to send a written reply when curiosity got the better of me, and I decided to attend the gathering on the assigned date, so that I might explain my principles to these gentlemen in person.

THE 'COMMITTEE MEETING' (section 9.2)

Wednesday came. The tavern in which the meeting was to take place was the Alte Rosenbad in the Herrnstrasse—a run-down place with very few guests. This wasn't very surprising in 1919, when the menus of even the larger restaurants were only very modest and scanty. But I had never before heard of this business.

I went through the badly-lighted guest room, where not a single guest was to be seen, and opened the door to the back room; there I found the 'session.' In the dim light of a grimy gas lamp, I could see four young people sitting around a table, one of them the author of the pamphlet. He greeted me cordially and welcomed me as a new member of the DAP.

I was somewhat taken aback. I was then informed that the 'national chairman' had not yet arrived; I decided that I would withhold my own ideas for the time being. Finally the chairman appeared. He was the same chairman as in the Sternecker Brewery, when Feder spoke.

My curiosity was growing, and I sat waiting for what was to come. Now at least I learned the names of the gentlemen. The chairman of the 'national organization' was a certain Herr Harrer;[7] and the leader of the Munich district was Anton Drexler.

The minutes of the previous meeting were read out, and a vote of confidence in the secretary was passed. Then came the treasurer's report.

---

[7] Karl Harrer (1890-1926) was a journalist and early founder of the DAP. He parted ways with Hitler not long after their initial meeting, and died soon thereafter at age 36.

— 7 —

The association possessed a total of seven marks and 50 pfennigs, whereupon the treasurer was assured that he had the confidence of the members. This was now inserted in the minutes. Then the chairman's replies to a number of letters were read: first, to a letter received from Kiel, then to one from Düsseldorf, and finally to one from Berlin. Everyone expressed approval. Then the incoming letters were read: one from Berlin, one from Düsseldorf, and one from Kiel—all resulting in great satisfaction. This was taken as the best and most obvious sign of the growing importance of the DAP. And then—there followed a long discussion of the replies to be given.

Terrible, terrible! This was tedious bureaucracy of the worst sort. And was I to join such a club?

Next came the question of new members—that is to say, the question of my capture.

I now began to ask questions. But I found that, apart from a few general principles, there was nothing: no program, no pamphlet, nothing at all in print, no membership cards, not even a party stamp; only clear good faith and good intentions.

I no longer felt like laughing—for what else was all this but a typical sign of the most complete helplessness and total despair of all political parties, their programs, and their activities?

The feeling that induced those few young men to join in what seemed such a ridiculous enterprise was nothing but the call of an inner voice. It told them, more intuitively than consciously, that the whole party system as it existed was incapable of raising up the German nation or repairing the inner wounds. I quickly read through the list of principles that formed the party platform. These were stated on typewritten sheets. Here again I found evidence of a spirit of longing and searching, but no sign whatsoever of a knowledge of the conflict that had to be fought.

I myself had experienced the feelings that inspired those people: it was the longing for a movement that would be more than a party, in the usual sense of that word.

When I returned to the barracks that evening, I had formed a definite opinion of that association.

I was facing the hardest question of my life: Should I join this party, or should I decline?

A FINAL DECISION (section 9.3)

Rationally, every consideration urged me to decline; but my feelings troubled me. The more I tried to prove to myself how senseless this club was, on the whole, the more my feelings inclined me to favor it.

In the days to follow, I was restless.

I began to consider all the pros and cons. I had long ago decided to take an active part in politics. It was clear that I could do so only through a new movement; but I had previously lacked the impulse to take concrete action. I'm not one of those people who will begin something one day and give it up the next, just for the sake of something new. That was the main reason why it was so difficult for me to decide to join such an organization. This would have to be the fulfillment of my goals, or else I shouldn't do it at all. I knew that such a decision would bind me forever, and that there could be no turning back. This was no idle game, but rather a serious and ardent cause. Even then I had an instinctive revulsion against people who took up everything, but never carried anything through to the end. I loathed these jacks-of-all-trades, and considered the activities of such people to be worse than doing nothing at all.

Fate itself now seemed to point the way. I would never have entered one of the big existing parties; I'll explain my reasons for this later on. This absurd little group, with its handful of members, seemed to have the unique advantage of not yet being frozen into an 'organization.' It still offered a chance for real personal activity on the part of the individual. Here it might still be possible to do some effective work; and, as the movement was still small, one could all the easier give it the proper shape. Here it was still possible to determine the character of the movement, the aims to be achieved, and the road to be taken; all of this would have been impossible in the big parties.

The longer I reflected on the situation, the more my opinion developed that just such a small movement could best serve to prepare the way for a national resurgence. This could never be done by the political parliamentary parties, which were too firmly attached to obsolete ideas or had an interest in supporting the new regime. What had to be proclaimed here was a new worldview, and not a new election slogan.

It was, however, infinitely more difficult to turn this intention into reality.

— 7 —

What qualifications did I bring to this task?

The fact that I was poor and without resources could, in my opinion, be the easiest to bear. But the fact that I was utterly unknown raised a more difficult problem. I was only one of the millions that Chance allowed to exist, whom even their next-door neighbors will not consent to know. And another difficulty arose from my lack of schooling.

The so-called 'intellectuals' still look down with limitless disdain on anyone who hasn't been through the prescribed schools, and had the necessary knowledge pumped into them. The question has never been, What can a man do?, but rather, What has he learned? 'Educated' people look upon any idiot who is plastered with diplomas as superior to the ablest young man who lacks these precious documents. I could therefore easily imagine how this 'educated' world would receive me, and I was wrong only insofar as I then believed men to be better than they proved to be, in the harsh light of reality. Because they are this way, the few exceptions stand out all the more brightly. I learned more and more to distinguish between the eternal students and those who are the true men of ability.

After two days of careful brooding and reflection, I became convinced that I must take the step.

It was the most fateful decision of my life.

There was and could be no turning back.

Thus I registered as a member of the German Worker's Party, and received a provisional membership card, with the number: seven.

— 8 —
CAUSES OF THE COLLAPSE

MORAL DISARMAMENT OF A DANGEROUS ACCUSER (section 10.4)

It required the entire bottomless falsehood of the Jews, and their fighting comrades the Marxists, to lay blame for the collapse [of Germany at the end of WWI] precisely on the man who alone had shown a superhuman will and energy in his effort to prevent the catastrophe that he had foreseen, and to save the nation from that time of humiliation and disgrace. By placing sole blame for the loss of the World War on Ludendorff, they took away the weapon of moral right from the only adversary dangerous enough to be likely to succeed against the betrayers of the Fatherland.[1]

All this was inspired by the unquestionably true principle that in the Big Lie there is always a certain degree of credibility, because the broad masses of a nation are always more easily corrupted in the very bottom of their hearts than consciously or voluntarily. And in the primitive simplicity of their minds, they more readily fall victims to the Big Lie than the small lie, since they themselves often tell small lies in little matters, but would be ashamed to resort to large-scale falsehoods. It would never occur to them to fabricate colossal untruths, and they would not believe that others could have the impudence to distort the truth so infamously.

Even though the facts that prove this are clear, they will still doubt and waver, and will continue to think that there must be some other explanation. The grossly impudent lie always leaves traces behind it, even after it has stuck—a fact that is known to all artful liars in this world, and to all who conspire together in the art of lying. These people know only too well how to use falsehood for the basest of purposes.

---

[1] Erich Ludendorff (1865-1937) was a leading German general during World War I. He was an early supporter of Hitler's, and participated with him in the failed putsch of 1923.

THE ESSENTIAL MEIN KAMPF

From time immemorial, however, the Jews have known better than any others how to exploit falsehood and calumny. Their very existence is based on one great lie, namely, that they are a religious community and not a race. And what a race. One of the greatest thinkers of mankind has branded them for all time with a statement that is profoundly and precisely true: he called them "The great master of the lie."[2] Those who don't realize the truth of that statement, or don't wish to believe it, will never be able to lend a hand in this world to help truth prevail.

It was a great stroke of fortune for the German nation that its period of lingering sickness was so suddenly ended by a terrible catastrophe. If things had gone on as they were, the nation would have slowly but surely come to ruin. The disease would have become chronic; whereas, in the acute form, it at least showed itself clearly to a considerable number of observers. It was no accident that man conquered the black plague more easily than tuberculosis. The first appeared in terrifying waves of death that shook the whole of mankind; the other advances insidiously. The first induces terror; the other, gradual indifference. The result is, however, that men opposed the first with all their energy, while they try to control tuberculosis by feeble means. Thus man has mastered the plague, while tuberculosis masters him.

The same applies to diseases in national bodies. As long as these diseases aren't of a catastrophic nature, people will slowly accustom themselves to them, and eventually succumb. It is then a stroke of luck—though a bitter one—when fate decides to intervene in this slow process of decay and suddenly brings the victim face to face with the final stage of the disease. More often than not, the result of a catastrophe is that a cure is undertaken immediately, and carried through with a firm determination.

But even in such a case, the prerequisite is always the recognition of the internal causes that created the disease in question.

---

[2] Hitler quotes the philosopher Arthur Schopenhauer. In his book *Parerga and Paralipomena* (1851), Schopenhauer remarks on the historically low opinion of the Jews: "We see also from the two Roman authors [Tacitus and Justinus] how much the Jews were at all times, and by all nations, loathed and despised. This may be due partly to the fact that they were the only people on earth who did not credit man with any existence beyond this life, and were therefore regarded as beasts... Scum of humanity—but great master of lies" (1851/2010, vol. 2, p. 357, revised translation). For further discussion of Schopenhauer's view of the Jews, see Dalton (2011b).

— 8 —

TOXINS AND SYMPTOMS (section 10.5)

The important question here is the differentiation of the root causes from the circumstances growing from them. This becomes all the more difficult the longer the toxins remain in the national body, and the longer they are allowed to become an integral part of that body. It may easily happen that, as time goes on, unquestionably harmful poisons will be accepted as belonging to the national being, or that they are tolerated as a necessary evil. In this case, it won't even be seen as necessary to locate the alien virus.

During the long period of peace prior to the last war, certain evils were evident here and there—although, with one or two exceptions, very little effort was made against the virus. Here again, these exceptions were first and foremost those economic phenomena of the nation that were more apparent to the individual consciousness than the harmful conditions existing in many other spheres.

There were many signs of decay that should have been given serious thought.

As far as economics were concerned, the following may be said:

The amazing increase of the German population before the war brought the question of providing daily bread into a more prominent position in all spheres of political and economic thought and action. Unfortunately, those responsible couldn't decide to arrive at the only correct solution, but preferred to reach their goal by cheaper methods. Renouncing the idea of acquiring fresh territory, and substituting for it a mad desire for global economic conquest, was bound to eventually lead to unlimited and harmful industrialization.

The first and most fatal consequence was a weakening of the agricultural class, whose decline was proportionate to the increase in the proletariat of the urban areas. In the end, the equilibrium was completely upset.

The big barrier dividing rich and poor now became apparent. Luxury and poverty lived so close together that the consequences were bound to be deplorable. Poverty and frequent unemployment began to wreak havoc with the people, leaving discontent and embitterment behind them. The result of this was to divide the population into political classes. Discontent increased despite commercial prosperity. Matters finally reached the point at which everyone felt that 'things can't go on as they are,' although no one seemed able to visualize what was really going to happen.

These were typical signs of the depths to which the prevailing discontent had reached.

THE RULE OF MONEY (section 10.6)

Far worse than these, however, were other consequences that became apparent as a result of the economization of the nation.

In proportion to the degree that commerce assumed definite control of the state, money became more of a god, to whom all had to serve and bow down. Heavenly gods became more and more old-fashioned, and were stuffed away in the corners to make room for the worship of Mammon. And thus began a period of utter degeneration. This was especially pernicious because it came at a time when the nation was at its critical hour, and more than ever needed an exalted ideal. Germany should have been prepared to protect with the sword her efforts to win her own daily bread through 'peaceful economic labor.'

Unfortunately, the domination of money was sanctioned in the very quarter that should have opposed it. His Majesty the Kaiser made a mistake when he raised representatives of the new finance capital to the ranks of nobility. Admittedly, it may be an excuse that even Bismarck failed to realize the looming danger in this respect. In practice, however, all ideal virtues became secondary considerations to those of money; it was clear that having once taken this road, the nobility of the sword would soon rank second to the nobility of finance.

Financial operations succeed easier than military ones. Hence it was no longer inviting for a true hero or even a statesman to be brought into touch with the nearest Jewish banker. Men of real merit weren't interested in cheap decorations, and declined them with thanks. But from the standpoint of blood-purity, such a development was deeply regrettable. The nobility began to lose more and more of the racial qualities that were a condition of its very existence. In many cases, the term 'ignobility' would have been more appropriate. . . .

— 8 —

JEWISH PRESS TACTICS (section 10.13)

The function of the so-called liberal press was to dig a grave for the German people and the German Reich. We need not mention the lying papers of the Marxist press; for them, lying is as much a vital necessity as the mouse is to a cat. Their sole task is to break the national backbone of the people, thus preparing the nation to become the slaves of international capital and its masters, the Jews.

And what did the state do to counteract this mass poisoning of the nation? Nothing, absolutely nothing at all! A few silly decrees, a few fines for criminality, and that was it. By this policy, they hoped to win the favor of this plague by means of flattery, with a recognition of the 'value' of the press, its 'importance,' its 'educational mission,' and similar nonsense. The Jews acknowledged all this with a knowing smile and a sly thanks.

The reason for this disgraceful failure on the part of the state lay not so much in its refusal to realize the danger, as in the cowardly way of meeting the situation through half-hearted decisions and measures. No one had the courage to employ any thoroughly radical methods. Everyone piddled around with halfway prescriptions. Thus, instead of striking at its heart, they only irritated the viper. The result was that not only did everything remain the same, but the power of the institutions that should have been combated grew stronger year by year.

The government's defense in those days, against a mainly Jewish-controlled press that was slowly corrupting the nation, followed no definite line of action; it was lacking in resolve and, above all, had no fixed goal in view. This is where official understanding of the situation completely failed: in estimating the importance of the struggle, in choosing the means, and in deciding on a definite plan. They merely tinkered with the problem. Occasionally, when bitten, they imprisoned a journalistic viper for a few weeks or months, but the whole snakes' nest was allowed to carry on unmolested. ...

SYPHILIS (section 10.15)

A further example of the weak and half-hearted way in which vital national problems were dealt with in pre-war Germany is the following:

Parallel to the political, ethical, and moral infection of the nation has been, for many years, an equally virulent process of poisoning the public health. Particularly in large cities, syphilis has steadily increased, and tuberculosis has steadily reaped its harvest of death in almost every part of the country.

Although in both cases the effect on the nation was alarming, it seemed as if no one was able to undertake any decisive measures against these scourges.

In the case of syphilis especially, the attitude of state and governmental leaders was one of absolute capitulation. To combat it, something far more sweeping was required. The discovery of a questionable remedy, and its commercial exploitation, were only of little assistance in fighting this plague. Here again, the only correct course is to attack the disease in its causes rather than its symptoms. The cause lies mainly in the prostitution of love. Even if it didn't directly bring about this frightful plague, it would still be deeply harmful to the people; the moral havoc resulting from this degeneracy would be sufficient to bring about the destruction of the nation, slowly but surely.

This Judaizing of our spiritual life and mammonizing of our mating instinct will sooner or later ruin our future offspring. The vigorous children of a natural, emotional bond will be replaced by miserable specimens of financial expediency. Economic considerations are more and more becoming the basis and sole prerequisite for marriage. And love must then find its outlet somewhere else.

Here, as elsewhere, one may defy Nature for a certain period of time; but sooner or later she will take her revenge. And when we realize this truth, it's often too late.

Our own nobility offers an example of the devastating consequences that follow from a persistent refusal to recognize the natural requirements for marriage. Here we have before us the results of those reproductive habits that, on the one hand, are determined by social pressure and, on the other, by financial considerations. The one leads to inherited weaknesses, and the other to poisoning of the blood. Just consider how every department store Jewess is viewed as an eligible mate for our royalty—and indeed, it shows. All this leads to absolute degeneration.

Today our bourgeoisie strive to follow the same path; they will come to the same end.

— 8 —

These unpleasant truths are hastily and nonchalantly brushed aside, as if by so doing the truth could be abolished. No: it can't be denied that our urban populations are tending more and more toward a prostituted love-life, and are thus becoming more and more contaminated by the scourge of syphilis. It simply is true. The most visible effects of this mass contamination can be seen, on the one hand, in our insane asylums and, on the other, unfortunately, in our children. They are the sad product of this steadily growing contamination of our sexual life; in their sicknesses, the children reveal the vices of their parents.

There are many ways of reconciling oneself to this unpleasant and terrible fact. Many people go about seeing nothing at all or, more precisely, not wanting to see anything. This is by far the simplest and easiest 'opinion.' Others cover themselves in the sacred mantle of prudery, as absurd as it is hypocritical. They describe the whole situation as sinful, and are profoundly indignant when brought face to face with a victim. They close their eyes in pious horror to this godless scourge, and pray to God that he might rain down fire and brimstone on this whole Sodom and Gomorrah—if possible, after their deaths. In doing so, God should once again make an instructive example of this shameless humanity. A third group, finally, are well aware of the terrible results that this scourge inevitably brings about, but they merely shrug their shoulders, fully convinced that nothing can be done against this danger. Hence the only thing to do is let matters take their own course.

THE SIN AGAINST BLOOD AND RACE (section 10.16)

Undoubtedly all this is very convenient and simple, but it must not be forgotten that a nation can fall victim to such convenience. The excuse that other nations are also faring poorly doesn't change the fact of our own deterioration, except that feelings of sympathy for others makes our own suffering easier to bear.

But the important question, then, is this: Which nation will be the first to take the initiative in mastering this plague, and which nations will succumb to it? This is the crux of the whole situation. Here again we see the touchstone of racial value: the race that cannot withstand the test will simply die out, making room for healthier, tougher, or more resistant races.

Because this question primarily concerns future generations, it is one of those cases where, with terrible justification, the sins of the fathers are visited upon their children, unto the tenth generation—a truism, but one that applies only to a desecration of blood and race.

The sin against blood and race is the original sin in this world. It brings an end to every nation that commits it.

The attitude towards this one vital problem in pre-war Germany was most regrettable. What measures were taken to halt the infection of our youth in the large cities? What was done to put an end to the contamination and mammonization of our love lives? What was done to fight the resultant syphilization of our national body?

The answer to this question can best be illustrated by showing what should have been done.

Instead of taking this problem lightly, the authorities should have realized that the fortunes or misfortunes of future generations depended on its solution. Yes—it would be decisive for the entire future of our people. But to admit this would have required ruthless measures and surgical operations. What was needed, first of all, was that the attention of entire country be concentrated on this terrible danger, so that everyone would realize the importance of fighting against it. It would be futile to impose definitive and often unbearable obligations, and to expect them to be effective, unless the public were thoroughly instructed on the need for such obligations. But this demands a widespread and systematic method of enlightenment, one that excludes any other daily problems that might distract the public's attention.

In every case where apparently impossible demands are involved, the entire public attention must be focused on this one question, as though its solution were a matter of life or death. Only in this way can the public be compelled to join in a great voluntary effort, and to achieve important results.

This principle applies also to the individual man, provided he wants to achieve some great end. He must always concentrate his efforts on one definitely limited stage of his progress, which has to be completed before the next step is attempted. Those who don't attempt to realize their aims step by step, and who don't concentrate their energy in reaching the individual stages, will never attain the final objective. At some point along the road, they will falter and fail. This systematic way of approaching an

— 8 —

objective is an art in itself, and always calls for expending every ounce of energy in order to conquer the road, step by step.

Therefore the most essential prerequisite for an attack on such a difficult stage of the pathway of humanity is that the authorities must succeed in convincing the masses that the immediate objective that is now being sought is the only one that deserves to be considered, and the only one on which everything depends. The broad masses are never able to clearly see the whole stretch of road ahead without becoming tired and thus losing faith in their ability to complete the task. A certain number will keep the objective in mind, but they are only able to survey the road in small stages, as in the case of the traveller who knows where his journey will end but who tackles the endless stretch far better by attacking it in degrees. This is the only way can he advance without losing enthusiasm.

THE TASK OF COMBATING SYPHILIS (section 10.17)

In this way, with the assistance of every form of propaganda, the problem of fighting syphilis should have been placed before the public—not as *a* task, but as the *main* task. Every possible means should have been employed to bring this truth to the minds of the people, until the whole nation has been convinced that everything depends on the solution to this problem; which is to say, a healthy future or national decay.

Only after such preparatory measures—spread over a period of many years, if necessary—will the public be fully aroused, and only then can serious and definite measures be taken. We could then do so without the risk of being misunderstood, or of being suddenly faced with a slackening of the public will.

It must be made clear to all that a serious fight against this plague calls for tremendous sacrifices and an enormous amount of work.

A war against syphilis means fighting against prostitution, against prejudice, against old-established customs, against current fashion, public opinion, and last but not least, against a false prudery in certain circles.

The first prerequisite to be fulfilled before the state can claim a moral right to fight against all these things is the facilitation of earlier marriages for the coming generations. Whatever way we view it, late marriages have the sanction of a custom that is, and will remain, a disgrace to humanity.

It's a cursed institution, ill-suited to a being who likes to regard himself as in the 'image' of God.

Prostitution is a disgrace to humanity, and cannot be removed simply by moralistic lectures, good intentions, etc. Its restriction and final elimination presupposes the removal of a whole series of contributory circumstances. The first remedy must always be to establish such conditions as will make early marriages possible, especially for young men—women are, after all, only passive subjects in this matter.

An illustration of the extent to which people have so often been led astray nowadays is shown by the fact that one often hears mothers in so-called 'good' society openly expressing their satisfaction at having found their daughter a man who has 'sown his wild oats,' etc. As there is no shortage of such men, the poor girl will be happy with one of these de-horned Siegfrieds, and the children will be a visible result of such supposedly sensible unions.

When one realizes that, apart from this, every possible effort is being made to hinder the process of procreation and that Nature is being wilfully cheated of her rights, there remains really only one question: Why does such an institution still exist, and what purpose does it serve? Isn't it little better than prostitution? Doesn't our duty to posterity play a part any more? Or don't people realize the curse they are inflicting on themselves and their offspring by such criminally foolish neglect of one of the primary laws of nature?

This is how civilized nations degenerate and gradually perish.

Marriage is not an end in itself, but must serve a higher goal, which is to increase and maintain the species and race. This is its only meaning and purpose.

This being the case, it's clear that the institution of marriage must be judged by the manner in which it fulfills its function. Therefore early marriages should be the rule, because only the young couple will still have the strength necessary for raising healthy offspring. Of course, early marriages cannot be made the rule without a whole series of social changes; otherwise a policy of early marriages cannot even be contemplated. In other words, a solution of this seemingly small question cannot occur without decisive social measures. Their importance should be clear, especially when the so-called 'social' Republic has shown itself unable to solve the housing problem, and thus has made it impossible for innumerable couples to get married. That only furthers the advance of prostitution.

Another reason why early marriages are impossible is our absurd method of regulating the scale of salaries, which pays far too little attention to the problem of family support.

Prostitution, therefore, can only be seriously tackled if, by means of a radical social reform, early marriage is made easier than at present. This is the first preliminary requirement for the solution of this problem.

SOUND MIND ONLY IN SOUND BODY (section 10.18)

Secondly, a whole series of evils must be eradicated through education and training—things that no one has yet worried about. First of all, our present educational system must establish a balance between mental instruction and physical training. The institution known today as *Gymnasium* is a positive insult to the Greek model. Our system of education entirely loses sight of the fact that, in the long run, a healthy mind can exist only in a healthy body. This statement, with few exceptions, applies particularly to the broad masses of the nation.

In pre-war Germany, there was a time when no one took the trouble to think over this truth. Training of the body was criminally neglected, and the one-sided training of 'the mind' was regarded as a sufficient guarantee for the nation's greatness. This mistake showed its effects sooner than anticipated. It's no accident that Bolshevik teaching flourishes in those regions whose population has been degenerated by hunger: in central Germany, Saxony, and the Ruhr Valley. In all these districts there is a marked absence of any serious resistance, even by the so-called intellectual classes, against this Jewish disease. And the simple reason is that the intellectual classes are themselves physically degenerate—not through privation, but through education. The exclusive intellectualism of education among our upper classes makes them incapable of defending themselves, let alone making their way in life. In nearly every case, physical weakness is the forerunner of personal cowardice.

The extreme emphasis on purely intellectual education, and the consequent neglect of physical training, necessarily leads to sexual thoughts in early youth. Those youth whose constitutions have been trained and hardened by sports and gymnastics are less prone to sexual indulgence than those stay-at-homes who have been fed exclusively with intellectual fare. A sensible system of education must bear this in mind. We must not forget that a healthy young man will have different expectations from a woman than those of a weakling who has been prematurely corrupted.

Thus, in every branch of our education, the daily curriculum must occupy a boy's free time in useful development of his physical powers. He has no right in those years to loaf about, becoming a nuisance in public streets and cinemas. But when his day's work is done, he should harden his young body so that he will not become soft later in life. To prepare for this, and to carry it out, should be the function of our educational system, and not exclusively to pump in so-called wisdom. Our school system must also rid itself of the notion that bodily training is best left to the individual himself. There is no such thing as freedom to sin against posterity, and thus against the race.

THE FIGHT AGAINST SPIRITUAL POISONING (section 10.19)

The fight against the poisoning of the mind must be waged simultaneously with the training of the body. Our whole public life today may be compared to a hothouse for sexual ideas and incitements. A glance at the bill-of-fare provided by our cinemas, playhouses, and theaters suffices to prove that this is not the right food, especially for our youth. In shop windows and advertisements, the most vulgar means are used to attract public attention. Anyone who hasn't completely lost contact with adolescent yearnings will realize that all this must cause great damage. This seductive and sensual atmosphere puts ideas into the heads of our youth that, at their age, should still be unknown to them.

Unfortunately, the results of this kind of education can best be seen in our contemporary youth. They mature too early and are therefore old before their time. The law courts occasionally throw a distressing light on the spiritual life of our 14- and 15-year-olds. Who, then, will be surprised to learn that syphilis claims its victims already at this age? And isn't it deplorable to see the number of physically weak and intellectually spoiled young men, who have been introduced to the rites of marriage by the big-city whores?

No; those who wish to seriously combat prostitution must first assist in removing its spiritual basis. They will have to ruthlessly clean up the

— 8 —

moral plague of our city 'culture,' and do so without regard for the outcry that will follow. If we don't lift our youth out of the morass of their present environment, they will drown in it. Those who refuse to see these things are deliberately encouraging them, and thus are guilty of spreading the effects of prostitution to the future—since the future belongs to the coming generation. This process of cleansing our culture must be applied in practically all spheres. Theater, art, literature, the cinema, the press, and advertisements, all must remove the stains of our rotting world and be placed in the service of a moral, political, and cultural idea. Public life must be freed from the asphyxiating perfume of our modern eroticism, as well as from all unmanly and prudish hypocrisy. In all these things, the aim and the method must be determined by thoughtful consideration for the preservation of our national well-being in body and soul. The right to personal freedom falls behind the duty of maintaining the race.

Only after such measures have been put into practice can a medical campaign against this plague begin with some hope of success. But here again, half-measures are worthless. Far-reaching and important decisions must be made. It's a half-measure if incurables are given the opportunity of infecting one healthy person after another. This would be that kind of humanitarianism that allows a hundred to perish in order to avoid hurting one individual.

The demand that defective people be prevented from producing defective offspring is one that's based on the most reasonable grounds, and its proper fulfillment is the most humane act of mankind. Unhappy and undeserved suffering of millions will be spared, with the result that there will be a gradual improvement in national health. A determination to act in this way will at the same time provide an obstacle against the further spread of venereal disease. It would then be a case, where necessary, of mercilessly isolating all incurables—a barbaric measure for those unfortunates, but a blessing for the present generation and for posterity. The temporary pain experienced in this century can and will spare millennia from suffering.

The fight against syphilis, and the prostitution that paves its way, is one of the gigantic tasks of humanity. It's not merely a case of solving a single problem but the removal of a whole series of evils that are the contributory causes of this plague. Disease of the body in this case is merely the result of a sickening of the moral, social, and racial instincts.

But if, for reasons of laziness or cowardice, this battle isn't fought to the finish, we can imagine what conditions will be like in 500 years. Little of God's image will be left in human nature, except to mock the Creator. ...

MODERN MASSES OF HUMANITY (section 10.24)

Still another critical symptom has to be considered.

In the course of the 19th century, our towns and cities began to lose their character as centers of civilization, and became more and more centers of habitation. In our great modern cities, the proletarian man doesn't show much attachment to the place where he lives. This feeling results from the fact that his town is nothing but an accidental abode. The feeling is also partly due to the frequent change of residence that's forced upon him by social conditions; there's no time to form a bond to the place in which he lives. And yet another reason lies in the cultural barrenness and superficiality of our present-day cities.

At the time of the Wars of Liberation,[3] our German towns and cities were not only small in number but also very modest in size. The few that could be called great cities were mostly the residential cities of princes; as such, they almost always had a definite cultural value and cultural aspect. Those few towns of more than 50,000 inhabitants were, in comparison with modern cities of the same size, rich in scientific and artistic treasures. At the time when Munich had not more than 60,000 souls, it was already well on the way to become one of the first German centers of art. Nowadays almost every industrial town has a population at least as large as that, without having anything of real value to call its own. They are masses of tenement houses and apartments, and nothing more. It's a mystery how anyone could grow sentimentally attached to such a meaningless place. No one can bond to a place that offers no more than any other place would offer, that has no character of its own, and where pains have obviously been taken to avoid everything that might have any resemblance to an artistic appearance.

But that's not all. Even great cities become more barren of real works of art the more they increase in population. They assume more and more a neutral atmosphere, and present the same aspect, though on a larger

---

[3] Circa 1813.

scale, as the poor little factory towns. Everything that our modern age has contributed to the civilization of our great cities is absolutely deficient. All our cities are living on the glory and the treasures of the past. If we take away from the Munich of today everything that was created under Ludwig I, we would be horror-stricken to see how meager has been the output of important artistic creations since that time.[4] One could say the same of Berlin and most of our other great cities.

But the following is the essential point: Our great modern cities have no outstanding monuments that dominate the city, ones that could be pointed to as symbols of a whole epoch. Yet almost every ancient town had a monument erected to its glory. It wasn't in private dwellings that the characteristic art of ancient cities was displayed, but in the public monuments, which were not meant to have a transitory interest but an enduring one. And this was because they didn't represent the wealth of some individual citizen, but rather the greatness and wealth of the community. Thus it was that those monuments arose that bound the individual inhabitants to their own town in a way that's almost incomprehensible to us today. What struck the eye of the ancient citizen wasn't a number of mediocre private buildings, but imposing structures that belonged to the whole community. Compared to them, private dwellings were of only very secondary importance.

When we compare the size of those ancient public buildings with that of the private dwellings, then we can understand the great importance that was given to the principle that communal works should take precedence over all others. What we today admire in the ruins of the ancient world aren't the former commercial palaces but rather temples and public structures. The community itself was the owner of those great works. Even in the pomp of late Rome, it wasn't the villas and palaces of some citizens that filled the most prominent place but rather the temples and the baths, the stadiums, the circuses, the aqueducts, the basilicas, etc., which belonged to the state, and therefore to the whole people.

In medieval Germany the same principle held sway, although the artistic outlook was quite different. In ancient times, that which found its expression in the Acropolis or the Pantheon was now cloaked in the forms of the Gothic cathedral. These monumental structures towered gigantically

---

[4] Ludwig I, King of Bavaria (1786-1868), made Munich a major art center during the time of his rule, from 1825 to 1848.

above the swarm of smaller buildings, with their framework walls of wood and brick. And they remain the dominant feature of these cities even today, although they are becoming more and more obscured by apartment buildings. They determine the character and appearance of the town. Cathedrals, city halls, corn exchanges, and defense towers are the outward expression of an idea that's based in the ancient world.

And how deplorable has the relationship become today between our state and private buildings! If a similar fate should befall Berlin as did Rome, future generations might gaze upon the ruins of some Jewish department stores or corporate hotels and think that these were the characteristic expressions of the culture of our time. In Berlin itself, just compare the shameful disproportion between the buildings of the Reich and those of trade and finance.

Funding for public buildings are, in most cases, inadequate and ridiculous. They aren't built for eternity, but mostly for responding to the need of the moment. No higher idea influenced such buildings. When the Berlin Palace was built, it had a quite different significance from what the new library has for our time. One battleship alone represents an expenditure of about 60 million marks, whereas less than half that sum was allotted for the building of the Reichstag—which is the most imposing structure erected for the Reich, and which should have been built to last for ages. Yet, when the question of internal decoration arose, the Upper House voted against the use of stone and ordered that the walls should be covered with stucco. For once, however, the parliamentarians made an appropriate decision; plaster heads would be out of place within stone walls.

The community per se is not the dominant characteristic of our contemporary cities, and therefore it's no surprise that the community finds itself architecturally underrepresented. Thus we must eventually arrive at a state of desolation—with the practical effect that the individual citizen is totally indifferent to the fate of his city.

This too is a sign of our cultural decay and general collapse. Our era is entirely preoccupied with pointless little things, or rather, with the service of money. Therefore it's little wonder that, with the worship of such an idol, a sense of heroism entirely disappears. But the present is only reaping what the past has sown.

— 9 —
NATION AND RACE

Certain truths are so obvious that, for this very reason, they are neither seen nor recognized by ordinary people. People are so blind to some of the simplest facts in everyday life that they are very surprised when someone calls attention to what everyone should know. Examples of the Columbus Egg surround us by the hundreds of thousands; but Columbuses are rare.[1]

Walking around in the garden of Nature, most men have the conceit to think that they know everything. Yet almost all are blind to one of the outstanding principles that Nature employs in her work: the inner separation of the species of all living beings on Earth.

Even a superficial glance shows that nature follows a rigid basic law in which all life-forms are restricted to definite limits when propagating and multiplying their own kind. Each animal mates only with one of its own species. The titmouse seeks the titmouse, the finch with the finch, the stork with the stork, the field mouse with the field mouse, the house mouse with the house mouse, the wolf with the she-wolf, etc.

Deviations from this law take place only in exceptional circumstances, such as the compulsion of captivity, or when some other obstacle makes intercourse impossible between members of the same species. But then nature resists such intercourse with all her might. Her protest is most clearly demonstrated by the fact that the hybrid is either sterile or its descendants have limited fertility. In most cases, they are denied the ordinary powers of resistance to disease or to hostile attacks.

---

[1] The Columbus Egg refers to an apocryphal tale in which Christopher Columbus allegedly challenged a group of Spanish noblemen to balance an egg on one end. After they fail, he takes the egg, taps it on the table to slightly crush one end, and then it stands. The moral is that a seemingly impossible task, once done in a certain way, becomes obvious. Many inventions and discoveries are precisely of this nature.

This is only too natural.

Every crossing between two breeds that aren't quite equal yields a product that holds an intermediate place between the levels of the two parents. This means that the offspring will indeed be superior to the racially inferior parent, but not as high as the higher parent. For this reason, it must eventually succumb in any struggle against the higher species. Such mating contradicts the will of nature towards the selective improvements of life in general. The precondition to this improvement is not to mate superior and inferior, but rather to allow the complete triumph of the higher order. The stronger must dominate and not mate with the weaker, thus sacrificing its own greatness. Only the born weakling can look upon this principle as cruel, but he is only a feeble and limited man; for if such a law did not prevail, then the higher development of organic life would be inconceivable.

The consequence of this urge for racial purity, universally valid in nature, is not only the sharply-defined outward distinction between the races but also their uniform character in themselves. The fox is always a fox, the goose is a goose, the tiger is a tiger, etc. The only difference that can exist within the species must be in the various degrees of force, strength, intelligence, efficiency, endurance, etc., of the individual specimens. It would be impossible to find a fox that is kindly and protective towards geese, just as no cat has a friendly disposition towards mice.

That's why the struggle between the various species doesn't arise from mutual antipathy but rather from hunger, and from love. In both cases, Nature looks on calmly, and even with satisfaction. The struggle for daily bread leaves behind all those who are weak or sickly or wavering, while the male struggle for the female gives to the healthiest the right to propagate. And this struggle is a means of furthering the species' health and powers of resistance, and therefore its higher development.

If the case were different, progress would cease, and even regression would occur. Since the inferior always outnumber the superior, the former would always increase more rapidly if they possessed the same capacities for survival and reproduction. The end result would be that the best would be driven into the background. Therefore a corrective measure in favor of the better must intervene. Nature supplies this by establishing rigorous living conditions, to which the weaker will have to submit and will thereby be numerically restricted. But even the portion that survives cannot reproduce indiscriminately, for here a new and rigorous selection takes place, according to strength and health.

THE RESULT OF RACIAL MIXING (section 11.1)

If Nature doesn't wish that weaker individuals should mate with the stronger, even less does she wish that a superior race should mix with an inferior one. In such a case, all her efforts, throughout hundreds of thousands of years, to establish an evolutionary higher type of being, might be rendered futile.

History provides countless proofs of this law. It shows, with a startling clarity, that whenever Aryans have mingled their blood with that of an inferior race, the result has been the downfall of the cultured people. In North America, where the population is predominantly Germanic, and where those elements intermingled with the colored peoples only to a very small degree, there is a different humanity and culture than those of Central and South America. In these latter countries, the Latin immigrants mated with the aborigines, sometimes on a large scale. In this case we have a clear and decisive example of the effect of racial mixing. But in North America, the Germanic element, which has remained racially pure and unmixed, has come to dominate the American continent. And it will remain master, as long as that element doesn't fall victim to a defiling of the blood.

In short, the results of racial mixing are always the following:

(a) The level of the superior race becomes lowered; and

(b) Physical and mental degeneration sets in, thus leading slowly but surely towards a progressive sickness.

Such a development is nothing other than a sin against the will of the eternal Creator.

And as a sin, this act will be avenged.

Man's effort to contradict the iron logic of nature brings him into conflict with those principles to which he himself owes his own existence. By acting against nature, he prepares the way for his own ruin.

THE ESSENTIAL MEIN KAMPF

MAN AND IDEA (section 11.2)

Here we meet an insolent pacifist objection, one that is Jewish in its inspiration: "Man can control even nature!"

There are millions who mindlessly repeat this Jewish nonsense, and end up imagining that somehow they themselves are the conquerors of nature. Yet their only weapon is just a mere idea, and a very preposterous one at that. If one accepted it, then it would be impossible even to imagine the existence of the world.

The real truth is that, not only has man failed to overcome nature in any sphere whatsoever, but that at best he has merely succeeded in getting hold of and lifting a tiny corner of the enormous veil she has spread over her eternal mysteries and secrets. He never creates anything. All he can do is to discover something. He doesn't master nature, but has only come to be the master of those living beings who lack the knowledge he has arrived at, by penetrating into some of nature's laws and mysteries. Apart from all this, an idea can never overcome the preconditions for the existence and development of mankind; the idea itself has come only from man. Without humanity, there would be no human idea in this world. The idea as such is therefore always dependent on the existence of man, and thus is dependent on those laws that created the conditions of his existence.

And not only that! Certain ideas are even confined to certain people. This holds particularly true with regard to those ideas that have roots not in objective scientific truth but in the world of feeling. In other words—to use a current phrase that expresses this truth—they reflect an 'innner experience.' All such ideas, which have nothing to do with cold logic per se but represent mere feelings, such as ethical and moral conceptions, etc., are inextricably bound up with man's existence. Such ideas owe their existence to the creative powers of man's imagination.

Now then, a necessary condition for the maintenance of such ideas is the existence of certain races and certain types of men. For example, anyone who sincerely wishes that the pacifist idea should prevail in this world should do everything possible to help the Germans conquer the world. If the opposite should happen, it may easily be the case that the last pacifist would disappear with the last German. I say this because,

— 9 —

unfortunately, no one else in the world has fallen prey to this nonsense like our own people. Whether we liked it or not, we would have to wage war in order to achieve pacifism. This, and nothing less, was the plan of the American world-savior, Wilson.[2] Or at least, that was what our visionaries believed—and thus his goal was achieved.

The pacifist-humanitarian ideal may indeed be an excellent one, but only when the most superior type of man has succeeded in subjugating the world to such an extent that he is the sole ruler of the Earth. This ideal would have evil effects only to the extent in which its application became difficult and finally impossible. So, first of all, the fight; and then perhaps pacifism.

If the case were different, it would mean that mankind has already passed the peak of its development, and thus the end wouldn't be the supremacy of some moral ideal, but degeneration into barbarism and chaos. People may laugh at this statement. But our planet once moved through the ether for millions of years without men, and it may do so once again—if we forget that, wherever humans have reached a superior level of existence, it wasn't due to the ideas of a few crazy visionaries, but by knowing and rigorously applying the iron laws of nature.

RACE AND CULTURE (section 11.3)

All that we admire in the world today—science, art, technology, and inventions—are the products of the creative activities of a few peoples; and perhaps even originally of one race. The maintenance of civilization is wholly dependent on them. Should they perish, all that makes this Earth beautiful will descend with them into the grave.

However much the soil, for example, can influence men, this influence will vary according the the particular race in question. Poor soil may stimulate one race to the highest achievements; in another race, it may be the cause of poverty and finally of malnourishment, with all its consequences. Though subject to external circumstances, it is the internal characteristics of a people that always determine the outcome. That which reduces one race to starvation drives another to hard work.

---

[2] Woodrow Wilson, American president during World War I. It was his administration, heavily populated with Jewish advisers, that dictated the harsh terms of the Versailles Treaty. Hitler never forgave him for that.

All the great civilizations of the past decayed because the originally creative race died out, as a result of poisoning of the blood.

The ultimate cause of such a decline is the fact that the people forgot that all culture depends on men, and not the reverse. In other words, to preserve a certain culture, the man that creates it must be preserved.

But this preservation is bound up with the inexorable law of necessity, and with the right of victory of the best and strongest.

He who would live must fight. And he who doesn't wish to fight in this world of permanent struggle has no right to live.

Such a saying may sound harsh—and so it is! Yet far harsher is the fate of he who believes that he can overcome nature, and thus in reality insults her. Distress, misery, and disease are her replies!

Whoever ignores or misjudges the laws of race deprives himself of the happiness that belongs to him. He places an obstacle in the victorious path of the superior race and, by doing so, interferes with a precondition of all human progress. Burdened with humanitarian sentiment, he falls back to the realm of the helpless beast.

THE ARYAN AS FOUNDER OF CULTURE (section 11.4)

It would be futile to attempt to determine which race or races were the original standard-bearers of human culture, and were thereby the real founders of all that we understand by the word 'humanity.' It's much simpler to deal with this question insofar as it relates to the present time. Here the answer is simple and clear. Every manifestation of human culture, every product of art, science, and technical skill that we see today, are almost exclusively the creative product of the Aryan. This very fact fully justifies the conclusion that it was the Aryan alone who founded a superior type of humanity; therefore he represents the archetype of what we understand by the term 'man.' He is the Prometheus of mankind, from whose shining brow the divine spark of genius has at all times flashed forth, always kindling anew the fire that, in the form of knowledge, illuminated the dark night by drawing aside the veil of mystery, showing man how to rise up and become master over all the other earthly beings. Exclude him—and a profound darkness will descend upon the Earth. Within a few thousand years, human culture will vanish and the world will become a desert.

— 9 —

If we divide mankind into three groups—founders of culture, bearers of culture, and destroyers of culture—the Aryan alone can be considered as representing the first group. It was he who erected the foundation and walls of every great structure in human culture. Only the shape and color of such structures can be attributed to the characteristics of the various peoples. The Aryan furnished the great building stones and plans for the edifices of all human progress; only the execution of these plans can be attributed to the qualities of each individual race.

Within a few decades, the whole of eastern Asia, for instance, will possess a culture was founded by the Greek mind and Germanic technology. Only the external form—at least partly—shows the traits of Asiatic inspiration. It isn't true, as some believe, that Japan adds European technology to its own culture. The truth rather is that European science and technology are just overlaid with the peculiar characteristics of Japanese civilization. The foundations of actual life in Japan today aren't those of native Japanese culture, although this colors daily life and thus appears striking to the European eye. Rather, the real foundations are the enormous scientific and technical achievements of Europe and America; that is, of Aryan peoples. Only on basis of these achievements can the Orient follow contemporary world progress. They provide the basis of the struggle for daily bread, and create weapons and implements for this; only the outward form is gradually adapted to Japanese ways of life.

If, from today onwards, the Aryan influence on Japan ceased—if Europe and America collapsed—then Japan's present progress in science and technology might still last for a short while. But within a few decades, the inspiration would dry up, native Japanese character would flourish, and present civilization would become fossilized and fall back into the sleep from which it was aroused seven decades ago by Aryan culture. Therefore, just as present Japanese development is due to Aryan influence, so in the distant past, foreign influence and spirit awakened Japanese culture of that day.

The best proof of this is the fact that ancient Japanese civilization actually became fossilized and petrified. This can happen only if a people loses the racial nucleus that was originally creative, or if an outside influence is withdrawn after having awakened and maintained the initial cultural developments. If it be shown that a people owes the fundamental elements of its culture to foreign races, assimilating and elaborating such elements, and if subsequently that culture becomes fossilized whenever the external influence ceases, then such a race may be called 'culture-bearing' but never 'culture-creating.'

Examining various peoples from this standpoint shows that practically none of them were originally culture-founding, but almost always culture-bearing.

This development nearly always happens in the following way:

Aryan tribes, often ridiculously small in number, subjugate foreign peoples and, stimulated by the conditions of life in the new territory (fertility, climatic abundance, etc.), and profiting also by the abundance of manual labor, they develop the intellectual and organizational faculties dormant in them. Within a few thousand years, or even centuries, they create cultures that reflect the inner characteristics of the founders—though modified by the special qualities of the soil and the subjugated people.

In the end, though, the conquering race offends against the principle of blood purity to which they initially adhered. They begin to mix with the subjugated people, thus ending their own existence. Mankind's Fall in Paradise has always been followed by expulsion.

After a thousand years or more, the last visible traces of the former master people may then be found in a lighter tint of the skin that the blood had bequeathed to the subjugated race, and in a petrified culture that it had originally created. Once the blood of the bodily and spiritual conqueror got lost in the blood of the subjected people, the fuel for the torch of human progress was lost! Just as the blood of the former ruling race left a light nuance of color in the blood of its descendants as a token memory, so too the night of cultural life is gently illuminated by the products of those who were the original bearers of light. Their radiance shines through the barbarism to which the subjected race has reverted. This often leads the superficial observer to believe that he sees before him an image of the present race, when in fact he is only gazing into a mirror of the past.

It may happen that, in the course of its history, such a people will come into contact a second time, or perhaps more, with the race of original founders of their culture. They may not even remember that distant association. Instinctively, though, the remnants of the master blood will be drawn towards this new phenomenon, and what had formerly been possible only under compulsion can now succeed through the people's own will. A new cultural wave flows in, and lasts until the blood of its standard-bearers once again submerges in the blood of the conquered peoples.

It will be the task of those who study the universal history of civilization to conduct research from this viewpoint, instead of allowing themselves to be smothered by a mass of external data—as is only too often the case with our present historical science.

This short sketch of the development of the culture-bearing nations gives a picture of the development and activity—and the decline—of those who are the true culture-founders on this Earth, the Aryans themselves.

Just as in our daily life the so-called man of genius needs a particular occasion, and sometimes indeed a special stimulus, to make him shine, so too with racial genius in the life of peoples. In the monotony of everyday life, even men of significance seem just like the others, and don't rise above the average of their fellow men. But as soon as such men find themselves in a situation in which others stray or become hopeless, the humble and ordinary man reveals traits of genius—often to the amazement of those who had, until then, only known him in the pettiness of everyday life. That's why a prophet only seldom counts for anything in his own country.

War offers an excellent occasion for observing this. In times of distress, when the others despair, apparently harmless boys suddenly spring up and become heroes, with death-defying determination and an icy-cool mindset. If such an hour of trial hadn't come, no one would have guessed that a hero lurked in the body of that beardless youth.

A special impulse is almost always necessary to bring genius into view. The sledge-hammer of fate, which strikes down the one so easily, suddenly strikes steel in another. And when the shell of everyday life is broken, the hidden core lay visible to an astonished world. The world resists. It refuses to believe that something seemingly so normal is suddenly so different. This process is repeated every time a man of outstanding quality appears.

Though an inventor, for example, doesn't establish his fame until the day of his invention, it would be a mistake to believe that the creative genius didn't become alive until that moment. The spark of genius lives within the man who has it from the moment of birth. True genius is an innate quality; it can never be cultivated or learned.

As stated already, this applies not merely to the individual but also the race. Peoples with creative abilities have always been fundamentally creative. It belongs to their very nature, even though this fact may escape the eyes of the superficial observer. Here, too, recognition from outside is only the consequence of practical achievement. The rest of the world is incapable of recognizing genius as such, and can only see the visible manifestations of genius in the form of inventions, discoveries, buildings, paintings, etc. But even here, a long time passes before recognition is given. Just as the individual person who has been endowed with the gift of genius, or at least talent of a very high order, cannot realize that endowment until prompted by special circumstances, so too in the life of nations; creative capacities and powers frequently have to wait until certain conditions stimulate them to action.

The most obvious example of this truth is furnished by that race that has been, and still is, the standard-bearer of human progress: the Aryans. As soon as fate confronts them with special circumstances, their powers begin to develop progressively and to be manifested in tangible forms. The cultures that they create are almost always conditioned by the soil, the climate, and the people they subjugate.

The last factor is the most decisive. The more primitive the technical conditions for cultural activity, the more necessary is the existence of manual labor that can be organized and employed to take the place of mechanical power. Had it not been possible to employ members of the inferior race, the Aryans would never have been in a position to take the first steps toward a future culture. Similarly, without the help of certain suitable animals that they were able to tame, they would never have come to a technology that has subsequently enabled them to do without these beasts. The phrase, 'The Moor has done his work, the Moor can go' has, unfortunately, a deep meaning.[3] For thousands of years, the horse has been the faithful servant of man, helping to lay the foundations of human progress; but now the motor car has made the horse superfluous. In a few years to come, the horse's function will cease entirely. And yet without its

---

[3] Quoting from Schiller's 1783 play *Die Verschwörung des Fiesko zu Genua* (Fiesco's Conspiracy at Genoa), Act III, Scene 4.

collaboration, man could scarcely have come to the stage of development where he is today.

For the establishment of superior types of cultures, the inferior races were one of the most essential prerequisites. They alone could compensate for the lack of mechanical means, without which no progress is possible. The first stages of human culture were certainly not based so much on tame animals as on the use of inferior human beings.

Only after subjugated races were used as slaves did a similar fate strike the animals, and not vice versa, as some people would like to believe. At first it was the conquered enemy who had to draw the plow—and only afterwards the horse. Only foolish pacifists can see this as a sign of human degradation. Such people fail to recognize that this development had to take place in order to reach that place where these apostles could force their drivel upon the world.

Human progress is like ascending an infinite ladder. One can't reach the higher levels without first having climbed the lower rungs. The Aryan therefore had to take the path to which reality directed him, and not that dreamt of by the modern pacifist. The path of reality, however, is difficult and hard; yet it's the only one that finally leads to the goal that others envisage in their dreams. In reality, the dreamers only lead man away from his goal, rather than towards it.

It was no accident that the first forms of culture arose where the Aryan came into contact with inferior races, subjugated them, and forced them to obey his command. The members of the inferior race became the first technical instrument in the service of a developing culture.[4]

EFFECTS OF BLOOD-MIXING (section 11.5)

Thus the road that the Aryan had to follow was clearly marked. As a conqueror, he subjugated inferior races and turned their physical powers into organized channels under his own leadership, forcing them to follow his will and aims. By imposing on them a useful, though hard, activity, he not only spared their lives but probably made their lives easier than they had been with their former so-called 'freedom.' While he ruthlessly

---

[4] This idea anticipates the later idea of the 'megamachine' as a systematic use of human labor to achieve social and cultural ends. See Mumford (1966).

maintained his position as their master, he not only remained master but he also maintained and advanced human culture. This depended exclusively on his inborn abilities and, therefore, on his preservation as such.

As soon, however, as his subject began to rise up and approach the level of their conqueror—probably at the point when they began to use his language—the dividing wall between master and servant broke down. The Aryan neglected his own racial purity and thereby lost the right to live in the paradise that he himself had created. He became submerged in the racial mixture and gradually lost his cultural creativeness, until he finally became, both mentally and physically, more like the subjugated aborigines rather than his own ancestors. For awhile he could continue to live on the cultural capital that still remained; but a condition of fossilization soon set in, and he sank into oblivion.

Thus cultures and empires declined, yielding their places to new formations.

Blood mixture and the subsequent racial deterioration are the only causes of the decline of ancient civilizations. It's never by war that nations are ruined, but by the loss of their powers of resistance, which are contained only in pure racial blood.

Everything in this world that is not racially good is like chaff.

Every historical event in the world is nothing but a manifestation of the instinct of racial self-preservation, whether for better or worse.

SERVICE TO THE COMMUNITY (section 11.6)

The question of the inner causes for the dominating importance of Aryanism can be answered by saying it isn't so much that they have a stronger survival instinct, but rather that this manifests itself in a special way. Considered subjectively, the will-to-live is equally strong everywhere; only the forms in which it is expressed are different.

Among the most primitive organisms, the survival instinct doesn't extend beyond concern for the individual ego. Egoism, as we call this passion, goes so far that it even includes *time*; the present moment is deemed the most important, and nothing is left to the future. The animal lives only for itself, seeking food when hungry and fighting only for its own self-preservation. As long as the instinct for self-preservation manifests itself in this way, there is no basis for the formation of a community—not even the most primitive form of family. Even a community of two, male and female, demands an extension of the instinct for self-preservation, since the readiness to fight for one's own ego must be extended to the mate. The male sometimes provides food for the female, but in most cases both parents provide food for the offspring. Almost always, they are ready to protect and defend each other; so that here we find the first, though infinitely simple, form of the spirit of sacrifice. As soon as this spirit extends beyond the narrow limits of the family, we have the conditions under which larger associations, and finally even states, can be formed.

The lowest peoples of this Earth display this quality only to a very small degree, so that often they don't go beyond the formation of the family. With an increasing readiness to subordinate their immediate personal interests, the capacity develops for organizing more extensive communities.

The readiness to sacrifice one's personal labor and, if necessary, even one's life, for others is most highly developed in the Aryan. The greatness of the Aryan is not his intellect, but rather his willingness to devote all his faculties to the service of the community. Here the instinct for self-preservation has reached its noblest form. The Aryan willingly subordinates his own ego to the common interest and, when necessary, even sacrifices it.

The Aryan's peculiar ability for the building up of a culture is not grounded in his intellectual gifts alone. If that were so, they could only be destructive and could never be able to organize; the innermost essence of organization demands that the individual renounce his own personal opinions and interests, and lay both at the service of the larger group. By serving the common interest, he receives his reward in return. For example, he doesn't work directly for himself but makes his productive work a part of the activity of the group to which he belongs—not only for his own benefit, but for all. The spirit underlying this attitude is expressed by the word 'work,' which to him doesn't mean earning one's daily livelihood but rather a productive activity that doesn't clash with the interests of the community. Whenever human activity is directed exclusively to the service of the instinct for self-preservation, it's called theft, usury, robbery, burglary, etc.

THE ESSENTIAL MEIN KAMPF

This state of mind, which forces self-interest into the background in favor of the community, is the first prerequisite for any true human culture. From this alone rises all the great works of humanity, that bring little reward to the creator but is a source of great blessings for posterity. It's this spirit alone that explains why a people can endure a harsh but honest existence, but at the same time consolidates the foundations on which the community exists. Every worker, every peasant, every inventor, state official, etc., who works without ever achieving fortune or prosperity for himself is a representative of this sublime idea—even though he may never become conscious of the profound meaning of his own activity.

That which applies to work as the fundamental condition of human sustenance and the means of human progress, applies even more so to work done in defense of man and his culture. Giving one's own life for the sake of the community is the crowning sense of sacrifice. Only in this way can we protect that which has been built by man, ensuring that it won't be overthrown by man or destroyed by nature.

PUREST IDEALISM, DEEPEST KNOWLEDGE (section 11.7)

Our German language has a word that admirably expresses this kind of activity: *Pflichterfüllung*, or the service of the community before individual self-sufficiency.

To distinguish it from egoism or selfishness, we call the basic attitude that arises from this kind of activity—idealism. By this we signify the willingness of the individual to make sacrifices for the community and his fellow men.

It's of the utmost importance to insist again and again that idealism is not merely a superfluous expression of emotion, but rather something that has been, is, and always will be a necessary precondition of human culture—yes, even that it created the very idea of the concept of 'human.' The Aryan owes his position in the world to this kind of mentality; and to the world, man. From this pure spirit has arisen the creative force that, combining brutal fist with intellectual genius, has created the monuments of human culture.

Were it not for idealism, all the faculties of the intellect, even the most brilliant, would be nothing but intellect itself—a mere external phenomenon without inner value, and never a creative force.

Since true idealism, however, is essentially the subordination of individual interests and life to the community, and since the community, for its part, represents the prerequisite of every form of organization, this corresponds, in its innermost essence, with the final will of nature. This feeling alone makes men voluntarily acknowledge the privilege of strength and power, and thus makes them a constituent particle in that order that shapes and forms the whole universe.

The purest idealism is unconsciously associated with the deepest knowledge.

How true this is, and how little genuine idealism has to do with fantastic imagination, becomes clear the moment we ask an unspoiled child—a healthy boy, for example—to give his opinion. The very same boy who listens to the rantings of an 'idealistic' pacifist without understanding them, and even rejects them, would readily sacrifice his young life for the ideal of his people.

Unconsciously, his instinct will obey the primal necessity of the preservation of the species, even at the cost of his individual life, and he will protest against the fantasies of pacifist ranters—who in reality are nothing better than cowardly but disguised egoists, and who contradict the laws of human development. Such development requires a willingness of the individual to sacrifice for the community, and not the morbid imaginings of cowardly know-it-alls and critics of nature.

Just at the time when the idealistic attitude threatens to disappear, we notice a weakening of the force that founds and maintains the community, and is thereby a necessary precondition of culture. As soon as egoism begins to prevail among a people, the bonds of social order break down; and man, by seeking his own personal happiness, falls out of heaven and right into hell.

Yes: Posterity will forget those who pursued only their own interests; but it will praise those heroes who have renounced their own happiness.

ARYAN AND JEW (section 11.8)

The most striking contrast to the Aryan is the Jew. There is probably no other people in the world who have so developed the instinct of self-preservation as the so-called chosen people. The best proof of this is the simple fact that this race still exists. Where are another people that, in the course of the last 2,000 years, have undergone so few changes in mental outlook and character as the Jews? What other people has been involved in greater revolutionary changes—and yet, even after the most gigantic catastrophes, has emerged unchanged? What an infinitely tenacious will-to-live, to preserve one's kind, is shown by that fact!

The intellectual faculties of the Jew have been trained over thousands of years. Today he passes as 'smart'; and in a certain sense, he has been so throughout the ages. But his intelligence is not the result of an inner evolution, but rather has been shaped by the object-lessons of others.

The human spirit cannot climb upwards without taking successive steps. For every step upwards, it needs the foundation of the past—which, in the comprehensive sense, only appears in general culture. All thinking originates, only to a very small degree, in personal experience. The largest part is based on the accumulated experiences of the past. The general level of culture subconsciously provides the individual with such an abundance of preliminary knowledge that he can thereby more easily take further steps of his own.

The boy of today, for example, grows up among such an overwhelming mass of technical achievements of the last centuries that he takes for granted many things that, a hundred years ago, were still mysteries even to the greatest minds. Yet these things are of enormous importance to those who would understand the progress we have made in these matters, and would like to carry on that progress. If a man of genius from the 1820s were to arise from his grave today, he would find it harder to understand our present age than the average 15-year-old boy. He would lack an extraordinary amount of preliminary information that our contemporary youth receive automatically, so to say, as they grow up among the products of our modern culture.

Since the Jew—for reasons that will become apparent—never had a culture of his own, he has always been supplied with a basis for his intellectual work by others. His intellect has always developed through the cultural achievements of those around him.

The process has never been the reverse.

Though the Jewish people's instinct for self-preservation hasn't been weaker but rather much stronger than among other peoples, and although one gets the impression that their intellectual powers are at least equal to those of other races, they completely lack the most essential prerequisite of a cultured people—the idealistic spirit.

With the Jewish people, the readiness for sacrifice doesn't extend beyond the simple instinct for individual preservation. The feeling of solidarity that they apparently manifest is nothing but a very primitive herd instinct, similar to that which is found among other organisms in this world. It's a remarkable fact that this herd instinct provides mutual support only as long as there is a common danger, which makes mutual assistance useful or inevitable. The same pack of wolves that just joined together in a common attack will dissolve into individuals as soon as their hunger is quenched. The same is true of horses, which unite to defend themselves against any aggressor but separate as soon as the danger is over.

CONSEQUENCES OF JEWISH EGOISM (section 11.9)

It's the same with the Jew. His spirit of sacrifice is only apparent. It is present only as long as the individual's existence makes this an absolute necessity. But as soon as the common foe is conquered, the danger that threatened is overcome, and the prey secured, then the apparent Jewish harmony disappears and the original conditions return. The Jews act in concord only when a common danger threatens, or when a common prey attracts them. Where these two motives are lacking, the most brutal egoism appears; and these people, who had previously lived together in unity, turn into a swarm of rats that bloodily fight among themselves.

If the Jews were the only people in the world, they would wallow in filth and mire. They would exploit and uproot one another in a bitter struggle—except insofar as their utter lack of the ideal of sacrifice, which shows itself in their cowardice, turned the struggle into comic theater.

It would therefore be a complete mistake to infer any sense of sacrifice in the Jews from the fact that they stand together in a common struggle against—or rather, to exploit—their fellow man.

Here again, the Jew merely follows the naked egoism of the individual.

That's why the Jewish State—which should be a vital organization to preserve or increase the race—has absolutely no territorial boundaries. The territorial delimitation of a state always demands a certain spirit of idealism on the part of the race in question, and especially a proper interpretation of the idea of work. A territorially delimited state cannot be established or maintained without a generally positive attitude towards work. If this attitude is lacking, then the necessary basis of a culture is also lacking.

That's why the Jewish people, despite their apparent intellectual powers, have no culture—and certainly no culture of their own. The present sham culture of the Jew is the product of the work of others, and this product is debased in his hands.

SHAM CULTURE OF THE JEWS (section 11.10)

In order to correctly evaluate Jewry's attitude toward the question of human culture, we must bear in mind the essential fact that there never has been any Jewish art, and consequently there is none today. Above all, in those two royal domains of art—architecture and music—Jewry has done nothing original. What they do achieve in the field of art is either a patchwork, or intellectual theft.[5] The Jew essentially lacks the qualities that are characteristic of those creative races that are the founders of culture.

To what extent the Jew appropriates foreign civilization—or rather corrupts it—is indicated by the fact that he chiefly cultivates the art that calls for the least original invention, namely, acting. And even here he is only a 'juggler,' or rather an imitative monkey; he lacks the final touch that's necessary for true greatness. Even here, therefore, he is not a creative genius but rather a superficial imitator who, in spite of all his twists and tricks, cannot disguise the fact that there's no inner vitality in his work. Here the Jewish press comes in and renders friendly assistance by shouting hosannas over even the most ordinary bungler—as long as he's a Jew—until the rest of the world is stampeded into thinking that the object of so much praise must really be an artist. In reality he's nothing more than a pitiful comedian.

No; the Jew has no culture-creating abilities of any kind. There is not, and has never been, in him any spirit of idealism that is a necessary

---

[5] This complaint is ancient. For centuries, observers have remarked on the inability of Jews to create their own culture or civilization. As far back as circa 75 AD, Apollonius Molon wrote that the Jews "are the only people who have contributed no useful invention to civilization"; for details, see Dalton (2011).

element in the higher development of mankind. His intellect will never be constructive, but always destructive. At best, it may serve as a stimulus in rare cases, but only as the archetype of "the power that always wants Evil and nevertheless creates the Good."[6] Human progress occurs not through him, but in spite of him.

THE JEW, A PARASITE (section 11.11)

Since the Jew has never had a state based on territorial limits, and therefore never a culture of his own, the idea arose that here was a people who had to be considered as nomads.[7] This is a great and dangerous error. The true nomad does actually possess a definite territory; but he merely doesn't cultivate it, as the settled farmer does. He lives on the products of his herds, with which he wanders over his domain. The natural reason for this mode of existence can be found in the infertility of the soil, which doesn't allow permanent settlement.

The deeper cause, though, lies in the fact that there is no technical culture at hand to make up for the natural poverty of the living space. There are territories where even the Aryan can establish fixed settlements only by means of his technology, developed over the course of more than a thousand years. Otherwise these territories would have to be abandoned, unless the Aryan were willing to wander about in nomadic fashion. But his technical tradition and his age-long experience in the use of technical means would probably make the nomadic life unbearable for him.

We should remember that, during the first period of American colonization, numerous Aryans earned their daily livelihood as trappers, hunters, etc., frequently wandering about in large groups with their women and children, very much like nomads. But as soon as their growing numbers and improved tools allowed the land to be cleared, and natives driven out, their established settlements rapidly grew.

The Aryan himself was probably at first a nomad, becoming a settler only in the course of ages. And therefore he was never a Jew! No, the Jew is not a nomad; the nomad already has a definite attitude towards the concept of 'work,' and this served as the basis of later cultural development, when

---

[6] Goethe's *Faust*, line 1336.
[7] What we would today call 'nomadic hunter-gatherers.'

the necessary intellectual conditions were at hand. There's a certain amount of idealism in the nomad, even though of a rather primitive kind. His whole character, therefore, may seem odd to the Aryan, but he will never be unsympathetic to it. The Jew, however, hasn't the slightest trace of idealism. He has never been a nomad, but always a parasite in the body of other peoples. If he occasionally abandoned regions where he had previously lived, he didn't do so voluntarily. He did it because, from time to time, he was driven out by those whom he had abused.[8] Jewish self-expansion is a typical parasitic phenomenon; he always seeks new feeding ground for his race.

But this has nothing to do with nomadism, because the Jew never thinks of leaving a territory that he has once occupied. He firmly stays where he is, with such tenacity that he can hardly be driven out, even by force. He expands into new territories only when certain conditions for his existence appear; but without them—unlike the nomad—he would never change his residence. He is and remains an eternal parasite, a sponger who, like a pernicious bacillus, spreads over wider and wider areas as they become favorable to him. The effect produced by his presence is also like that of a sponger; wherever he establishes himself, the host people die out, sooner or later.

JEWISH 'RELIGIOUS COMMUNITY' (section 11.12)

Thus the Jew has, at all times, lived in states belonging to other people, and there he has formed his own state. It remains hidden behind the mask of 'religious community,' as long as external circumstances make it inadvisable to reveal its true nature. But as soon as he feels strong enough to do without a disguise, he lifts the mask and suddenly becomes that which many others didn't wish to believe or see: the Jew.

The Jew's life as a parasite thriving on the body of other nations and states explains a characteristic that caused Schopenhauer to describe the Jew as "the great master of lies."[9] Existence compels the Jew to lie, and to lie systematically—just as it compels the inhabitants of northern climates to wear warm clothes.

---

[8] For millennia, Jews have been driven out by their host populations. The Nazi expulsion of Jews was only the latest in a long history of such actions, reaching back at least to the ancient Egyptians.

[9] See note 2, p. 162.

— 9 —

He can live among other peoples only as long as he succeeds in persuading them that he is not a people but a 'religious community'—though of a special sort.

This is but his first great lie.

In order to continue his existence as a parasite of other peoples, he is obliged to conceal his inner nature. The greater the intelligence of the individual Jew, the better will he succeed in deceiving others. It may go so far that his host people will actually believe that the Jew really is a Frenchman or Englishman, a German or Italian, who happens to belong to a special religious faith. State authorities in particular, who generally have only a minimal historical sense, fall victim to his notorious deception. In these circles, independent thinking is considered a sin against the sacred rules by which official promotion takes place. It's therefore unsurprising that even today, in the Bavarian government offices, for example, there isn't the slightest suspicion that the Jews form a people and not a 'religion.' One glance, though, at the Jewish press should provide sufficient proof for even those of the most modest intelligence. The *Jewish Echo*, however, is not an official gazette and therefore not authoritative in the eyes of those government potentates.

JEWISH RELIGIOUS DOCTRINE (section 11.13)

Jewry has always been a nation of a definite racial character, and never a religion. Early on, and driven by a desire to get ahead, they began to seek for a means that would distract from any inconvenient attention. What could be more effective, and at the same time more above suspicion, than the idea of a religious community? Here, too, everything is copied, or rather stolen—the Jew could not possess any religious institution that developed from his own nature, seeing that he lacks any kind of idealism. As well, any belief in the afterlife is foreign to him.[10] To the Aryan mind, religion is unimaginable unless it embodies the conviction that life somehow survives after death. As a matter of fact, the Talmud is not a book that prepares one for the afterlife; it only supplies rules for a practical and profitable life in this world.

---

[10] The Old Testament—that is, the Jewish Bible—is almost completely lacking in reference to an immortal soul, an afterlife, heaven and hell, etc. The focus is strictly on the present physical, material realm. This is partly why material concerns—money, material goods, sensual pleasure, power, etc—weigh so heavily within Judaism.

Jewish religious doctrine is principally a collection of instructions for maintaining the blood purity of Jewry, and for regulating intercourse between Jews, themselves, and the rest of the world—which is to say, their relation with non-Jews. But this teaching isn't concerned with moral problems. Rather, it's concerned with petty economic problems.

Of the moral value of Jewish religious teaching, there are, and have always been, exhaustive studies (not by Jews; Jewish drivel on this subject is always self-serving) that show this kind of religion to be utterly monstrous, from the Aryan perspective. The Jew himself is the best example of the product of this religious training. His life is only of this world, and his mentality is as foreign to the true spirit of Christianity as his character was to the great Founder of this new creed, 2,000 years ago.[11] The Founder made no secret of his estimation of the Jewish people. When necessary, he drove those enemies of the human race out of the temple of God; then, as always, they used religion as a means of advancing their commercial interests. In return, Christ was nailed to the cross. Our modern Christians, on the other hand, enter into party politics and, when elections are being held, they debase themselves to beg for Jewish votes. They even enter into political swindles with the atheistic Jewish parties, against the interests of their own nation.

On this first and greatest lie—that Jewry is not a race but a religion—other subsequent lies are based. One of these relates to the language of the Jew. For him, language is not a means for expressing his inner thoughts but rather a means of concealing them. When he speaks French, he thinks Jewish; and when writing German verses, he only gives expression to the character of his own nationality.

As long as the Jew has not succeeded in mastering other peoples, he's forced to speak their language—whether he likes it or not. But as soon as they become his slaves, they would have to learn another language (Esperanto, for example!), so that by this means Jewry could more easily dominate them!

---

[11] Hitler seems unaware that Jesus, Mary, Joseph, and all 12 Apostles were Jews. For a detailed analysis of the relationship between Judaism and early Christianity, from Nietzsche's perspective, see Dalton (2010, 2011c).

— 9 —

THE 'ELDERS OF ZION' (section 11.14)

How much the whole existence of this people is based on a permanent lie is proved in a unique way by *The Protocols of the Elders of Zion*, so infinitely hated by the Jews.[12] With groans and moans, the *Frankfurter Zeitung* repeats again and again that these are forgeries: the best proof of their authenticity. Here, what many Jews unconsciously wish to do is clearly set forth, and that's what counts. It doesn't matter from what Jewish brain these revelations sprang; the important thing is that they disclose, with an almost terrifying precision, the nature and activity of the Jewish people, exposing both their inner contexts and final aims.

---

[12] The *Protocols* are a series of 24 short essays purporting to describe Jewish plans for world domination. Of uncertain origin, they emerged in Russia in the early 1900s, and were "exposed" as a hoax in 1921. From Hitler's standpoint, however, it's irrelevant who wrote it; what matters is whether it is a true account of the activities of international Jewry. Copies are widely available on the Internet—for example, at www.islam-radio.net and www.jewwatch.com. Radio Islam includes this brief and fairly accurate synopsis:

"Goyim are mentally inferior to Jews and can't run their nations properly. For their sake and ours, we need to abolish their governments and replace them with a single government. This will take a long time and involve much bloodshed, but it's for a good cause. Here's what we'll need to do:
- Place our agents and helpers everywhere.
- Take control of the media and use it in propaganda for our plans.
- Start fights between different races, classes, and religions.
- Use bribery, threats, and blackmail to get our way.
- Use Freemasonic Lodges to attract potential public officials.
- Appeal to successful peoples' egos.
- Appoint puppet leaders who can be controlled by blackmail.
- Replace royal rule with socialist rule, then communism, then despotism.
- Abolish all rights and freedoms, except the right of force by us.
- Sacrifice people (including Jews sometimes) when necessary.
- Eliminate religion; replace it with science and materialism.
- Control the education system to spread deception and destroy intellect.
- Rewrite history to our benefit.
- Create entertaining distractions.
- Corrupt minds with filth and perversion.
- Encourage people to spy on one another.
- Keep the masses in poverty and perpetual labor.
- Take possession of all wealth, property, and (especially) gold.
- Use gold to manipulate the markets, cause depressions, etc.
- Introduce a progressive tax on wealth.
- Replace sound investment with speculation.
- Make long-term interest-bearing loans to governments.
- Give bad advice to governments and everyone else.

Eventually the Goyim will be so angry with their governments that they'll gladly have us take over. We will then appoint a descendant of David to be king of the world, and the remaining Goyim will bow down and sing his praises. Everyone will live in peace and obedient order under his glorious rule." Even this brief summary demonstrates the relevancy of the document.

THE ESSENTIAL MEIN KAMPF

The best way of judging them, however, is reality. If historical developments of the last few centuries are studied in light of this book, we will immediately understand the constant outcry of the Jewish press. The moment that the general public gets hold of this book, the Jewish danger will be stamped out.

THE WAY OF JEWRY (section 11.15)

In order to properly know the Jew, it's necessary to study the road that he has followed among other peoples during the last few centuries. One example will suffice to give clear insight here. Since his way has been the same for all epochs—just as that of the people degraded by him has remained the same—it will be best, for present purposes, to mark his development by stages. For the sake of simplicity, I will indicate these stages by letters of the alphabet.[13]

The first Jews came into ancient Germany during the time of the Roman invasion; as usual, they came as merchants. During the turmoil caused by subsequent great migrations, the Jews seem to have disappeared. The period of the first Germanic state formation may be seen as the beginning of a process whereby Central and Northern Europe was again, and this time permanently, Judaized. A development began that has always been the same, or similar, wherever Jews came into contact with Aryan peoples.

(a) As soon as the first permanent settlements were established, the Jew was suddenly 'there.' He arrived as a merchant, and in the beginning didn't bother to disguise his nationality. He still remained openly a Jew, partly because of the large racial difference between himself and his host people, partly because he knew too little of the language, and partly because the social cohesion of the host people was too strong; he couldn't appear as anything other than a foreign merchant. His cunning, combined with inexperience on the part of the host people, meant that it was no disadvantage to openly retain his Jewish character. Rather, it would have been an advantage; the foreigner was often well-received.

(b) Slowly but steadily, he began to take part in economic life—not as a producer, but only as a middleman. His commercial cunning, acquired over

---

[13] The remainder of this chapter is organized around 12 distinct points, designated 'a' through 'l'.

thousands of years of negotiation as an intermediary, made him superior to the Aryans, who were still quite helpless and boundlessly honest. After a short time, commerce threatened to become a Jewish monopoly.

He began to lend money at usurious interest. It was he who first introduced the payment of interest.[14] The danger of this innovation was not initially recognized; rather, it was welcomed, because it offered momentary advantages.

(c) At this stage, the Jew became firmly settled. He inhabited special quarters of the cities and towns, gradually coming to form a State within a State.[15] He regarded the commercial domain and all financial transactions as his own exclusive privilege, which he ruthlessly exploited.

(d) Finance and trade became his complete monopoly. His usurious interest rates finally aroused opposition; his impudence gave rise to indignation; his wealth, to envy. His cup ran over when he included land among his commercial objects, and degraded it to the level of a commodity to be sold, or rather traded. Since he himself never cultivated the soil but considered it only as an object to be exploited—something on which the peasant could still live, but only by submitting to the miserable extortions of his new master—public antipathy grew into open hatred. His blood-sucking tyranny became so unbearable that excessive actions were taken against him. People began to scrutinize this foreigner more closely, discovering more and more repulsive traits and characteristics in him, until the cleft became unbridgeable.[16]

---

[14] Indeed, "the earliest roots of the concept [of usury] are found in the Old Testament and [later] in Aristotle" (Taeusch 1942: 291). And as Houkes (2004: 15) points out, Jews were prohibited from loaning at interest only to their fellow Jews, and not to strangers: "Lending to foreigners not only was permissible, but it was regarded a blessing of God." This is explicit in the Jewish Bible: "Thou shalt not lend upon usury to thy [Jewish] brother... To a foreigner you may lend upon usury, but to your brother you shall not lend upon usury" (Deut 23:19). And God indeed promised to the Jews that usury would lead to power over nations; "For the Lord your God will bless you, as he promised you, and you shall lend to many nations, but you shall not borrow; and you shall rule over many nations, but they shall not rule over you" (Deut 15:6).

[15] See note 6, p. 111.

[16] Compare to this observation by the ancient Greek writer Philostratus: "The Jews have long been in revolt not only against the Romans, but against all humanity... [They] are separated from ourselves by a greater gulf than divides us from Susa or Bactra or the more distant Indies" (*Life of Apollonius*, V.33.4). Notably, this was written circa 225 AD. For details, see Dalton (2011).

THE ESSENTIAL MEIN KAMPF

In times of distress, a wave of public anger has usually arisen against him, and the plundered and ruined masses began to defend themselves against what they considered to be a scourge of God. They came to know him though the course of centuries, eventually viewing his mere existence as something comparable to the plague.

(e) Now the Jew begins to reveal his true character. He pays court to governments with servile flattery, using his money to ingratiate himself further and thus securing the privilege of exploiting his victims. Although public wrath occasionally flares up against this eternal blood-sucker, driving him out, after a few years he reappears in those same places and carries on as before. No persecution can force him to give up this type of human exploitation, and none can drive him away; he always returns after a short time, and it's the same old story.

In an effort to at least prevent the worst from happening, people begin to withdraw the land from his usurious hands by making it illegal for him to own land.

(f) As the power of kings and princes grows, so in proportion does he cozy up to them. He begs for 'charters' and 'privileges,' which those gentlemen, who are generally in financial difficulty, gladly supply in return for suitable payment. However high a price he has to pay, he succeeds in getting it back within a few years from interest and compound interest. He is a true blood-sucker who clings to the body of his unfortunate victims and cannot be removed; and when the princes find themselves again in need, they draw from his blood with their own hands.

This game is repeated unendingly. And the role of the so-called 'German princes' is nearly as bad as that of the Jews themselves. This royalty is God's punishment for their people. The only equivalent can be found in some of the government ministers of our present time.

It was due to the German princes that the German nation couldn't succeed in permanently freeing itself from the Jewish danger. Unfortunately nothing changed as time went on. All that the princes received from the Jews was their thousand-fold reward for the sins committed by them against their own people. They made a pact with the devil and found themselves in his embrace.[17]

---

[17] The parallels to modern-day American politicians, dominated as they are by AIPAC and the money of the American Jewish Lobby, are striking.

— 9 —

(g) His ensnaring of the princes leads to their downfall. Slowly but surely, their standing among the people declines as they not only overlook the public interest but actually exploit them. The Jew knows very well how it will end for them, and works to hasten it. He increases their financial hardship by hindering their effective duty toward their people, by slithering around them with servile flattery, and by encouraging their vices—thus making himself all the more indispensable. His astuteness, or rather his unscrupulousness, in financial affairs allows him to squeeze new income from the princes, to grind the money out of them, and then to quickly spend it.

Thus every court has its 'court Jews,' as these monsters are called, who torture their innocent victims until they're driven to despair, while at the same time preparing eternal pleasures for the princes. Who, then, can be surprised that these ornaments of the human race received official honors, and were even admitted into the hereditary nobility, not only making that institution ridiculous but serving to poison it? Now, he can naturally exploit his position for his own advancement.

Finally he needs only to become baptized to possess all the rights and privileges of the native peoples. Not rarely does he avail himself of this business—to the great joy of the Church, having won over a new son, and also to the joy of Israel, which rejoices at pulling off such a swindle.

(h) A change now begins to take place within Jewry. Until now they have been Jews; that is, they hadn't previously put much value on pretending to be something else. And in any case, they couldn't easily overcome the distinctive racial characteristics that separated them from others. Even as late as the time of Frederick the Great,[18] no one looked upon the Jews as other than a 'foreign' people, and Goethe revolted at the thought that marriage between Christians and Jews might no longer be prohibited. And Goethe, by God, was certainly no reactionary or zealot; his words came from the voice of the blood and of reason. Notwithstanding the disgraceful happenings in court circles, the people instinctively recognized that the Jew was a foreign body in their own flesh, and they took the corresponding attitude toward him.

But all this was now to change. In the course of more than a thousand years, he has learned to master the host language so thoroughly that he

---

[18] That is, circa the 1780s.

can now downplay his Jewishness and place his 'Germanism' in the foreground. Though it seems ridiculous, or even absurd, he is impudent enough to call himself a 'Teuton,' which in this case means 'German.' With this he begins one of the most infamous deceptions imaginable. He doesn't possess the slightest bit of Germanism; he only has acquired the art of twisting the German language—and in the most disgusting way—to his own uses. Apart from this, he never mixes with the German character; his whole Germanism rests on language alone.

Race, however, doesn't lie in language, but only in the blood. No one knows this better than the Jew, seeing that he attaches so little importance to the preservation of his own language, while at the same time strives to maintain the purity of his own blood. A man may change his language without much trouble; but it's only his old ideas that he expresses in the new language. His inner nature is not thereby changed.

The Jew himself is the best proof of this; he can speak a thousand languages and yet he remains a Jew. His distinguishing characteristics are the same when he spoke Latin at Ostia 2,000 years ago as a grain merchant, as they are today when he profits from grain-selling with his garbled German. He's always the same Jew. And it's self-evident that this obvious fact goes unrecognized by the typical ministerial secretary or police official; there is scarcely anyone with less instinct or intelligence than these civil servants of our modern German state authority.

The reason why the Jew suddenly decides to transform himself into a 'German' is obvious. He senses that royal power is slowly crumbling, and he therefore looks around to find a new platform on which to stand. Furthermore, his financial domination over all spheres of economic life has become so powerful that he can no longer sustain or expand that enormous structure unless he earns full 'civil rights.' He desires both preservation and expansion; the higher he climbs, the more alluring becomes the prospect of reaching that ancient goal, promised to him long ago: the dream of world domination. He now anticipates this with feverish eyes. Therefore all his efforts are now directed toward full possession of 'civil rights.'[19]

This was the reason for his emancipation from the ghetto.

---

[19] Jews began to gain civil rights in Germany in 1812, with partial political emancipation in Prussia. Rights for all German Jews came in 1870, upon German unification.

— 9 —

(i) And thus the Court Jew slowly develops into the national Jew. But naturally he still remains associated with the upper circles, and he even attempts to push his way in even further. But at the same time, others of his race curry favor with the beloved public. If we remember the crimes he has committed against the masses over the centuries, how repeatedly and ruthlessly he has exploited them, how he sucked out their very blood; and further, when we remember how they gradually came to hate him, and finally considered him as a punishment from the heavens—then we can well understand how difficult the Jew must have found this final transformation. Yes, it must be an arduous task to present themselves as 'friends of humanity' to their flayed victims.

He therefore begins by making amends for his previous sins. He begins his career as a 'benefactor' of humanity. Since his new philanthropy has a very concrete aim in view, he cannot very well apply to himself the biblical recommendation, not to allow the left hand to know what the right hand is giving.[20] No, he is obliged to let as many people as possible know how deeply the sufferings of the masses have grieved him, and to what a degree of personal sacrifice he is ready to make in order to help them—whether he likes it or not.

With this innate 'modesty,' he trumpets his virtues before the world, until finally people actually begin to believe him. Anyone who doubts him is considered unjust. Thus after a little while, he begins to twist things around, so as to make it appear that it was he who suffered the injustices, and not vice versa. The particularly stupid ones believe him, and they can't help but pity 'the unfortunate.'

A remarkable fact is that, despite his proclaimed readiness to make personal sacrifices, the Jew never becomes impoverished. He knows how to make ends meet. Occasionally his benevolence might be compared to manure; it isn't spread around merely for love of the field, but rather with a view to future produce. Anyhow, after a comparatively short period of time, the Jew has come to be known as a 'benefactor and friend to mankind.' What an amazing transformation!

That which is more or less natural for others thus becomes an object of astonishment, and even admiration. That's why he receives more credit for his acts of benevolence than the rest of humanity.

---

[20] Matthew (6:3).

And even more: The Jew becomes a liberal all at once, and begins to talk enthusiastically of the necessity of human progress.

Gradually he becomes the spokesman of a new age.

Yet at the same time he continues to destroy the foundations of that part of the economy that might truly benefit people. Through the purchase of stock, he pushes his influence into the circuit of national production, turning it into an object of trade, and thus ruining the basis on which personal ownership alone is possible. There then arises a feeling of estrangement between worker and employer, which eventually leads to political class struggle.

Finally, Jewish influence on all economic activities increases with a terrible speed via the stock exchange. He becomes the owner, or at least the controller, of the national labor force.

In order to strengthen his political position, he seeks to remove the racial and civil barriers that had previously hindered his advance. With a characteristic tenacity, he champions the cause of religious tolerance for this purpose. And in Freemasonry, which has completely fallen into his hands, he finds a magnificent weapon to achieve his ends.[21] Government circles, as well as the higher circles of the political and commercial bourgeoisie, fall prey to his net of Masonic strings, though they themselves never suspect what is happening.

Only the people as such, or rather the masses who were just becoming conscious of their own power and were beginning to use it to fight for their rights and liberties, had escaped his grasp. But this influence is more necessary than anything else. The Jew realized that, in his efforts to attain a dominant public role, he would need a 'pace-maker.' And he thought he could find this in broad sections of the bourgeoisie. But the Freemasons failed to catch the glove-makers and linen-weavers in their fragile nets. It thus became necessary to find a coarser and more effective means.

Thus Freemasonry became joined with a second weapon in the service of Jewry: the press. The Jew exercises all his skill and tenacity in getting

---

[21] The Freemasons were originally a guild of stone workers that was established in the 15th century. Because of its influence in medieval society, it expanded to become a private club of local or regional civic leaders. Over time it became known as a 'secret society' composed of powerful and hidden rulers of government. As Jews became wealthier and more influential in European society, they sought membership, and thus Freemasonry gradually became associated with Jewish power.

— 9 —

hold of it. By means of the press, he gradually begins to control the whole of public life. He drives it along a road that he has chosen to reach his own ends; he is now in a position to create and direct that force which, under the name of 'public opinion,' is better known today than it was a few decades ago.

In this, he gives himself the air of thirsting after knowledge. He praises every step of progress, particularly those phases that lead to the ruin of others. He judges all progress and development from the standpoint of his own advantage. And when it brings him no such advantage, he is the mortal enemy of enlightenment; he hates all true culture. He uses all the knowledge acquired in the schools of others exclusively in the service of his own race.

He guards his nationality more than ever. Though overflowing with 'enlightenment,' 'progress,' 'liberty,' 'humanity,' etc., his first concern is to preserve his own racial integrity. He occasionally bestows one of his women on an influential Christian; but the racial stock of his male descendants is always pure. He poisons the blood of others, but preserves his own. The Jew rarely marries a Christian girl, but the Christian marries a Jewess.[22] The resulting mongrels always fall on the Jewish side. Thus a part of the higher nobility becomes completely degenerate. The Jew is well aware of this fact, and thereby systematically 'disarms' the intellectual leaders of his racial adversaries. To mask his tactics and fool his victims, he speaks of the equality of all men, no matter their race or color.[23] And the fools begin to believe him.

Since his whole nature still has too foreign an odor for the broad masses to allow themselves to be caught in his nets, he uses the press to construct a picture of himself that is entirely untrue but well-designed to serve his purpose. In the comic papers, special efforts are made to represent the Jews as a harmless little people that, like all others, has its peculiarities. Despite their manners, which may seem a bit strange, the comics present them as

---

[22] Orthodox Judaism is matrilinial; that is, a Jewish woman bears Jewish children, even if the father is non-Jewish. From a biological perspective, of course, a child of mixed parentage is half of each. But in Hitler's view, the Jewish (lower) half always prevails.

[23] Though it is hard to believe today, there is a long philosophical and sociological legacy on behalf of the inequality of men. Thinkers as diverse as Plato, Aristotle, Gobineau, and Nietzsche held such a view.

fundamentally honest and benevolent souls. Attempts are generally made to make them appear more insignificant than dangerous.

During this phase of his progress, the chief goal of the Jew is the victory of democracy, or rather: rule of the parliamentary system. This is most compatible with his purposes; the personal element is excluded—and in its place we have the stupidity of the majority, incompetence, and last but not least, cowardice.

The final result must necessarily be the overthrow of the monarchy, which has to happen sooner or later.

STANDING OF THE FACTORY WORKER (section 11.16)

(j) A tremendous economic development transforms the social structure of a nation. The small artisan class slowly disappears and the factory worker, who took its place, has scarcely any chance of establishing an independent existence of his own; he sinks more and more to the level of a proletariat. An essential characteristic of the industrial 'factory worker' is that he is scarcely ever able to support himself, now or later in life. He becomes propertyless, in the truest sense of the word. His old age is miserable and can hardly be called life at all.

In earlier times, a similar situation was created that demanded a solution; and one was found. Together with the peasant and the artisan, a new class was gradually formed, along with officials and salaried workers—especially from the state. All of them were propertyless, in the truest sense of the word. But the state found a remedy for this unhealthy situation by providing an old-age pension for its officials. Private enterprises slowly followed this example in increasing numbers, so that today every regular non-manual worker receives a pension in his later years, provided that the firm in which he works surpasses a certain size. Only by caring for the state official in old age could they develop a high degree of unselfish devotion to duty; in pre-war times, this was one of the distinguishing characteristics of German officials.

Thus an entire propertyless class was saved from destitution, and found a place in the social structure of the national community.

The question is once again put before the state and nation, but this time in a much larger form. More and more, millions of people left the countryside and the villages to take up employment in the big city factories. The working and living conditions of this new class were worse than miserable. The more or less mechanical transformation of prior methods of artisan and peasant work didn't fit well. The way that the peasants and artisans formerly worked had nothing comparable to the intensive labor of the new factory worker. In the old trades, time did not play an important role, but it became an essential element in the new industrial system. The formal transfer of the old working hours into the large-scale industrial enterprises had fatal results. The actual amount of work previously accomplished within a certain time was comparatively small, because the modern methods of intensive production were then unknown. Therefore, though in the older system a working day of 14 or even 15 hours was bearable, now it was beyond the limits of human endurance because every minute was utilized to the extreme.

This absurd transfer of the old working hours to the new industrial system proved unfortunate in two respects: it ruined the workers' health, and it destroyed their faith in a higher law of justice. To this was finally added, on the one hand, miserable wages; and on the other side, the employer held a much more lucrative position than before.

In the country, there could be no social problem because the master and the farmhand were doing the same kind of work, and even ate out of the same dish. But this, too, changed.

The division between employer and employees seems now to have extended to all branches of life. How far this Judaizing process of our people has been allowed to extend is illustrated by the low standing, if not contempt, of the manual worker. This isn't German. It's due to the introduction of a foreign element into our lives—in truth, a Judaizing process. One effect has been to transform the old respect for manual work into a definite feeling of contempt for all physical labor.

Thus a new social class has grown up, one that stands in low esteem. The day must come when we will have to face the question of whether the nation will be able to make this class an integral part of the social community, or whether the difference of status will become a permanent gulf separating this class from the others.

One thing, however, is certain: This class doesn't include the worst elements in its ranks, but rather the most energetic. The sophistication of so-called culture hasn't yet exercised its disintegrating and degenerating influence. The broad masses of this new lower class haven't yet been infected with the poison of pacifist weakness. They are still robust and can be, if necessary, even brutal.

While our bourgeoisie pay no attention at all to this question, and indifferently allow events to take their course, the Jew seizes upon the many possibilities for the future. While on the one hand he organizes capitalistic methods of exploitation to their ultimate degree, he curries favor with the victims of his policy and power, and in a short while becomes the leader of their struggle *against himself*. 'Against himself' is here only figuratively speaking; for this Great Master of Lies knows how to appear in the guise of the innocent, and throw the guilt on others.[24] Since he has the impudence to lead the masses, they never for a moment suspect that they are falling prey to one of the most infamous betrayals of all time.

And yet that's what it was.

JEWISH TACTICS (section 11.17)

The moment this new class arises from the general economic situation, the Jew clearly sees where to find the necessary pacemaker for his own progressive march. First he uses the bourgeoisie as a battering-ram against the feudal order; and then the worker against the bourgeois world. Just as he succeeded in obtaining civil rights in the protection of the bourgeois class, he now hopes to use the workers' struggle for existence as his path to obtain full control over them.

From that point on, the workers' only task is to fight for the future of the Jewish people. Without knowing it, the worker places himself at the service of the very power against which he believes he is fighting. The worker thinks he's fighting *against* capital, and thus is all the more easily brought to fight *for* capitalist interests. Outcries are raised against

---

[24] "Great Master of Lies" again recalls Schopenhauer; see note 2, p. 162. The idea that Jews cast themselves as innocents to hide their danger was already recognized by Nietzsche: "People of the basest origin, in part rabble, outcasts not only from good but also from respectable society, raised away from even the smell of culture, without discipline, without knowledge, without the remotest suspicion that there is such a thing as conscience in spiritual matters; simply—Jews: with an instinctive ability to create an advantage, a means of seduction out of every superstitious supposition... When Jews step forward as innocence itself, then the danger is great." (*Will to Power*, sec. 199.)

international capital, but in reality such actions are directed against the structure of national economics, in the hope that the international stock exchange can triumph over its dead body.

The Jew's procedure is as follows:

He approaches the worker, hypocritically pretending to feel pity for him and his lot of misery and poverty, thus gaining his confidence. He shows himself eager to study the workers' various hardships—and strives to awaken a yearning to change the conditions under which they live. He artfully encourages the desire for social justice, which is a typical Aryan characteristic, and this is then transformed into a hatred of the more fortunate ones. Next he turns the struggle for the elimination of social ills into a precise worldview. And thus he establishes the Marxist doctrine.

THE CORE OF THE MARXIST WORLDVIEW (section 11.18)

By presenting his doctrine as a series of socially just demands, he propagates the doctrine all the more effectively. But he also provokes the opposition of decent people who refuse to admit these demands that seem fundamentally unjust and impossible to realize. Under this cloak of purely social ideas are hidden truly diabolic purposes, which are proclaimed with a boundless impudence. This doctrine is an inseparable mixture of reason and absurdity—but in such a way that only the absurdity can be realized, never the reason.

By categorically repudiating the value of the individual and also the nation and its racial content, this doctrine destroys the fundamental basis of all culture; for culture depends on these very factors. Such is the true core of the Marxist worldview—insofar as the term 'worldview' can be applied at all to this phantom product of a criminal brain. The shattering of the concept of personality and of race removes the chief obstacle that barred the way to domination by society's inferior element—and this is the Jew.

The significance of this doctrine lies precisely in its economic and political absurdity. For this reason, intelligent people refuse to support it, while all those who are less intellectual, or who are poorly educated in economic principles, join it with flying colors. The intelligence behind the movement—for even this movement needs intelligence to exist—is 'served up' by the Jews themselves, from their own ranks.

THE ESSENTIAL MEIN KAMPF

Thus arises a movement that's composed exclusively of manual workers under Jewish leadership. By all appearances, this movement strives to improve the workers' living conditions; but in reality its aim is the enslavement, and thereby the destruction, of all non-Jewish people.

The Freemasons carried out a program of pacifistic paralysis of the instinct for national self-preservation among our so-called intelligentsia, which was then extended to the broad masses of the workers and bourgeoisie by means of the always-Jewish press.

To these two instruments of disintegration, a third and still more ruthless one was added, namely, organized brute force. As a shock- and storm-troop, Marxism seeks to finish off those parts of the social order left standing, after the two former weapons do their work.

The combined activity of all these forces has been wonderfully managed. And it won't be surprising if we find that those institutions which have always presented themselves as the organs of the more or less traditional state authority should now fail. Among our high and highest state officials (with very few exceptions), the Jew has always found the most complacent backers of his destructive work. An attitude of cringing submissiveness towards 'superiors,' and a condescending arrogance towards 'inferiors,' are the characteristics of this class, along with a degree of narrow-mindedness that is truly frightening. All this is exceeded only by a towering and utterly amazing self-conceit.

But these qualities are of greatest use to the Jew. Therefore they are the ones that he appreciates most.

ORGANIZATION OF MARXIST WORLD-DOCTRINE (section 11.19)

The practical struggle, only now beginning, may be described as follows:

Consistent with the ultimate goals of the Jewish struggle—goals that are not exhausted by economic domination of the world—the Jew divides the organization of his Marxist world-doctrine into two parts. Though apparently distinct, these parts in truth form an indivisible unity: the political movement and the trade union movement.

The trade union movement gathers recruits. It offers assistance and protection to the workers in the hard struggle they must wage for the bare means of existence—a struggle that's due to the greediness and narrow-mindedness of many of the employers. Unless the workers are ready to surrender all claims to their vital human rights, and unless they are ready to submit to those who are irresponsible and heartless, then the worker must necessarily take matters into his own hands. The organized national community—that is to say, the state—pays no attention to his needs.

The so-called national bourgeoisie, blinded by its own financial interests, opposes this life-or-death struggle of the workers, and places the heaviest obstacles in their way. Not only do they hinder all efforts at shortening the inhumanly long work hours, prohibiting child-labor, granting security and protection to women, and improving the hygienic conditions of the workshops and the dwellings of the working-class, but they actually sabotage them. All the while, the clever Jew takes the cause of the oppressed into his own hands. He gradually becomes the leader of the trade union movement. This is an easy task for him, because he doesn't genuinely intend to eliminate social evils; rather, his objective is to establish an economic stormtroop who will follow his commands and thereby destroy national economic independence. For while a sound social policy has to move between the two aims of securing public health and of safeguarding an independent national economy, the Jew gives no consideration to these goals at all. Rather, their elimination is his life's goal. He desires, not the preservation, but rather the destruction of an independent national economy.

Therefore, as leader of the union movement, he has no scruples about putting forth demands that not only exceed the declared purpose of the movement, but couldn't be carried out without ruining the national economy. Furthermore, he has no interest in seeing a healthy and sturdy population develop; he would prefer a degenerate, unthinking herd that can more easily be subjugated. Because these are his final objectives, he can afford to propose the most senseless demands—demands that are unrealizable, and that therefore couldn't lead to any real change. At best, they can arouse a spirit of unrest among the masses. And that's precisely his purpose—and not a real and honest improvement of social conditions.

The leadership of Jewry will thus remain unquestioned, at least until an enormous effort is undertaken to enlighten the masses, so that they can better understand the causes of their misery. Or until the state got rid of the Jew and his work. As long as the masses remain as ill-informed as they actually are today, and as long as the state remains as indifferent to their lot as it now is, the masses will follow whatever leader makes them the most extravagant promises in economic matters. And the Jew is a master at this. His entire activities are unhampered by moral considerations of any kind.

Naturally, then, it takes him only a short time to defeat all his competitors in this field and drive them from the scene. In accordance with his general brutality and rapacity, he teaches the union movement the most brutal use of physical violence. Those who, using their intelligence, are able to resist the Jewish lures are now broken by terror. The success of that kind of activity is enormous.

By means of the union—which ought to be a blessing for the nation—the Jew shatters the foundation of the national economy.

Parallel to this runs the political organization.

It operates hand-in-hand with the union movement, inasmuch as the latter prepares the masses for political organization, and even forces them into it. This is also the source of the money that the political organization needs to keep its enormous apparatus in action. It is the organ of control for the political activity of its members, and recruits the masses at all big political demonstrations. In the end it ceases to struggle for economic interests, but places its chief weapon—the refusal to work, in the form of a general strike—at the disposal of a political idea.

By means of a press whose contents are adapted to the intellectual horizon of the most ignorant readers, the political and trade union organizations obtain an instrument that prepares the lowest stratum for a campaign of ruthless action. Its purpose isn't to lead people out of the swamp of baseness and to lift their minds up, but to cater to their lowest instincts. Among the lazy-minded and self-seeking sections of the masses, this kind of speculation turns out to be quite profitable.

Above all, it's this very press that carries on a fanatical campaign of slander, striving to tear down everything that might be considered as a support for national independence, and sabotaging all cultural values and the autonomy of the national economy along the way.

Above all, it attacks all men of character who refuse to yield to Jewish efforts to dominate, or who appear dangerous to the Jews merely because of their superior ability. In order to be hated by the Jew, it isn't necessary to openly combat him; it's quite sufficient if one be considered *capable* of opposing the Jew at some point in the future, or of using his talents to enhance the power and position of a nation hostile to the Jew.

His unfailing instinct readily sniffs out the inner spirit of all those he meets; and those who aren't of a kindred spirit with him may be sure to earn his hostility. Since the Jew is not the attacked but the attacker himself, he considers as enemies not only those who attack him but also those who resist him. He then uses dishonorable means to break such upright people, including lies and slander.

He stops at nothing. His vileness is so appalling that one really cannot be surprised if, in the imagination of our people, the Jew is pictured as the personification of the devil and the symbol of all evil.

The ignorance of the broad masses about the inner character of the Jew, and the lack of instinct and narrow-mindedness of our upper classes, make our people an easy victim of this Jewish campaign of lies.

While the upper classes, with their innate cowardice, turn away from anyone whom the Jew attacks with lies and slander, the common people believe everything—either from ignorance or simple-mindedness. State authorities either wrap themselves in a robe of silence, or more frequently, they persecute the unjustly victimized ones in order to stop the campaign in the Jewish press. In the eyes of some official ass, such action appears to uphold the authority of the state and preserve public order.

Slowly, fear of the Marxist weapon of Jewry descends like a nightmare on the mind and soul of innocent people.

They begin to quiver before this fearful enemy, and thereby become his victims.

PALESTINE AS ORGANIZATIONAL CENTER (section 11.20)

(k) Jewish domination in the state seems now so fully assured that not only can he afford to call himself a Jew again, but he even openly acknowledges his ideas on national and political questions. A part of his race avows itself quite openly as an alien people, but even here they lie. When the Zionists try to make the rest of the world believe that the new national consciousness of the Jews will be satisfied by the establishment of a Palestinian state,[25] the Jews thereby cleverly dupe the simple-minded

---

[25] That is, Israel—which only came into being in 1948, and then illegally.

goyim. They haven't the slightest intention of building up a Jewish state in Palestine so as to live there. What they really want is a central organization for their international world-swindle, one with sovereign rights and freedom from outside control—in other words, a refuge for convicted low-lifes and a training ground for budding criminals.

As a sign of their growing confidence and sense of security, a certain portion of them openly and impudently proclaim their Jewish race, while another part hypocritically pretends that they are still German, French, or English.

Their blatant behavior in their relations with other people shows how close they see the approaching victory.

The black-haired Jewish youth lies in wait for hours, satanically glaring at the unsuspecting girl whom he plans to seduce, adulterating her blood and stealing her from her own people. He uses every possible means to undermine the racial foundations of a subjugated people. In his systematic efforts to ruin girls and women, he strives to break down the last racial barriers for other peoples, even on a large scale. The Jews were and are responsible for bringing Negroes into the Rhineland, with the ultimate idea of bastardizing the hated white race, and thus lowering its cultural and political level so that he himself might dominate.

A racially-pure people who are conscious of their blood can never be overcome by the Jew. In this world, he will only be the master over a bastardized people.

That's why he systematically tries to lower the racial quality of a people by a continuous poisoning of the individual.

DICTATORSHIP OF THE PROLETARIAT (section 11.21)

In the field of politics, he now begins to replace the idea of democracy with a dictatorship of the proletariat.

In the organized mass of Marxism he has found a weapon that makes it possible for him to discard democracy, so as to subjugate and rule in a dictatorial fashion by the aid of brute force.

He systematically works to bring about this revolution in two ways: economically and politically.

Aided by international influences, he forms a ring of enemies around those nations that have proven too sturdy for him to attack from within.

He incites them to war, and if necessary, plants the flag of revolution amidst the battlefield.

Economically he undermines the state, until social programs become so unprofitable that they are taken from the state and turned over to his financial control.

Politically he works to withdraw the means of subsistence from the state, undermines the foundations of national resistance and defense, destroys confidence in leadership, reviles the past and its history, and drags everything truly great down into the gutter.

Culturally he contaminates art, literature, and the theater, scorns national sentiment, overturns all concepts of the sublime and beautiful, the worthy and the good, and ultimately drags the people down to the level of his own base nature.

Religion is mocked, and ethics and morality are portrayed as antiquated prejudices; until the last pillars have fallen, on which the national being depends, in its struggle for existence in this world.

FROM NATIONAL JEWS TO RACIAL JEWS (section 11.22)

(l) Now begins the last great revolution. As soon as the Jew gains political power, he drops the last few veils. Out of the democratic national Jew arises the blood-Jew, the tyrant of the peoples. In the course of a few years, he tries to root out all those who represent the national intelligence. By thus depriving the people of their natural intellectual leaders, he makes them ripe for a slave's lot of permanent subjugation.

Russia offers the most terrible example of such slavery, where he killed or starved 30 million people in a bout of savage fanaticism, and partly by means of inhuman torture.[26] He did this so that a gang of Jewish journalists and stock exchange bandits could dominate a great people.

The final result is not merely the loss of freedom of people oppressed by the Jews, but also the end of this parasite of nations. The death of the victim is followed, sooner or later, by that of the vampire.

---

[26] The total number of people killed by the Bolsheviks and Stalin is hard to estimate, but Hitler's figure is surely within reason. Russian scholars have long tossed around a figure of 20 million, but that is almost certainly an underestimate. If we count deaths into the late Soviet period, some researchers have identified an overall toll of 50 to 60 million—an astounding figure that is rarely discussed in the West. It's an open question how many had died by 1925, when *Mein Kampf* was initially published.

THE ESSENTIAL MEIN KAMPF

BASTARDIZED PEOPLE (section 11.23)

If we review all the causes of the German collapse, we find that the most profound and decisive cause remains the failure to recognize the racial problem, and especially the Jewish danger.

It would have been easy enough to endure the defeats suffered on the battlefields in August 1918. They were nothing compared to the military victories that our nation achieved. Our downfall was not the result of those defeats. Rather, we were overthrown by a force that had prepared those defeats by systematically operating, for several decades, to steal the political and moral instincts and stamina that alone make a nation capable, and thus fit to exist.

By neglecting the problem of preserving the racial foundations of our nation, the old Reich disregarded the sole right that allowed it to survive in this world. Nations that make mongrels of their people, or allow their people to be turned into mongrels, sin against the will of eternal Providence. And thus their overthrow at the hands of a stronger opponent cannot be looked upon as a wrong but, on the contrary, as a restoration of justice. If a people refuses to guard and uphold the nature-given qualities that have their roots in the blood, then such a people has no right to complain over the loss of its earthly existence.

Everything on this Earth can be improved. Every defeat can be the foundation of a future victory. Every lost war can be the cause of a later resurgence. Every hardship can give a new impetus to human energy. And from every oppression, forces can emerge that bring about a new spiritual rebirth—provided that the blood is kept pure.

But the loss of racial purity will wreck inner happiness forever. It degrades men for all time. And the consequences can never be removed.

If this single problem is studied and compared with the other problems of life, we will easily recognize how insignificant they are. They are all limited in time; but the problem of the maintenance or loss of the purity of the blood lasts as long as man himself.

All symptoms of decline in the pre-war period can be traced back to racial causes.

— 9 —

FAILURE TO RECOGNIZE THE INNER ENEMY (section 11.24)

Whether one is dealing with questions of general law or excesses of economic life, of symptoms of cultural decline or political degeneration, of defective schooling or the evil influence of the press over the adult population—always and everywhere, it's a fundamental disregard for the racial needs of the nation. That is, the failure to recognize the danger posed by a foreign race.

That's why all attempts at reform, all institutions for social relief, all political striving, all economic progress, and all apparent increase in the general stock of knowledge, were futile, practically speaking. The nation and the organization that enables it to exist—the state—weren't becoming healthier but, on the contrary, were languishing more and more. The false prosperity of the old Reich couldn't disguise its inner weakness. And every attempt to invigorate it failed because the most important problem was disregarded.

It would be a mistake to think that the followers of the various political parties that tried to fix the condition of the German people, or even all their leaders, were bad or malevolent in themselves. Their activity was doomed to failure simply because of the fact that they saw nothing but the symptoms of our general malady, and tried to treat the symptoms while overlooking the real cause of the disease. If one makes a methodical study of the political development of the old Reich, one cannot help seeing that, after a careful political analysis, a process of inner degeneration had already set in even at the time of German unification. The general situation was declining year by year, despite the apparent political success and increasing economic wealth.

At the Reichstag elections, the growing number of Marxist votes indicated that the internal breakdown and political collapse were then rapidly approaching. All the victories of the so-called bourgeois parties were worthless—not only because they couldn't prevent the numerical increase in the growing mass of Marxist votes, but mainly because they themselves were already infected with the ferment of decay. Though quite unaware of it, the bourgeois world was infected from within with the deadly poison of Marxist ideas. Their occasional resistance was due to the competitive strife among ambitious political leaders, rather than any principled opposition between adversaries who were determined to fight to the bitter end.

During all those years, only one protagonist fought with steadfast perseverance, and that was the Jew. The Star of David steadily ascended as the will to national self-preservation declined.

Therefore, in August 1914, it wasn't a unified people resolved to attack that rushed to the battlefields. Rather, it was the last flicker of an instinct for national self-preservation against the creeping pacificist-Marxist paralysis of the national body. Even in those days of destiny, we didn't recognize the internal enemy; therefore all external efforts were bound to be in vain. Providence didn't grant her reward to the victorious sword, but followed the eternal law of retribution.

A profound recognition of all this was the source of those principles and tendencies that inspire our new movement. We were convinced that, only by recognizing such truths, could we halt the German national decline and lay a granite foundation on which the state could again be built—one that would not be an alien mechanism alien for economic purposes and interests, but a national organism:

A Germanic State
for the German Nation.

— 10 —
THE FIRST PERIOD OF DEVELOPMENT OF THE NATIONAL SOCIALIST GERMAN WORKERS' PARTY

If, at the close of this [first] volume, I describe the first stage in the progress of our movement and give a brief account of the problems raised, it's not because I seek to expound on the ideals of the movement. These are so momentous that they require a whole volume. Therefore I will devote the second volume of this book to a detailed survey of the principles that form the program of our movement, and attempt to draw a picture of what we mean by the word 'state.'

When I say 'we,' I mean to include all those hundreds of thousands who have fundamentally the same longing, though in the individual cases they cannot find adequate words to describe their inner vision. It's a noteworthy fact of all great reforms that, in the beginning, there is only one single champion to come forward on behalf of several million. The goal has often been the object of profound longing on the part of hundreds of thousands for many centuries, until finally one man comes forward to proclaim the will of the masses and become the standard-bearer of the old yearning—which he now leads to victory as a new idea.

The fact that millions yearn at heart for a radical change in our present conditions is proven by their profound discontentment. This feeling is manifest in a thousand ways: in some as discouragement and despair, in others as resentment, anger, and indignation. One man reacts with indifference, another with violent excess. Other witnesses to this feeling are those who abstain from voting, as well as the many who tend to side with the fanatical leftwing extremists.

It was to the latter that our young movement was intended to appeal. It wasn't meant to be an organization for the contented and satisfied, but rather to embrace all those who were suffering from profound anxiety and could find no peace, the unhappy and the discontented. It wasn't meant to float on the surface of the nation but rather to push its roots deep among the masses....

NATIONALIZATION OF THE MASSES (section 12.4)

Thus, as early as 1919, we were convinced that accomplishing the nationalization of the masses would constitute our highest aim.

From a tactical standpoint, a number of obligations followed.[1]

(1) No social sacrifice could be considered too great, in order to win over the masses for a national revival.

Any economic concessions granted today to employees are negligible when compared with the benefit to the whole nation if they contribute to bringing back the masses of the people to their own nation. Nothing but meanness and shortsightedness—which, unfortunately, are prevalent characteristics of our employers—could prevent people from recognizing that, in the long run, no economic improvement, and therefore no rise in profits, are possible unless the internal national solidarity of our people is restored.

If the German unions had defended the interests of the working-classes uncompromisingly during the war; if, even during the war, they had used the labor strike a thousand times over to force the dividend-hungry industrialists to grant the workers' demands; if at the same time they had stood up as good Germans for the national defense as stoutly as for their own claims; and if they had given to their country what was their country's due—then the war would never have been lost. How ridiculously insignificant would all, and even the greatest, economic concessions have been in comparison with the tremendous importance of winning the war!

For a movement that plans to restore the German worker to the German people, it's absolutely necessary to understand clearly that economic sacrifices should be utterly disregarded—provided, of course,

---

[1] What follows are 14 numbered sections, constituting Hitler's program of nationalization—although some have been edited out here.

— 10 —

that they don't go as far as endangering the independence and stability of the national economic system.

(2) The nationalistic education of the masses can be carried out only indirectly, by improving their social conditions. Only in this way can the economic conditions be created that enable everyone to participate in the cultural life of the nation.

(3) The nationalization of the broad masses can never be achieved by half-measures—that is, by feebly insisting on a so-called objective standpoint—but only by a ruthless and devoted insistence on the one goal to be attained. This means that a people cannot be made 'national' in the sense of that word given by our bourgeois class today—with so many limitations—but rather in the vehement and extreme sense. Poison can be overcome only by an antidote, and only a shallow bourgeois mind could think that the middle way is the road to heaven.

The broad masses of a nation are neither professors nor diplomats. They are only poorly acquainted with abstract ideas; their reactions lie more in the domain of the feelings. That's where their positive or negative attitude lies. They respond only to an expression of force from one of the two extremes, and never to any half-measure that wavers between the two. Their emotional grounds also account for their extraordinary stability. Faith is stronger than knowledge; love is less changeable than respect; hate is more permanent than aversion. And the driving force that has brought about the most tremendous revolutions on this Earth has never been a scientific teaching that has gained power over the masses, but always a fanaticism that has inspired them—and sometimes even a hysteria that has driven them forward.

Anyone who wishes to win over the masses must know the key that opens the door to their hearts. It's not objectivity—meaning, weakness—but rather will and power.

(4) The soul of the people can be won only if we carry through the positive struggle for our own aims, and also destroy the enemy that opposes them.

When they see a ruthless attack on a foe, the people take it as proof of the rightness of such action. Conversely, when the aggressor renounces the destruction of the foe, this makes their rightness seem uncertain, if not an injustice.

THE ESSENTIAL MEIN KAMPF

The masses are but a part of nature itself. Their feelings don't allow them to understand hand-shaking between avowed enemies. They desire the victory of the stronger and the destruction of the weaker, or at least his unconditional submission.

The nationalization of the masses will succeed only if, in the positive struggle to win the soul of the people, those international poisoners who oppose it are rooted out.

(5) All the great questions of our time are questions of the moment, and are only the results of certain definite causes. And among all those, there is only one that has a profoundly causal significance, namely, the question of the racial preservation of the people. Human strength and weakness depends on the blood alone. Nations that are unaware of the importance of their racial stock are like men who try to educate the poodle to do the work of the greyhound—not understanding that both the speed of the greyhound and the docility of the poodle are inborn qualities, and these cannot be learned. A people that fails to preserve its racial purity thereby renounces the unity of the soul of the nation, in all its manifestations. A disintegrated national character is the inevitable result of a disintegration of the blood. And the change in the spiritual and creative forces of a people is only an effect of the change in their racial foundations.

Whoever would free the German people from their vices of today— which did not spring from their original nature—must first rid them of the foreign viruses in the national body.

The German nation will never be restored unless the racial problem, and hence the Jewish problem, is clearly understood.

The racial problem supplies the key, not only to human history, but also to every kind of human culture.

(6) By incorporating the internationalist masses into the national community, we don't intend to neglect a safeguarding of trade and professional interests. Divergent professional interests are not the same as class division, but are inherent in our economic life. Professional grouping doesn't clash at all with the idea of a national community, for this means national unity in regard to all those problems that affect the life of the nation as such.

The integration of a professional group or class into the national community, or into the state, cannot be accomplished by lowering the higher classes, but only by raising up the lower classes. The class that carries through this process is never the higher class, but rather the lower—the one that's fighting for equal rights. The bourgeoisie of today was not incorporated in the state through measures of the nobility, but only by its own energy and leadership.

The German worker cannot be raised and incorporated into the German national community via ineffectual talk of brotherhood, but by a systematic improvement in the social and cultural life of the worker—until the most serious differences are bridged. A movement that has this for its aim must try to recruit its followers mainly from the ranks of the workers. It may include members of the intellectual classes only insofar as they completely understand the goal to be achieved. This process of transformation and reunion cannot be completed within 10 or 20 years; it will take several generations, as experience has shown.

The most difficult obstacle to the reunion of our contemporary worker with the national community doesn't consist so much in the fact that he fights for the interests of his fellow workers, but rather in the international ideas with which he is imbued, and which are hostile to nationhood and fatherland. If inspired by the same leadership, the trade unions could turn millions of workers into the most valuable members of the national community, without thereby affecting their own struggles for their economic demands.

A movement that sincerely tries to bring the German worker back into his people, and rescue him from the folly of internationalism, must wage a vigorous campaign against certain notions that are prevalent among the industrialists. One of these is that the employee is obliged to surrender all his economic rights to the employer and, further, that the workers would come into conflict with the national community if they attempted to defend their own justified interests. This assertion is a deliberate lie; the idea of a national community doesn't impose any obligations on the one side that aren't imposed on the other.

A worker certainly sins against the spirit of the national community if he acts entirely on his own initiative and puts forward exaggerated demands without regard for the common good or the survival of the national economy. But an industrialist also does so if he adopts inhuman methods of exploitation and misuses the working forces of the nation, to make millions for himself unjustly from the sweat of the workers. He has no right to call himself 'national,' and no right to talk of a folk community; he's only an unscrupulous egoist who sows the seeds of social discontent and provokes a spirit of conflict that sooner or later must harm the interests of the nation.

The reservoir from which the young movement has to draw its members will primarily be the working masses. Those masses must be delivered from the clutches of the international delusion. They must be freed from social distress. They must be raised above their present cultural misery and transformed into a united and valuable factor in the folk community, inspired by nationalist ideas and sentiment.

If, among nationalist intellectual circles, men can be found who genuinely love the people and eagerly anticipate the future of Germany, and at the same time have a sound grasp of the importance of a struggle for the soul of the masses, such men are cordially welcomed in the ranks of our movement. They can serve as a valuable intellectual force. But this movement can never aim at recruiting its membership from the herd of bourgeois voters. If it did so, the movement would be burdened with a group of people whose whole mentality would only paralyze our campaign to win over the masses.

In theory, it may be true that the broad masses ought to be influenced by a combined leadership of the upper and lower social strata within the framework of the movement. But notwithstanding all this, the fact remains that, though it may be possible to exercise a psychological influence on the bourgeois classes and to arouse some enthusiasm or even awaken some understanding among them by our public demonstrations, their traditional characteristics—or better, vices—cannot be changed. Such vices are part of a tradition that has developed over centuries. The difference between the cultural levels of the two groups, and between their attitudes towards economic questions, is still so great that it would become an obstacle as soon as the initial enthusiasm of our demonstrations subsided.

Finally, it's not part of our program to transform the nationalist camp itself, but rather to win over those who are anti-nationalist.

The strategy of the whole movement must finally be determined from this viewpoint.

(7) This one-sided but clear approach must be manifested in the propaganda of the movement; and on the other hand, this is absolutely necessary on propagandist grounds.

If propaganda is to be of service to the movement, it must be addressed to one side alone. If it varies, the direction of its appeal won't be understood in the one camp or may be rejected by the other, as merely obvious and uninteresting; for there is a great difference in the intellectual training of the two camps in question.

Even the style and tone can't have the same effect in those two opposite extremes of the social structure. If the propaganda refrains from using primitive forms of expression, it won't appeal to the sentiments of the masses. If, on the other hand, it conforms to the crude sentiments of the masses in its words and gestures, it will be rejected by the so-called intellectual circles as coarse and vulgar.

Among a hundred so-called orators, there are scarcely ten who are capable of speaking with effect before an audience of street-sweepers, locksmiths, sewer-cleaners, etc. today, and then lecturing with equal effect tomorrow before an audience of university professors and students. Among a thousand public speakers, there may be only one who can speak to locksmiths and professors in the same hall in such a way that his statements can be fully comprehended by each group, while at the same time he effectively influences both and awakens enthusiasm, to hearty applause. But it must always be remembered that even the most beautiful theory, in most cases, can reach the public only through smaller minds.

What matters is not the vision of the man of genius who created the great idea, but rather the success that his prophets achieve in transmitting this idea to the broad masses.

Social Democracy and the whole Marxist movement were particularly attractive because of the uniformity of the public to which they addressed their appeal. The more limited and narrow their ideas and arguments, the easier it was for the masses to grasp and assimilate them; those ideas and arguments were well-adapted to a low level of intelligence.

These considerations led the new movement to adopt a clear and simple line:

THE ESSENTIAL MEIN KAMPF

In both its message and forms of expression, propaganda must be kept on a level with the intelligence of the masses, and its value must be measured only by the actual results.

At a public meeting of all classes, the best speaker is not the one who is closest to the intellectuals, but the one who knows how to win the hearts of the masses.

An educated man who is present, and who finds fault with an address because of its low intellectual level—even though he sees its effect on the lower groups to be won over—only proves the incapacity of his thinking and his worthlessness to the new movement. The only useful intellectuals are those who understand its mission and its aims so well that they have learned to judge the propaganda exclusively by the success obtained, and never by the impression made on the intellectuals themselves. Our propaganda isn't meant to serve as entertainment for those national-minded people, but to win over the enemies of nationalism—those who, nevertheless, are of our own blood.

In general, those trends that I briefly summarized in the chapter on 'War Propaganda' determined the approach that we adopted in our campaign, and the manner in which we put it into practice.[2]

Success proves that the decision was right.

(8) The goal of any political reform movement can never be reached by trying to educate the public or influence those in power, but only by gaining political power. Every world-changing idea has not only the right but also the obligation to secure those means that enable it to be carried out. In this world, success is the only basis for judging right or wrong. And by 'success' we don't mean the mere conquest of power—as in 1918—but an exercise of power that is beneficial to the nation. A coup d'etat cannot be considered successful if, as many empty-headed government lawyers in Germany now believe, the revolutionaries succeed in getting control of the state into their hands. It's successful only if, in comparison with conditions under the old regime, the lot of the nation has been improved. This certainly does not apply to the German revolution, as that movement was called, which brought a gang of bandits into power in the fall of 1918.

But if the conquest of political power is a prerequisite for the practical realization of the ideals that inspire a reform movement, then any

---

[2] See volume one, chapter 6 (not included in the present work).

movement that aims at reform must, from the very first, be considered as a movement of the masses—and not as a literary tea club, or a shopkeepers' bowling society. ...

EDUCATION FOR STRUGGLE (section 12.9)

(13) The movement must educate its adherents about the principle that struggle isn't to be considered a necessary evil but rather as desired in itself. Therefore they must not fear the hostility of their adversaries, but they must take it as a necessary condition for their whole right to existence. They must not try to avoid the hatred of the enemies of our people and our worldview, but must welcome it. Lies and slander are among the manifestations of this hatred.

The man who is not opposed, vilified, and slandered in the Jewish press is not a staunch German, and no true National Socialist. The best rule to measure the sincerity of his convictions, his character, and his strength of will is the hostility that his name arouses among the mortal enemies of our people.

The followers of the movement, and indeed the whole nation, must be reminded again and again of the fact that the Jew and his newspapers are always spreading lies. If he tells the truth on some occasions, it's only for the purpose of masking some greater deception, which turns the apparent truth into a deliberate falsehood. The Jew is the great master of lies.[3] Lies and deception are his weapons in struggle.

Every Jewish slander and every Jewish lie is a scar on the bodies of our warriors.

He whom they revile the most is nearest to us, and he whom they mortally hate is our best friend.

Anyone who opens a Jewish newspaper in the morning and doesn't find himself vilified there, has spent yesterday to no account. If he had achieved something, he would be persecuted, slandered, derided, abused, and besmirched. Those who effectively combat this mortal enemy of our people, who is at the same time the enemy of all Aryan peoples and culture, can only expect to arouse opposition on the part of this race and become the object of its slanderous attacks.

---

[3] Again recalling Schopenhauer; see note 2, p. 162.

When these truths become part of the flesh and blood of our members, then the movement will be impregnable and invincible.

EDUCATION FOR RESPECT OF THE PERSON (section 12.10)

(14) The movement must use all possible means to cultivate respect for the individual personality. It must never forget that all human values are based on *personal* values, and that every idea and achievement is the fruit of the creative power of one man. Admiration for everything great is a tribute to one creative personality, and all those who feel such admiration become thereby united.

Nothing can take the place of the individual. This is especially true when the individual embodies in himself not the mechanical but the creative and cultural element. No pupil can take the place of the master in completing a great picture that was left unfinished; and just in the same way, no substitute can take the place of the great poet or thinker, or the great statesman or military general. Their activity lies in the realm of art. It can never be mechanically acquired, because it's an innate product of divine grace.

The greatest revolutions and the greatest achievements of this world, its greatest cultural works and the immortal creations of great statesmen, are inseparably bound up with one name, and are represented by it. The failure to pay tribute to one of those great spirits signifies a neglect of that enormous source of power that lies in the names of all great men and women.

The Jew knows this best of all. He, whose great men have always been great only in their efforts to destroy mankind and its culture, worships them as idols. But he attempts to stigmatize respect for a nation's own great spirits as unworthy; this he labels a 'personality cult.'

As soon as a people has so lost its courage as to submit to this Jewish arrogance and defamation, it renounces the most important source of its own inner strength. This is not a pandering to the masses, but a veneration of genius, ennoblement, and enlightenment.

When men's hearts are breaking and their souls despair, their great forebears turn their eyes towards them from the dim shadows of the past—they who knew how conquer anxiety and affliction, despair and misery, mental servitude and physical bondage—and extend their eternal hands to despairing souls!

Woe to the nation that is ashamed to grasp them!

DANGER OF OBSCURITY (section 12.11)

During the initial phase of our movement, our greatest handicap was the fact that none of us were known and our names meant nothing—a fact that then seemed to diminish our chances for success. Our most difficult task then—when it was often only six, seven, or eight of us—was to make everyone in this tiny circle believe that there was a tremendous future in store for the movement.

Consider that only six or seven poor devils, who were entirely unknown, came together to found a movement that would succeed in doing what the great mass parties had failed to do: namely, to reconstruct a German Reich of greater power and glory. We would have been very pleased if we were attacked or even ridiculed. But the most depressing fact was that no one paid any attention to us at all. This utter lack of interest in us caused me the greatest suffering at the time.

When I entered the circle of those few men, there was no question of a party or a movement. I already described my initial impressions of that small organization. Subsequently, I had time and the occasion to study the form of this so-called party, which at first looked so impossible. By God, the picture was quite depressing and discouraging. There was nothing; absolutely nothing at all. There was only the name of a party. And the committee consisted of all the party members. Somehow or other, it seemed just like the kind of thing we were fighting against—a miniature parliament. The voting system ruled. When the great parliament cried until they were hoarse, at least they shouted about problems of importance. Here, this small circle engaged in interminable discussions as to how they might answer the letters that they were delighted to have received!

Needless to say, the public knew nothing of all this. In Munich, nobody knew of our party, not even by name, except our few members and their few friends.

Every Wednesday, a so-called committee meeting was held in one of the cafés, and a lecture was arranged for one evening each week. In the beginning, all the members of the movement were also members of the committee; therefore all the faces were the same. Now the task was to extend the narrow limits of this small circle and get new members; but above all, to make the movement known at any price.

We chose the following technique:

Monthly—and later, every two weeks—we decided to hold a 'meeting.' Some of the invitations were typewritten, and others were written by hand. For the first few meetings, we distributed them in the streets and delivered them personally. Each solicited among his own acquaintances and tried to persuade some of them to attend our meetings.

The result was lamentable.

I still remember how I once personally delivered 80 of these invitations, and how we waited in the evening for the crowds to come.

After an hour, the 'chairman' finally had to open the 'meeting.' Again there were only seven men: the same old seven.

THE FIRST MEETING (section 12.12)

We then changed our methods. We had the invitations typed in a Munich stationery shop, and then mimeographed them. The result was that a few more people attended our next meeting. The number increased gradually: from 11 to 13, then to 17, to 23, and finally to 34.

We collected some money within our own circle, each poor devil giving a small contribution. In that way, we raised sufficient funds to be able to advertise one of our meetings in the *Munich Observer*, which was still an independent paper. This time we had an astonishing success. We chose the Munich Hofbräuhaus Keller (not to be confused with the Munich Hofbräuhaus Festsaal) as our meeting place. It was a small hall and would accommodate scarcely more than 130 people. To me, however, the hall seemed enormous, and we were all worried that this 'mighty' edifice might remain partly empty on the night of the meeting.[4]

At 7:00 pm, 111 people were present, and the meeting was opened.

A Munich professor delivered the principal address, and I spoke after him. That was my first time speaking in public.

The whole thing seemed very daring to Herr Harrer, who was the first

---

[4] This was on 16 October 1919.

chairman of the party. He was a very decent fellow; but he believed that I, despite a number of good qualities, had no talent for public speaking. Even later, he couldn't be persuaded to change his opinion.

Things turned out differently. I was allotted 20 minutes for my speech on this occasion, which might be looked upon as our first public meeting.

I spoke for 30 minutes. And something that I always felt deep down in my heart, without really knowing, was here proven to be true: I could speak! After my 30 minutes, the people in the little hall were electrified. Their enthusiasm found its first expression in the fact that my appeal to those present brought us donations of 300 marks. That was a great relief for us. Our finances at that time were so meager that we couldn't afford to have our party slogans printed, or even distribute leaflets. Now we at least possessed the nucleus of a fund from which we could pay our most urgent and necessary expenses. ...

SECOND MEETING (section 12.14)

Around October 1919, the second larger meeting took place in the Eberlbräu Keller. Theme: 'Brest-Litovsk and Versailles.' There were four speakers. I spoke for almost an hour, and the success was even more striking than at our first meeting. The number of people who attended had grown to more than 130. An attempted disturbance was immediately stopped by my comrades. The would-be disrupters were thrown down the stairs, with gashed heads.

Two weeks later, another meeting took place in the same hall. The attendance had now increased to more than 170, and the room was fairly well filled. I spoke again, and once more it was more successful than at the previous meeting.

I then proposed a larger hall. After looking around, we found one at the other end of the town, in the 'Deutschen Reich' on Dachauer Strasse. The first meeting there had a smaller attendance than the previous meeting: barely 140 people. The committee members got discouraged; those who had always been skeptical were now convinced that this drop-off was due to the fact that our events were held too frequently. There were vociferous discussions, in which I defended my own view, that a city with 700,000 inhabitants should be able to stand not one meeting every couple weeks, but ten every week. I held that we shouldn't be discouraged by a setback, that the tactics we had chosen were correct, and that sooner or later success would be ours—if we only continued with determined perseverance to push ahead on our path. This whole winter of 1919–20 was one continual struggle to strengthen confidence in our ability to carry the movement through to success, and to instill a burning faith that could move mountains.

The next meeting in the small hall proved me correct. Our audience increased to more than 200. The publicity effect and financial success were spectacular.

I immediately urged that a further meeting be held. It took place in less than two weeks, and there were more than 270 people there.

Two weeks later, we invited our followers and their friends, for the seventh time, to attend our meeting. The same hall was scarcely large enough for the number that came. They amounted to more than 400....

'INTELLECTUAL WEAPONS,' 'SILENT WORKERS' (section 12.18)

I don't put much value on the friendship of people who don't succeed in getting hated by their enemies. Therefore, we considered the friendship of such people as not only worthless, but even dangerous to our young movement. That was the main reason why we first called ourselves a 'party.' We hoped that, by giving ourselves such a name, we might scare away a whole host of folkish dreamers. And secondly, that was why we named ourselves The National Socialist German Workers' Party.

The first term, 'party,' kept away all those dreamers who live in the past and all the lovers of bombastic nomenclature, those advocates of the so-called 'folkish idea.' Secondly, the full name of the party kept away all those knights of the 'intellectual sword'—all those wretches whose 'intellectual weapons' hid their cowardice.

It was only to be expected that this latter class would attack us the hardest—not actively, of course, but only with their pens. This is the only weapon of the folkish goose-quills. To them, our principle "We shall meet violence with violence in our own defense," was terrifying. They reproached us bitterly, not only for what they called our crude worship of the cudgel, but also because, according to them, of our lack of spirit as such. They didn't realize for a moment that even a Demosthenes[5] could be reduced to silence at a mass-meeting by 50 idiots who had come there to shout him down and use their fists against his supporters. Their innate cowardice prevents them from exposing themselves to such a danger; they always work 'silently' and never dare to make 'noise,' or to come forward in public.

Even today, I must warn our young movement in the strongest possible terms to guard against falling into the snare of those so-called 'silent workers.' They are not only cowards but also, and always will be, incompetents and do-nothings. A man who is aware of certain things and knows that danger threatens, and at the same time sees the possibility of a certain remedy, has an obligation not to work 'in silence' but openly and publicly. He must fight against the evil, and for its cure. If he does not, then he is a timid weakling who fails from cowardice, laziness, or incompetence.

Most of these 'silent workers' generally pretend to know God-knows-what. They do nothing but try to fool the world with their tricks. Though quite indolent, they try to create the impression that their 'silent' work keeps them very busy. In short, they are sheer swindlers—political crooks who hate the honest work of others. When you find one of these folkish moths buzzing over the value of his 'silence,' you may bet a thousand-to-one that you are dealing with someone who does nothing productive at all, but steals—steals the fruits of others' labor.

Additionally, one should note the arrogance and conceited impudence with which these obscurantist idlers try to tear to pieces the work of other people—criticizing it with an air of superiority, and thus aiding the mortal enemy of our people.

Every last agitator, who has the courage to stand on a beerhall-table amid his enemies and manfully and openly defend his position, achieves a thousand times more than these lying, treacherous sneaks. He will at least convert one or another to the movement. One can examine his work and test its effectiveness by its actual results. Only those cowardly swindlers—who praise their own 'silent' work and shelter themselves under the despicable cloak of anonymity—are just worthless and, in the truest sense of the term, useless drones, for the purpose of our national reconstruction.

---

[5] Famed orator and stateman of ancient Athens, contemporary of Aristotle. Lived circa 350 BC.

THE ESSENTIAL MEIN KAMPF

FIRST GREAT MASS MEETING (section 12.19)

In the beginning of 1920, I put forward the idea of holding our first mass meeting. There were differences of opinion amongst us. Some leading members of our party thought that the time was not ripe for such a meeting, and that the outcome might be detrimental. The Red press began to take notice of us, and we were lucky enough to arouse their hatred. We had begun to appear at other meetings and to ask questions or contradict the speakers, and naturally we were shouted down. But still we thereby gained some success. People got to know us; and the better they understood us, the stronger was their aversion and their enmity. Therefore we expected that a large contingent of our friends from the Red camp would attend our first mass meeting.

I fully realized that our meeting would probably be broken up. But we had to face the fight; if not now, then some months later. Since the first day of our founding, we were resolved to secure the future of the movement by fighting our way forward in a spirit of blind faith and ruthless determination. I was well-acquainted with the mentality of all those on the Red side, and I knew quite well that if we opposed them, not only would we make an impression but we might even win new followers. Thus we had to be resolved to put up resistance.

Herr Harrer was then chairman of our party. He didn't support my view as to the opportune time for our first mass meeting. Accordingly, as an honest and upright man, he resigned from the leadership of the movement. Herr Anton Drexler took his place. I kept the work of organizing the propaganda in my own hands and uncompromisingly carried it out.

We decided on 24 February 1920 as the date for the first great mass meeting of the still-unknown movement.

I made all the preparatory arrangements personally. They were very brief. The whole apparatus of our organization was designed to make rapid decisions. Within 24 hours, we had to decide on the attitude we would take in regard to the questions that would be put forth at the mass meeting. They would be announced on posters and leaflets, whose content followed the guidelines that I have already laid out regarding propaganda in general:[6] appeal to the broad masses; concentration on a few points; constant

---

[6] See volume one, chapter 6 (not included here).

— 10 —

repetition; concise and dogmatic expression of ideas; perservance in distribution; and patience in awaiting the effect.

For our principal color, we chose red; it has an exciting effect on the eye and was therefore calculated to arouse and provoke our opponents. Thus they would have to remember us—whether they liked it or not.

Subsequently, the inner fraternization in Bavaria between the Marxists and the Center Party became clear. The ruling Bavarian People's Party[7] did its best to counteract the effect that our posters had on the Red working masses. Later they moved to prohibit them. If the police could find no other grounds for doing so, then they could claim that we were 'disturbing the traffic' in the streets. And thus the so-called German National People's Party pleased their inner, silent Red ally by completely banning those posters—posters that brought back hundreds of thousands of workers to their own people, who had been incited and seduced by internationalism. These posters—appended to the first and second editions of this book[8]— bear witness to the bitterness of the struggle in which the young movement was then engaged. Future generations will find in them a documentary proof of our determination and the justice of our own cause. And they show the despotism of our so-called national officials, who acted against us because we were nationalizing the broad masses of the people....

DRAFTING THE PROGRAM (section 12.21)

Before holding our first great mass meeting, it was necessary not only to have our propaganda material ready but also to have the main points of our program printed.

In the second volume of this book, I'll develop the guiding principles that we then followed in drawing up our program. Here I will only say that the program was arranged, not merely to set forth the form and content of the young movement, but also with the goal of making it understood among the broad masses.

The so-called intellectual circles made jokes and sneered at it, and then tried to criticize it. But the effectiveness of our program has proven that the ideas of that time were right.

---

[7] They were affiliated with the Center Party.

[8] Not included here.

THE ESSENTIAL MEIN KAMPF

During these years, I saw dozens of new movements arise and disappear without leaving a trace. A single one remains: the National Socialist German Workers' Party. Today I am more convinced than ever before that, though they may combat us and try to paralyze our movement, and though petty party ministers may forbid us to speak, they cannot prevent the triumph of our ideas.

When both the present system of state administration and the names of its advocates are forgotten, the fundamentals of the National Socialist program will supply the basis for a future state.

Our four months of meetings held before January 1920 slowly enabled us to collect the financial means necessary to have our first leaflets, posters, and programs printed.

A MOVEMENT ON THE MARCH (section 12.22)

I'll bring the first part of this book to a close by referring to our first great mass meeting, because it marked the occasion on which it burst the bounds of a small club and began to exert an influence on the most powerful factor of our time: public opinion.

I myself had but one concern at that time: Will the hall be filled, or will we speak to a gaping void? I was firmly convinced that if only the people would come, this day would turn out to be a great success for the young movement. And so I waited impatiently for the evening to come.

The meeting would begin at 7:30 pm. At 7:15, I walked through the chief hall of the Hofbräuhaus on the Platz in Munich, and my heart nearly burst with joy. The great hall—for at that time, it seemed very big to me—was filled to overflowing, shoulder to shoulder. Nearly 2,000 people were present. And above all, those people had come whom we had always wished to reach. More than half of the audience seemed to be communists or independents. Our first great demonstration was destined, in their view, to come to an abrupt end.

But things happened otherwise. When the first speaker finished, I got up to speak. After a few minutes, I was met with a hailstorm of interruptions, and violent encounters broke out in the hall. A handful of my loyal war comrades and some other followers wrestled with the disturbers and gradually restored order. I continued my speech. After half an hour, applause began to drown the interruptions and the shouting.

— 10 —

I now took up the program, and began to explain it for the first time.

Minute by minute, the interruptions was increasingly drowned out by shouts of applause. I finally came to explain the 25 points, and laid them out, point after point, before the masses.[9] As I asked them to pass their own judgment on each point, one after another was accepted with increasing enthusiasm—unanimously and again unanimously. When the last point was reached and found its way to the heart of the masses, I had before me a hall full of people united by a new conviction, a new faith, and a new will.

After nearly four hours, the hall began to clear. As the masses streamed towards the exit, crammed shoulder to shoulder, shoving and pushing, I knew that a movement was now set afoot among the German people that would never be forgotten.

A fire was kindled, from whose flame the sword would be fashioned that would restore freedom to the German Siegfried, and bring life back to the German nation.

And alongside the coming revival, I sensed that the Goddess of Inexorable Vengeance was now getting ready to redress the treason of 9 November 1918.

The hall slowly emptied.

The movement was on the march.

---

[9] Listed in Appendix.

FROM
VOLUME
TWO

— 11 —
WORLDVIEW AND PARTY

On 24 February 1920, the first great mass meeting of our young movement took place. In the Banquet Hall of the Munich Hofbräuhaus, the 25 theses of our new party program were explained to an audience of nearly 2,000 people; each thesis was enthusiastically received.

Thus we made the public aware of those first principles and lines of action by which the new struggle would abolish a mass of confused and obsolete ideas and opinion—things that had led to obscure and pernicious ends. A new force now appeared among the timid and feckless bourgeoisie. This force was destined to resist the triumphant advance of the Marxists and, at the last minute, bring the wheel of destiny to a halt.

It was self-evident that this new movement could gain the significance and support that are necessary pre-requisites in such a gigantic struggle only if it succeeded from the very outset in awakening a sacred conviction in the hearts of its followers. This was not a case of introducing a new electoral slogan into the political field, but rather that an entirely new worldview—one of fundamental significance—had to be promoted....

MARXISM AND DEMOCRATIC PRINCIPLES (section 1.2)

On such a spiritual ground, it's impossible for the bourgeois camp to develop the necessary strength to carry on the fight against the organized power of Marxism.

Indeed, they have never seriously thought of doing so. Though these parliamentary quacks of the white race are generally recognized as mentally inferior men, they are shrewd enough to know that they could not seriously entertain the hope of being able to use the weapon of Western democracy to fight a doctrine—namely, Marxism—which employs this very democracy for its own end. Democracy is exploited by the Marxists for the purpose of paralyzing their opponents and gaining a free hand for themselves, in order to put their own methods into action. When certain groups of Marxists use all their ingenuity for the time being to give the impression that they are inseparably attached to the principles of democracy, it's good to recall the fact that, on critical occasions, these same gentlemen showed no regard for the democratic principle of majority rule! Such was the case in those days when the bourgeois parliamentarians, in their monumental small-mindedness, believed that the security of the Reich was guaranteed because it had an overwhelming numerical majority in its favor; meanwhile the Marxists didn't hesitate to suddenly grasp power, backed by a mob of loafers, deserters, party bosses, and Jewish journalists. That was a slap in the face of the democracy that so many parliamentarians believed in. Only those credulous parliamentary wizards of a bourgeois democracy could have believed that the Marxist world-plague, and the brutal determination of its carriers, could for a moment—now or in the future—be banished by the magical formulas of Western parliamentarianism.

Marxism will march shoulder to shoulder with democracy until it succeeds in indirectly winning the support of even the nationalist world that it strives to root out. But if the Marxists ever came to believe that there was a danger that, from this witch's cauldron of our parliamentary democracy, a majority vote might be concocted that could seriously attack Marxism—even if only on the basis of its ruling majority—then the whole parliamentarian hocus-pocus would be at an end. Instead of appealing to the democratic conscience, the standard bearers of the Red International would immediately emit a furious rallying-cry among the proletarian masses, and the ensuing fight would take place not in the sedate atmosphere of Parliament but in the factories and the streets. Then democracy would be finished at once; that which the intellectual agility of the parliamentarian apostles had failed to accomplish would now be successfully carried out by the crowbar and the sledgehammer of the exasperated proletarian masses, just as in the fall of 1918. At a single blow, they would awaken the bourgeois world to the madness of thinking that Jewish world domination could be opposed by means of Western democracy.

— 11 —

WORLDVIEW AGAINST WORLDVIEW (section 1.3)

As I have said, only a very credulous mind could think of complying with the rules of the game when he has to face a player for whom those rules are nothing but a mere bluff or a means of serving his own interests—which he will quickly discard when they are no longer to his advantage.

All the parties that profess so-called bourgeois principles look upon political life as, in reality, a struggle for seats in Parliament. The moment that their principles and convictions are of no further use in that struggle, they are thrown overboard like sand ballast. And the programs are constructed in such a way that they can be dealt with in a like manner. But such a practice has a correspondingly weakening effect. The parties lack the great magnetic attraction that alone draws in the broad masses; these masses always respond to the compelling force that emanates from absolute faith in the ideas put forth, along with the fanatical fighting courage to defend them.

At a time in which the one side, armed with all the weapons of a thousand-times criminal worldview, makes an attack against the established order, the other side will be able to resist only when it draws its strength from a new faith, which in our case is a political faith. This faith must replace the weak and cowardly command to defend with the battle-cry of a courageous and ruthless attack. If our present movement is accused, especially by the so-called national bourgeois cabinet ministers—the Bavarian Center, for example—of heading towards a 'revolution,' we have only one answer to those political midgets: We are trying to make up for that which you, in your criminal stupidity, failed to do. By your parliamentarian cattle-trading, you helped to drag the nation into the abyss; but we, by our aggressive policy, are setting up a new worldview, one that we shall defend with indomitable devotion. Thus we are building the steps upon which our nation may once again ascend to the temple of freedom.

Hence during the founding time of our movement, we had to take special care that our militant group, which fought for a new and exalted political faith, shouldn't degenerate into a mere society for the promotion of parliamentarian interests.

The first preventive measure was to create a program that would, by itself, tend towards developing a certain inner greatness that would scare away all the small and weak minds of our present party politicians.

THE ESSENTIAL MEIN KAMPF

The fatal defects that finally led to Germany's collapse [in 1918] offer the clearest proof of how correct we were in considering it absolutely necessary to set up programmatic goals that were sharply and distinctly defined.

Because we recognized these defects, we realized that a new conception of the State had to be formed. This in itself became a part of our new world-conception.

— 12 —
THE STATE

THE STATE IS NOT AN END IN ITSELF (section 2.3)

The Jew Marx was able to draw the final conclusions from these false concepts and ideas on the nature and purpose of the State: By eliminating from the State-concept all thought of racial obligation, without finding any other formula that might be equally accepted, the bourgeois world prepared the way for a doctrine that rejects the State as such.

Even in this field, therefore, the bourgeois world's struggle against Marxist internationalism is absolutely doomed to failure. The bourgeoisie have already sacrificed the basic principles that alone could furnish a solid footing for their ideology. Their crafty opponent has perceived the defects in their structure and now assaults it with those weapons that they themselves have provided—though without meaning to do so.

It's therefore the first obligation of any new movement based on a folkish worldview, to put forth a clear and logical doctrine of the nature and purpose of the State.

The fundamental principle is that the State is not an end in itself, but the means to an end. It's the pre-condition of a higher form of human civilization, but it's not the cause. This cause is found exclusively in the existence of a culture-creating race. There may be hundreds of excellent States on this earth, and yet if the Aryan culture-bearer died out, no culture would exist that corresponds to the spiritual level of the highest peoples today. We may go still further and say that the fact that States have been created by human beings does not in the least exclude the possibility of the destruction of the human race, because the superior intellectual faculties and flexibilities of the racial bearers would be lost.

THE ESSENTIAL MEIN KAMPF

If, for example, the surface of the globe were shaken today by some seismic convulsion and if a new Himalaya emerged from the ocean waves, this one catastrophe alone might destroy human civilization. No State could exist any longer. All order would be shattered. And all vestiges of cultural products developed over thousands of years would disappear—nothing but one tremendous field of death submerged in water and mud. If, however, just a few people survived this horrible chaos, and if these people belonged to a culture-producing race, then, when the commotion had passed, even if after thousands of years, the earth would again bear witness to the creative power of the human spirit. Only with the destruction of the last culture-creating race and its individual members would the Earth definitely be turned into a desert.

On the other hand, modern history gives examples showing that state institutions that owe their beginnings to a race that lacks creative genius won't endure. Just as many varieties of prehistoric animals gave way to others and left no trace behind them, so man will also have to give way, if he loses that definite spiritual force that enables him to find the weapons necessary for his self-preservation.

It's not the State per se that brings about a certain definite advance in cultural progress; it can only protect the race that is the cause of such progress. The State per se may well exist unchanged for hundreds of years, though the cultural faculties and the general life of the people—which is shaped by these faculties—may have suffered profound changes because the State didn't prevent a racial mixture from taking place. The present State, for instance, may continue to exist in a merely mechanical form, but the racial poisoning of our national body brings about a cultural decay that, even now, manifests itself in terrifying ways.

Thus the indispensable precondition for the existence of a superior humanity is not the State but the nation, which alone possesses the essential ability.

This capacity is always there, though it lies dormant until external circumstances awaken it to action. Nations, or rather races, that are endowed with the faculty of cultural creativeness possess this faculty in a latent form, even if conditions are temporarily unfavorable to their realization. It's therefore outrageously unjust to speak of the pre-Christian Germans as 'cultureless,' as barbarians. They never have been that. But the severity of the prevailing climate of their northern homeland hampered development of their creative faculties. If they had come to the fairer climate of the south without any culture whatsoever, and if they had acquired the necessary tools from inferior nations, then the dormant cultural faculty would have blossomed radiantly—as happened in the case of the Greeks, for example. But this primordial culture-creating force wasn't solely due to their northern climate. The Laplander would not have become creators of a culture if they were transplanted to the south, nor would the Eskimo. No, this glorious creative faculty was only bestowed on the Aryan; it becomes active or lies dormant depending on whether there are favorable circumstances or whether adverse Nature prevents it.

From these facts the following conclusions may be drawn: The State is a means to an end. Its end is to preserve and promote a community of people who are physically and mentally akin. First it must preserve the existence of the race, which thereby permits the free development of all the forces dormant in this race. A part of these forces will always have to serve primarily to maintain the physical existence of the race, and only the remaining portion will be free to promote intellectual progress. But as a matter of fact, the one is always the necessary precondition of the other.

States that don't serve this purpose have no justification for their existence; they are monstrosities. The fact that they do exist is no more of a justification than the success of a band of pirates can be considered a justification of piracy. ...

CONSEQUENCES OF OUR RACIAL DIVISION (section 2.6)

And if we ask what kind of state structure we Germans need, we must first clearly understand which kind of people it should contain and what purpose it should serve.

Unfortunately the German nationality is no longer based on a unified racial core. The mixing process of the original elements, however, has not gone so far as to justify speaking of a new race. On the contrary: The blood-poisoning of our national body, especially since the Thirty Years' War,[1] has degraded not only our blood but also our soul. The open borders of our

---

[1] The Thirty Years' War was a religious war in central Europe—mainly within present-day Germany—that ran from 1618 to 1648. Some 8 million lives were lost.

fatherland, the association with non-German foreign elements in these borderlands, and especially the strong influx of foreign blood into the interior of the Reich itself, have prevented any complete assimilation of those various elements because of the steady influx. No new race arose from this melting-pot. Rather, the various racial elements continue to exist side by side, with the result that—especially in times of crisis, when the herd usually sticks together—the Germans disperse in all directions. The fundamental racial elements are not only scattered by district, but also within single districts. Aside the Nordic type we find the East-European, aside the Easterner there is the Dinaric,[2] the Westerner intermingles with both—with cross-breeds among them all.

This is, on the one hand, a grave disadvantage: The Germans lack a strong herd instinct that arises from unity of blood and saves nations from ruin in dangerous and critical times; on such occasions, all petty differences disappear, and a united herd faces the enemy. The word 'hyper-individualism' arises from the fact that our primordial racial elements exist side by side without ever truly combining. During times of peace, such a situation may offer some advantages, but all things considered, it has prevented us from gaining world dominion. If the German people had historically possessed the herd unity that other peoples enjoyed, then the German Reich would today likely be mistress of the globe. World history would have followed another course, and in this case no one can tell if we might have reached, in this way, that which many blind pacifists hope to gain by begging, whining, and crying: namely, a peace based not upon the waving of olive branches by tearful, mournful, pacifist women, but a peace guaranteed by the triumphant sword of a master people, administering the world in the service of a higher culture.

The fact that our people do not have a nationality of unified blood has brought us untold misery. It gave capital cities to many petty German potentates, but it deprived the German people of their master right.

Even today our nation still suffers from this lack of inner unity; but the cause of our past and present misfortunes may turn out to be a future blessing for us. Though on the one hand it was a drawback that our racial elements were not mixed together, so that no homogeneous national body

---

[2] 'Dinaric' refers to the indigenous people of the Dinaric Alps, a mountain range running across the former Yugoslavia—present-day Serbia, Croatia, and Bosnia especially. Dinarics were seen as a mixture of the northern European and the southern.

— 12 —

could develop, on the other hand it was fortunate that at least a part of our best blood was thus kept pure and escaped racial degeneration.

A complete assimilation of all our racial elements would certainly have brought about a homogeneous national organism; but, as has been proven in every case of racial mixture, it would have been less capable of creating a civilization than the highest of its original elements. This is the benefit of incomplete mixing: that even now we have large groups of unmixed German Nordic people within our national body, and that they are our most precious treasure for the future.

During that dark period of absolute ignorance in regard to all racial laws, when each individual was considered equal to every other, there could be no clear appreciation of the difference between the various fundamental racial characteristics. Today we know that a complete assimilation of all the various national elements might have resulted in giving us a larger share of external power; but the highest of human aims would not have been attained, because the only kind of people that fate has clearly chosen to bring about this perfection would have perished in such a racial mish-mash. ...

DANGERS OF RACIAL MIXING (section 2.9)

Nature generally takes certain corrective measures with respect to racial purity. She has little love for the bastard. The products of cross-breeding suffer bitterly, especially the third, fourth, and fifth generations. Not only are they deprived of the higher parental qualities of the cross-breeding, but their lack of blood-unity also means a lack of unified will-power and vigorous vital energies. At all critical moments in which a racially-unified person makes correct—that is, coherent—decisions, the racially-mixed person becomes confused and takes half-measures. Taken together, this means not only the relative inferiority of the mixed-race person, but also in practice the possibility of a more rapid decline. In innumerable cases where race holds up, the bastard breaks down. In this we see the corrective action of nature. But often she goes further. She restricts the possibilities of procreation— thereby hindering the fertility of cross-breeds and driving them to extinction.

For instance, if an individual member of a race were to mix with someone of a lower race, the first result would be a lowering of the racial level, and furthermore the descendants of this cross-breeding would be weaker than those who remained racially unmixed. If new blood from the superior race is blocked, and if the bastards continue to cross-breed among themselves, they will either die out because they have insufficient powers of resistance, which is Nature's wise provision, or in the course of many thousands of years they will form a new mixture in which the original elements will become so wholly mixed through this thousand-fold crossing that the original elements will be no longer recognizable. And thus a new people would be developed that possessed a certain herd resistance, but its intellectual and cultural significance would be markedly inferior to that of the first cross-breeds. But even in this last case, the mongrel product would succumb in the mutual struggle for existence, as long as a higher racial group remained unmixed. The herd solidarity of this new national body, even though developed over thousands of years, would still be no match in the struggle with an equally unified, but spiritually and culturally superior, race; it would lack the elasticity and creative capacity to prevail.

Hence we can establish the following valid principle: Every racial mixture necessarily leads, sooner or later, to the downfall of the mongrel product, as long as the higher part of this cross-breed still exists with any kind of racial unity. The danger to the mongrels ceases only with the bastardization of the last remaining elements of the higher race.

This principle is the source of a slow but steady process of regeneration in which all racial poisoning is gradually eliminated, as long as there remains a basic stock of pure racial elements that resists further bastardization.

Such a process may begin automatically among those people with a strong racial instinct, particularly those who have been thrown off the track of normal, racially-pure reproduction by some special condition or special compulsion. As soon as this compulsion ceases, that part of the race that has remained intact will tend to mate with its own kind, thus halting further mixture. Then the mongrels will recede quite naturally into the background, unless their numbers have increased so much that they can withstand all serious resistance from those who have remained racially pure.

When men have lost their natural instincts and ignore the obligations imposed on them by nature, then there's no hope that nature will correct the loss that has occurred until a recognition of the lost instincts has been restored; then the task of restoring what has been lost must be accomplished.

— 12 —

But there's a serious danger that those who have become blinded once in this respect will repeatedly continue to break down racial barriers and finally lose the last remnants of what is best in them. What then remains is nothing but a uniform mish-mash, which seems to be the dream of today's famous world-reformers; but that mish-mash would soon banish all ideals from the world. Indeed: a great herd could thus be formed, a herd-animal produced by all sorts of ingredients. But a mixture of this sort could never produce a breed of men who were culture-bearers—or better, culture-founders and culture-creators. The mission of humanity might then be seen as at an end.

Anyone who doesn't wish for the Earth to fall into such a condition must realize that it's the task of the Germanic states in particular to bring a halt to this bastardization.

Our contemporary generation of weaklings will naturally decry such a policy, and whine and complain about it as an assault on the most sacred of human rights. No, there's only one right that is sacrosanct, and this right is at the same time a most sacred duty, namely: that the purity of the blood should be preserved, thus preserving the best types of human beings and rendering possible a nobler development of humanity itself.

THE FOLKISH STATE AND RACIAL HYGIENE (section 2.10)

A folkish State should begin by raising marriage above the level of being a constant scandal to the race. The State should consecrate it as an institution to produce creatures made in the likeness of the Lord, and not to create monsters that are a mixture of man and ape.

Protest against this on so-called humane grounds is inappropriate for a generation that makes it possible for the most depraved degenerates to propagate themselves, thereby imposing unspeakable suffering on their own offspring and their contemporaries—while on the other hand, contraceptives are permitted and sold in every drug store, and even by street venders, so that babies might not be born even among the healthiest parents. In our present state of law and order, this brave, bourgeois-national world looks upon it as a crime to make procreation impossible for those who suffer with syphilis, tuberculosis, hereditary diseases, and also cripples and cretins. But the actual prevention of procreation among millions of our very best people is not considered an evil, nor does it offend against the noble morality of this social class, but rather encourages their short-sighted mental laziness. For otherwise they would at least rack their brains to figure out how to create the conditions for the feeding and maintenance of those future beings who, as the healthy representatives of our nation, will someday serve the same function with respect to future generations.

How boundlessly unideal and ignoble is this whole system! People no longer bother to breed the best for posterity, but rather let things slide along, as best they can. The fact that the churches join in committing this sin against the image of God, even though they continue to emphasize the dignity of that image, is quite consistent with their present activities. They talk about the Spirit, but they allow man, as the embodiment of the Spirit, to become a degenerate proletarian. Then they are amazed at how little influence the Christian faith has in their own country, and at the depraved 'ungodliness' of this physically and therefore morally degenerate riff-raff. They then try to make up for it by converting the Hottentots and the Zulu Kaffirs, and to grant them the blessings of the Church. While our European people—God be praised—are left to become the victims of physical and moral depravity, the pious missionary goes out to Central Africa and establishes missions for Negroes. Eventually even there, healthy—though primitive and backward—people will be transformed, in the name of 'higher culture,' into a foul breed of bastards.

It would better accord with noble human aspirations if our two Christian churches would cease to bother the Negroes with missions that they don't want and don't understand. Instead, they should kindly but seriously teach the people of Europe that it's much more pleasing to God for a couple that is not healthy to show loving kindness to some poor orphan and become a father and mother to him, rather than give birth to a sickly child who will be a cause of suffering and unhappiness to all.

The folkish State will have to make up for everyone else's neglect in this area. It must put race at the center of all life. It must ensure its purity. It must declare that children are a people's most valuable treasure. It must see to it that only those who are healthy shall beget children. There is only one disgrace: for ill or defective parents to bring children into the world; and one highest honor: to refrain from doing so. Conversely, it must be considered reprehensible to refrain from giving healthy children to the nation. Here the State must assert itself as the trustee of a millennial future, by which the selfish desires of the individual count for nothing and must yield. To this end, the State must employ the most modern medical technologies. It must proclaim as unfit for procreation all those who are inflicted with some visible hereditary disease or are the carriers of it, and then must put this policy into actual practice. Conversely, it must ensure that the normally fertile woman is not restricted by the financial irresponsibility of a political regime that sees the blessing of children as a curse to their parents. The State will have to abolish the cowardly and even criminal indifference by which it handles the problem of social amenities for large families, and it will have to be the supreme protector of this greatest blessing of a people. Its attention and care must be directed more towards the child than the adult.

Those who are physically and mentally unhealthy and unfit must not perpetuate their own suffering in the bodies of their children. From an educational point of view, this is the greatest task for the folkish State to accomplish. Someday this work will appear greater and more significant than the most victorious wars of our present bourgeois era. Through education, the State must teach individuals that being sickly and ill is not a disgrace but rather an unfortunate accident, one to be pitied. But it's a crime and a disgrace to make this affliction all the worse by passing it on to innocent creatures out of mere egotism. And by comparison, it's an expression of a truly noble nature, and an admirable humanitarian act, if an innocently sick person refrains from having a child of his own but gives his love and affection to some unknown child who, through its health, promises to become a robust member of a healthy community. In accomplishing such an educational task, the State integrates its function by this activity in the moral sphere. It must act without regard to the question of whether its conduct will be understood or misconstrued, blamed or praised.

If only for a period of 600 years, those individuals who are physically degenerate or mentally ill were to be prevented from procreating, humanity would not only be freed from an immense misfortune but also restored to such a condition as we at present can hardly imagine.

If the fertility of the healthiest portion of the nation were to be conscientiously and methodically promoted, the result would be a race that, at least, would have eliminated the germs of our present moral and physical decay.

Once a people and a State have started on this course, developing the most valuable racial core of the nation and increasing its fertility, the people as a whole will subsequently enjoy the blessings of a highly-bred racial stock.

To achieve this, the State should first of all not leave to chance the colonization of newly acquired territory, but should do so according to special norms. Specially-constructed racial committees should issue colonization certificates to individuals; these certificates should guarantee their racial purity. In this way, border colonies could gradually be founded, whose inhabitants would be of the purest racial stock and hence of the highest racial quality. This will make them a valuable asset to the whole nation; their development would be a source of pride and confidence to each citizen because they would contain the kernel for a great development of our nation—yes, and even of mankind itself.

The folkish worldview must finally succeed in bringing about a nobler era in which men will no longer pay exclusive attention to breeding dogs, horses, and cats, but will improve the breed of the human race itself.[3] It will be an era in which one class knowingly and silently renounces, while the other joyfully sacrifices and gives.

That such a thing is possible cannot be denied in a world where hundreds and thousands voluntarily accept the principle of celibacy, without being obliged or bound to do so by anything except religious injunction.

Why wouldn't it be possible to induce people to make this sacrifice if, instead of such a precept, they were simply told that they ought to put an end to this original sin of racial poisoning? And further, if they realized their duty to give to the Almighty Creator beings such as he himself created?

Naturally, our wretched army of contemporary bourgeois won't understand this. They will ridicule the idea, or shrug their shoulders and

---

[3] Such passages recall the similar intentions of Plato who, in the *Republic*, argued that wise rulers would breed the best possible citizens, not unlike the process with animal-breeders, who always try to breed "from the best." Plato explains: "And do you think that if they weren't bred in this way, your stock of birds and dogs would get much worse? What about horses and other animals? Are things any different with them? ... If this also holds true of human beings, our need for excellent rulers is indeed extreme." (459a-c)

— 12 —

groan out their eternal excuses: "Of course it's a fine thing, but it can't be done!" And we reply, true, it can't be done by *you*—your world isn't fit for it! You have only one concern: your own life; and only one God: your money! Thus we turn not to you for help, but to the great army of those who are too poor to consider their personal lives as the highest good on Earth. They place their trust not in gold but in other gods. Above all we turn to the vast army of our German youth. They are growing up in a great epoch, and they will fight against the evils that were due to the laziness and indifference of their fathers. Either the German youth will one day create a new folkish State or they will be the last witnesses of the complete collapse and end of the bourgeois world.

For if a generation suffers from defects that it recognizes and admits, and is nevertheless quite pleased with itself—as the bourgeois world is today—and is satisfied with the cheap excuse that nothing can be done, then such a society is doomed. A marked characteristic of our bourgeois is that they can no longer deny the failings that exist. They must admit that much is foul and wrong, but they're no longer able to fight against the evil, which would mean mobilizing the forces of 60 or 70 million people to oppose this danger. On the contrary: When such an effort is made elsewhere, they only indulge in silly comments and try, from a safe distance, to show that such an approach is theoretically impossible and doomed to failure. No argument is too absurd to be employed in the service of their own dwarfishness and moral attitude. If, for example, a whole continent wages war against alcoholism, so as to free a people from this devastating vice, our bourgeois European offers nothing better than an incredulous stare and head-shaking, a superior ridicule—something appropriate for this ridiculous society.[4] But when all this ridicule comes to nothing, and in that part of the world this sublime and intangible attitude is effective and successful, then such success is questioned or deprecated. Even moral principles are used in this slanderous campaign against a struggle that aims at suppressing the greatest immorality.

No—we must have no mistake about this: Our contemporary bourgeoisie has become worthless for any such noble human task because it has lost all sense of quality, and is evil. Evil, not so much—I'd say—

---

[4] Hitler refers to the then-recent American experiment with prohibition, which was enacted in 1920. (It was subsequently repealed in 1933.)

because evil is desired but rather because of an incredible laziness and all that comes with it. That's why those political societies that call themselves 'bourgeois parties' are nothing but associations to promote the interests of certain professional groups and classes. Their highest aim is to defend their own selfish interests as best they can. It's obvious that such a politicized 'bourgeois' guild is fit for anything other than a struggle; especially when the adversaries are not small businessmen but the proletarian masses, incited to extremes and determined to do their worst.

— 13 —
WORLDVIEW AND ORGANIZATION

The folkish State, which I have tried to sketch in general outline, won't become a reality simply due to the fact that we know what's necessary for it. It's not enough to know how such a State should appear. The problem of its foundation is far more important. The existing parties benefit from the State, and they cannot be expected to bring about a change in the regime or to willingly modify their attitude. This is rendered all the more impossible because the leading elements are always Jews and yet more Jews. The present trend of development would, if allowed to go on unhampered, lead to the realization of the pan-Jewish prophecy—that the Jews will one day devour the other nations of the Earth and become their master.[1]

In contrast to the millions of 'bourgeois' and 'proletarian' Germans—who are stumbling to their ruin, mostly through timidity and stupidity—the Jew persistently pursues his way and keeps his mind fixed on his future goal. Any party that's led by him can fight for no other interests than his, and his interests certainly have nothing in common with those of the Aryan nations.

---

[1] In fact there has been some suggestion in recent years that Jews have become de facto masters of other nations. In late 2003, after the initiation of the second Iraq war that was heavily promoted by the American Jewish Lobby, Malaysian president Mahathir Mohamad said this in a public address: "Today Jews rule the world by proxy. They get others to fight and die for them" (AP, 16 Oct 2003). American foreign policy is almost entirely oriented toward the promotion of Jewish and Israeli interests, due to the overwhelming—and primarily monetary—influence of Jews on the US government. Unfortunately, this influence goes unquestioned and unexamined, thanks to dominant Jewish influence in American media. Through their decisive influence on the lone global superpower, Jews effectively are the masters of other nations.

THE ESSENTIAL MEIN KAMPF

If we wish to transform our ideal picture of the folkish State into reality, we must stay independent of the forces that now control public life, and seek out new forces that will be ready and capable of taking up the fight for such an ideal. It will be a struggle, insofar as the first objective isn't the creation of a folkish State-conception, but rather, above all: the elimination of the Jewish one. As so often happens in history, the main difficulty isn't establishing a new order but clearing the ground for it. Prejudices and special interests join together in forming a common front, attempting by all means to prevent the victory of any new idea that's disagreeable or threatening to them.

That's why the fighter for a new idea is unfortunately, and despite his desire for positive work, compelled to wage a negative battle first—in order to abolish the existing state of affairs.

STRUGGLE AND CRITICISM (section 5.1)

As displeasing as it may be to the individual, a young doctrine of great and essential importance must adopt the sharp probe of criticism as its weapon.

It displays a very superficial insight into historical development when the so-called folkists emphasize again and again that they won't adopt the use of negative criticism, but will engage only in constructive work; this absurd, childish stammering is 'folkish' in the worst sense of the word. It's further proof that the history of our own times has made no impression on these minds.

Marxism too has had its aims to pursue constructive work (if only the establishment of despotic rule by international Jewish world-finance!); nevertheless, for the prior 70 years, its principal work was criticism—destructive, disintegrating criticism, over and over, until this corrosive acid ate into the old State so thoroughly that it finally collapsed. Only then did the so-called 'construction' begin. And that was natural, right, and logical.

An existing order isn't abolished merely by proclaiming and insisting on a new one. It mustn't be presumed that adherents or beneficiaries of the existing order will be converted and won over to the new movement simply by demonstrating its necessity. On the contrary, it may easily happen that two different situations exist side by side, and that a so-called worldview is transformed into a party, unable to rise above its limitations. A worldview is intolerant and cannot exist as 'one party among many.' It imperiously demands its own recognition as unique and exclusive, and also a complete transformation of all public life in accordance with its views. It can never allow the previous condition to continue in existence.

The same holds true of religions.

Christianity was not content with erecting an altar of its own, but rather first had to destroy the pagan altars. It was only from this passionate intolerance that an apodictic faith could take form; intolerance is an indispensable precondition.

It may be objected here that such phenomena in world history arise from mostly a specifically Jewish mode of thought; indeed, that such fanaticism and intolerance embody the specifically Jewish mentality. This may be a thousand-times true, and it's a deeply regrettable fact. The appearance of fanatical intolerance in human history may be both deeply regrettable and foreign to human nature—but this doesn't change the fact it exists today. The men who want to liberate our German nation from its present condition shouldn't worry their heads with thinking how wonderful it would be if this or that had never arisen; rather, they must find ways to eliminate it. A worldview that's inspired by infernal intolerance can only be broken by the same spirit, by a doctrine driven by the same determined will, and which is itself a pure and absolutely true new idea.

One may today regret the fact that the advent of Christianity marked the appearance of the first spiritual terror into the much freer ancient world.[2] But the fact cannot be denied that, ever since then, the world has been pervaded and dominated by this kind of coercion, and that violence has been broken only by violence, and terror only by terror. Only then can a new condition be constructively created.

Political parties are prone to compromises, but worldviews never. Political parties tend to reckon with their opponents, but worldviews proclaim their own infallibility.

---

[2] There is good reason to view Christianity as a specifically Jewish form of religious "terror." This was certainly Nietzsche's view; see Dalton (2010) or (2011c) for details.

— 14 —
STRUGGLE IN EARLY TIMES

Memories of our first great meeting, in the banquet hall of the Hofbräuhaus on 24 February 1920, had not yet died away when we began preparations for our next meeting.[1] Up to that time, we had carefully considered the holding of a small meeting every month, or at most every two weeks, in a city like Munich, but now it was decided that we should hold a mass meeting every week. I needn't say that, assuredly, we faced one fear over and over again: Will the people come, and will they listen? — though I was personally convinced that, once they came, they would stay and listen.

FIGHT AGAINST POISONOUS PROPAGANDA (section 6.1)

During that time, the hall of the Munich Hofbräuhaus acquired an almost sacred significance for us National Socialists. There was a meeting every week, almost always in that hall, and each time it was fuller than before, and the people more attentive!

Starting with 'War Guilt'—which no one at that time cared about—and the peace treaties, we addressed almost everything that either stirred up the audience or seemed ideologically necessary. We gave greatest attention to the peace treaties. Again and again, the young movement made prophecies to those great masses, and now nearly all of them have been fulfilled! Today it's easy to speak and write about these things. But in those days, a public mass meeting—not of petty bourgeoisie but agitated proletarians—with the topic 'The Peace Treaty of Versailles' meant an attack on the Republic and evidence of reactionary or monarchist

---

[1] See sections 12.19-12.22 above.

tendencies.[2] The moment someone uttered the first criticism of the Versailles Treaty, one could expect an immediate and almost stereotyped reply: 'And Brest-Litovsk?' 'Brest-Litovsk?'[3] Again and again the crowd would murmur this, gradually swelling into a roar, until the speaker would have to give up his attempt to persuade them. One wanted to pound one's head against a wall in despair over these people! They would neither listen nor understand that Versailles was a scandal and a disgrace, a dictate that marked an unprecedented thievery of our people. The destructive work of the Marxists and the enemy's poisonous propaganda had robbed these people of their reason.

And we had no right to complain. The guilt on the other side was enormous! But what had our bourgeoisie done to call a halt to this terrible disintegration, to oppose it, and to open a way to the truth by giving a better and more thorough explanation? Nothing, and again nothing! At that time, the great folkish apostles of today were not to be seen. Perhaps they spoke to select groups at tea parties, or in their own little circles, but they never appeared where they should have been, namely, among the wolves; that is, unless there was a chance to howl with the pack.

As for myself, I then saw clearly that the question of war guilt had to be cleared up for the small kernel of our movement—and cleared up in light of historical truth. A pre-condition for future success of our movement was that it should impart knowledge of the peace treaty to the broadest masses. At the time, the masses viewed this peace as a success of democracy. Therefore we had to form a united front against it, and engrave ourselves into men's minds as an enemy of this treaty. Then, later on, when the harsh reality of this despicable swindle would be disclosed in all its naked hatred, a recollection of our earlier position would earn us their confidence.

---

[2] The Treaty of Versailles was signed on 28 June 1919, and signaled the formal end of World War One. It imposed humiliating and onerous conditions on Germany, and was a source of never-ending disdain by many Germans.

[3] The Treaty of Brest-Litovsk was signed on 3 March 1918. It marked Russia's withdrawal from World War One, and was cast in very favorable terms for Germany.

— 14 —

AGAINST THE TIDE (section 6.2)

Even then I took my stand on those important fundamental questions where public opinion had gone completely wrong, and I opposed these wrong notions without regard for popularity, hatred, or struggle. The NSDAP shouldn't be the servant of public opinion, but rather must dominate it. It shouldn't become a slave of the masses, but rather master!

Especially for a weak movement, there's a natural temptation to conform to the tactics of a more powerful enemy, particularly when his tactics have succeeded in leading the people to insane conclusions or to adopt mistaken attitudes. This is particularly strong when reasons can be found—though they may be entirely illusory—that seem, to the young movement, to point towards the same ends. Human cowardice will then all the more readily adopt those arguments that give it a semblance of justification, from 'its own viewpoint,' for participating in such a crime.

On several occasions I have experienced such cases, in which the greatest energy was required to keep the ship of our movement from being swept into an artificial public tide, and indeed from being driven by it. The last time was when our infernal press—the Hecuba of the existence of the German nation[4]—succeeded in bringing the question of South Tyrol into a prominent position that was catastrophic for the German people. Without considering what interests they were serving, several so-called 'national' men, parties, and organizations joined in the general outcry, simply for fear of Jew-incited public opinion, and foolishly helped to support the struggle against a system that we Germans should, particularly in these days, consider as the sole ray of light in this degenerating world.

While the international world-Jew slowly but surely strangles us, our so-called patriots shout against a man and his system with the courage to free themselves from the shackles of Jewish Freemasonry, at least in one corner of the Earth, and to oppose nationalist resistance against this international world-poison. But weak characters were too tempted to sail with the wind and capitulate to the clamor of public opinion. And a capitulation it was! These men are such base liars that they won't even

---

[4] Hecuba was the wife of Trojan King Priam in Homer's *The Iliad*. Hitler's phraseology here is unclear; perhaps it refers to the fact that Hecuba pleaded with her son Hector not to fight Achilles, thus mirroring the press' support for German capitulation. Both cases ended in disaster.

admit it to themselves, but it remains true that only cowardice and fear of public sentiment, aroused by the Jews, induced them to join in. All other reasons are only miserable excuses of little sinners who are conscious of their own guilt.

Thus it was necessary to grasp the movement with an iron hand, in order to save it from a path of ruin. Certainly an attempt at such change wasn't popular at the time, because the great flame of public opinion was burning in only one direction; and such a decision could sometimes be fatal. Not a few men in the course of history have been stoned for an act that posterity would later kneel down and thank them for.

It's on this posterity that a movement must depend, and not on the praises of the moment. It may well be that, in such hours, individuals have to endure anguish; but they shouldn't forget that, after such hours, salvation will come, and that a movement that wants to renew the world must serve the future and not the present.

POLITICS OF THE WIDE VIEW (section 6.3)

On this point, it may be asserted that the greatest and most enduring successes in history are mostly those that were least understood at the beginning, because they were in strongest contrast to public opinion, to its views and will.

We experienced this when we made our own first public appearance. It can truthfully be said that we didn't 'court the favor of the masses' but rather always opposed the nonsense of these people. In those years, it nearly always happened that I faced an assembly of men who believed the oppose of what I wanted to say, and who wanted the opposite of what I believed. Then it took a couple hours to persuade two or three thousand people to give up their former opinions—to shatter, blow by blow, the foundation of their views, and to eventually lead them over to our convictions and our worldview.

I quickly learned something important, namely, to snatch the enemy's weapons of reply from his own hands. One could soon see that our adversaries—especially the discussion leaders—were furnished with a definite 'repertoire' of arguments that were being constantly repeated. The uniform character of this procedure pointed to a deliberate and unified training. And so it was. We were thus able to recognize the incredible discipline of the enemy's propaganda, and I'm proud to this day that I discovered a means, not only of making this propaganda ineffective, but of beating its makers with it. Two years later I was a master of this art.

In every speech that I made, it was important to clearly anticipate the probable form and matter of the counter-arguments to be expected in the discussion, and to dismantle them in the speech. It was thereby necessary to mention all the possible objections and show their inconsistency; this made it easier to win over an honest listener by disposing of all the doubts that had been imprinted on his memory. That which he had learned was automatically refuted, and this made him all the more attentive to the speech.

ENLIGHTENMENT ABOUT THE PEACE TREATIES (section 6.4)

That was the reason why—after my first lecture on the 'Peace Treaty of Versailles' that I delivered to the troops while still a so-called 'instructor'—I changed the lecture and henceforth spoke of the 'Treaties of Brest-Litovsk and Versailles.' In the discussion after my first lecture, I quickly determined that people really knew nothing about the Treaty of Brest-Litovsk, and that clever party propaganda had succeeded in presenting it as one of the most scandalous acts of violence in the world. The persistent repetition of this lie to the broad masses caused millions of Germans to see the Treaty of Versailles as a just retribution for the crime that *we* had committed at Brest-Litovsk. They considered all opposition to Versailles as unjust, and in many cases there was honest moral indignation. And this was also the reason why the shameless and monstrous word 'reparations' came into common use in Germany. This hypocritical lie appeared to millions of our exasperated fellow countrymen as the fulfillment of a higher justice. Terrible, but true.

The best proof of this was the propaganda that I initiated against Versailles by my enlightenment on the Treaty of Brest-Litovsk. I compared the two treaties with one another, point by point, showing the immense humanity of the one treaty and the inhuman barbarity of the other—and the result was striking. When I spoke on this theme at meetings of 2,000 persons, I often saw 3,600 hostile eyes fixed on me. And yet, three hours later, I had in front of me a swaying mass of righteous indignation and fury. A great lie had once again been torn from the hearts and minds of a crowd of thousands, and a truth implanted in its place.

I considered the two lectures—'The True Causes of the World War' and 'The Peace Treaties of Brest-Litovsk and Versailles'—to be the most important of all. I therefore repeated them dozens of times, always giving them a new form until, at least on those points, a definitely clear and unanimous opinion emerged among those from whom our movement recruited its first members.

Furthermore, these gatherings gave me the benefit of gradually transforming myself into a speaker at mass meetings, and I became skilled in the pathos and gesture demanded by large halls with thousands of people.

Outside of the small circles that I mentioned, at that time I found no party engaged in explaining things to the people in this way. And yet today they speak as if *they* were the ones to bring about the change in public opinion. If a so-called nationalist politician spoke somewhere or other on this theme, it was only to circles of those who were already of the same conviction, and for whom his words were, at best, only a confirmation of their opinions. What was really needed was not this, but rather, by enlightenment and propaganda, to win over those whose education and opinion placed them firmly in the enemy camp.

The leaflet was also put to use in this enlightenment. While still a soldier, I had written a leaflet in which I contrasted the Treaty of Brest-Litovsk with that of Versailles, and it was distributed in large numbers. Later on I used it for the party, again with good success. The first meetings were distinguished by the tables covered with leaflets, newspapers, and pamphlets of every kind. But we relied mainly on the spoken word. And in fact, this is the only means of producing really great changes, for fundamental psychological reasons.

— 15 —
CONFLICT WITH THE RED FRONT

Old and New Black-Red-Gold (section 7.8)

The organization of our security troop cleared up a very difficult question. Until then the movement possessed no party symbol and also no party flag. The lack of these symbols was not only a disadvantage at the time but was intolerable for the future. The disadvantages were chiefly that party members possessed no outward sign of their common bond, and it was absolutely unthinkable for the future that they should remain without a symbol of the movement that could be opposed to the International.

More than once in my youth, I recognized the psychological importance of such a symbol, and it was emotionally advisable as well. After the War, I was at a Marxist mass-demonstration in Berlin, in front of the Royal Palace and the Lustgarten. A sea of red flags, red scarves, and red flowers was in itself sufficient to give that huge assembly of about 120,000 persons an outward appearance of strength. I could feel and understand how easily the man in the street succumbs to the hypnotic magic of such a grandiose spectacle.

The bourgeoisie—which, as a party, neither represents nor advocates any worldview—had therefore no flag of its own. Their party consisted of 'patriots' who went around in the Reich colors. If these colors were the symbol of a definite worldview, then one could understand the rulers of the State regarding this flag as expressive of it, seeing that, through their efforts, the official Reich flag came to symbolize their own worldview.

But this wasn't the case.

The Reich was formed without the aid of the German bourgeoisie, and the flag itself was born of the War. Hence it was merely a State flag, possessing no importance in the sense of any particular philosophical mission.

THE ESSENTIAL MEIN KAMPF

Only in one part of the German-speaking territory—in German-Austria—was there anything like a bourgeois party flag in evidence. Here a section of the national bourgeoisie selected the 1848 colors—black, red, and gold—for their party flag, and thereby created a symbol that, though of no importance from a philosophical viewpoint, nevertheless had a revolutionary political character. The sharpest opponents of this black-red-gold flag at that time—and this shouldn't be forgotten today—were the Social Democrats and the Christian Socialists or Clericals. It was those in particular who degraded and besmirched these colors, in the same way that they dragged the black-white-red into the gutter in 1918.[1]

In any case, the black-red-gold of the German parties in the old Austria were the colors of 1848—that's to say, of a period likely to be regarded as somewhat idealistic, but it was represented by honest German souls. Although even then, the Jew was lurking in the background as an invisible wire-puller. It was thus high treason and a shameful sell-out of the German people and German treasure that initially made these colors so attractive to the Marxists and the Center; so much so that today they revere them as their most cherished possession, and use them as a protection of the flag they once spat on.

Until 1920, then, there was no flag to confront Marxism that would have represented its philosophical polar opposite. After 1918, even the best parties of the German bourgeoisie were loath to accept the suddenly-discovered black-red-gold colors as their symbol. They themselves were incapable of counteracting this with a future program of their own that would oppose this new development. At best, they had in mind a reconstruction of the old Reich.

The black-white-red banner of the old Reich is indebted to this idea for its resurrection, as the flag of our so-called national bourgeois parties.

It's obvious that the symbol of a State that was overthrown by the Marxists under inglorious circumstances is now unworthy to serve as a

---

[1] The black-red-gold colors were originally adopted by the Frankfurt Parliament in 1848—essentially identical to the present-day flag. When Bismarck became Chancellor of the German Reich in 1871, he adopted the North German Confederation colors of black-red-white. The Weimar regime reverted to the black-red-gold in 1919, following defeat in WWI. Hitler restored the black-red-white scheme, in the form of the swastika insignia, from 1933 until Germany's defeat in 1945. The post-war German government then switched back, yet again, to the black-red-gold.

banner under which this same Marxism is to be destroyed in turn. As sacred and beloved as these old colors must be, in their youthful freshness, to every decent German who has fought under them and witnessed the sacrifice of so many lives, that flag is worthless as a symbol for a struggle for the future.

Unlike our bourgeois politicians, I've always adopted the standpoint in our movement that it was true good fortune for the German nation to have lost its old flag. It doesn't matter to us what the Republic does under its flag. But let us be deeply grateful to Fate for having so graciously spared the most glorious war flag for all time from becoming a bed sheet for prostitution. The [Weimar] Reich of today, which sells-out itself and its people, must never be allowed to adopt the honorable and heroic black-white-red colors.

As long as the November outrage endures, let it continue to bear its own external sign and not steal that of an honorable past. Our bourgeois politicians should awaken their consciences to the fact that whoever desires this black-white-red flag for the State is pilfering from the past. The old flag was suitable only for the old Reich, just as—thank God—the Republic chose the colors best suited to itself.

THE NATIONAL SOCIALIST FLAG (section 7.9)

This was also the reason why we National Socialists recognized that hoisting the old flag would not symbolize our own activity. We had no wish to resurrect the old Reich from the dead, which had been ruined through its own blunders, but to build up a new State.

The movement that's fighting Marxism today along these lines must display the symbol of the new State on its banner.

The question of the new flag—that's to say, its appearance—kept us very busy in those days. Suggestions poured in from all sides, which, although well-meant, were more or less impractical. The new banner not only had to symbolize our own struggle, but on the other hand it had to prove effective as a poster. Anyone who concerns himself with the masses will recognize the great importance of these apparently petty matters. In thousands of cases, a striking emblem may be the first cause of awakening interest in a movement.

THE ESSENTIAL MEIN KAMPF

For this reason, we declined all suggestions, by means of a white flag, for identifying our movement with the old State; or rather, with those decrepit parties whose sole political objective is the restoration of past conditions. Besides, white is not a stirring color. It's suitable only for young women's associations and not for ground-breaking movements in a revolutionary time.

Black was also suggested: certainly well-suited to the times, but nothing to embody the will of our movement. In the end, this color is also not stirring enough.

White and blue were discarded, despite their admirable aesthetic appeal as the colors of an individual German State, because of their orientation toward a particularist narrow-mindedness that had a bad reputation. And here too, it would have been hard to attract attention to our movement. The same applies to black and white.

Black-red-gold were completely out of the question.

So were black-white-red, for reasons already stated—at least, in the form previously used. But the effectiveness of these colors is far superior to all the others. They are the most strikingly harmonious combination to be found.

I myself was always for keeping the old colors, not only because I, as a soldier, regarded them as my most sacred possession, but because in their aesthetic effect, they are the most compatible with my own feeling. Accordingly I had to discard all the innumerable designs that had been proposed for the new movement, including many that had incorporated the swastika into the old banner. I, as leader, was unwilling to make public my own design, as it was possible that someone else could come forward with one that was just as good, if not better, than my own. As a matter of fact, a dentist from Starnberg submitted a good design, very similar to mine, with only one mistake, in that his swastika with curved arms was set upon a white background.

After innumerable trials, I myself decided upon a final form: a banner of red material with a white disc, and a black swastika in the middle. After many trials, I found the correct proportions between the dimensions of the flag and the white disc, as well as the shape and thickness of the swastika.

And this is how it has remained.

Along the same lines, we immediately ordered armbands for our security squad: similar red material with a white disc and black swastika.

— 15 —

The party emblem was also designed along the same lines: a white disk on a red field, and a swastika in the middle. Herr Füss, a Munich goldsmith, supplied the first practical and permanent design.

The new flag appeared in public for the first time in midsummer 1920. It suited our young movement admirably. It was young and new, like the movement itself. No one had seen it before; it had the effect of a blazing torch. We ourselves experienced an almost childlike delight when one of the party women made the flag and handed it over to us. Just a few months later, we had half a dozen of them in Munich, and the new symbol of the movement was spread by the growing strength of the security troops.

And what a symbol it truly is! Not only because of those revered colors that express our glorious past and which once brought so much honor to the German people, but this symbol was also an embodiment of the movement's will. As National Socialists, we see our program in our flag. In *red*, we see the social ideal of the movement; in *white*, nationalism; in the *swastika*, the mission of Aryan humanity to fight for victory, and at the same time, for the victory of the idea of creative work, which has always been anti-Semitic and always will be anti-Semitic.

Two years later, when our security troops had long since grown into storm troops,[2] incorporating many thousands of men, it seemed necessary to give this defensive organization of a young worldview a special symbol of victory: the Standard. I also designed this, and entrusted it to an old party comrade, master goldsmith Herr Gahr. Since then, this Standard has been the distinctive symbol and battle sign of the National Socialist struggle.

FIRST MEETING IN THE CIRCUS (section 7.10)

Meeting activity increased, particularly during 1920, compelling us at times to hold two meetings a week. Crowds gathered around our posters, the largest meeting halls in town were always filled, and tens of thousands of misled Marxists found their way to us and became warriors for the liberation of the German Reich. The Munich public got to know us. We were being spoken about, and the words 'National Socialist' became familiar to many, and already implied a program. Our host of supporters

---

[2] The *Sturmabteilung*, or SA, literally means 'storm detachment,' but was more commonly referred to as storm troops or, informally, as 'brown shirts.'

and members was constantly growing, so that by the winter of 1920-21 we could already be regarded as a strong party in Munich.

Apart from the Marxist parties, there was at that time no party in Munich—certainly no nationalist party—that could hold such mass demonstrations as ours. The Munich Kindl Keller, which held 5,000 people, was more than once overcrowded, and there was only one other hall that we hadn't yet used; this was the Circus Krone.[3]

At the end of January 1921 there was again great cause for anxiety in Germany. The Paris Agreement, at which Germany pledged to pay the insane sum of a hundred billion gold marks, was to be confirmed in the form of the London Dictate.[4]

Thereupon a long-established Munich working committee, representing so-called folkish groups, wanted to call a public meeting of protest. I became nervous when I saw that time was being wasted and nothing undertaken. At first, a demonstration was suggested in the Königsplatz, but this was rejected for fear of being broken up by the Reds. Another demonstration was proposed in front of the Feldherrn Hall, but this too came to nothing. Finally a combined demonstration in the Munich Kindl Keller was suggested. Meanwhile, day after day went by, the big parties entirely ignored the terrible event, and the working committee couldn't decide on a definite date for holding the intended demonstration.

On Tuesday, 1 February 1921, I urgently demanded a final decision. I was put off until Wednesday. On Wednesday I demanded a clear determination regarding if and when the meeting was to take place. The reply was again uncertain and evasive; they said they 'intended' to arrange a demonstration the following Wednesday.

With that, I lost all patience and decided to conduct a protest demonstration of my own. At noon on Wednesday I dictated in ten

---

[3] The Circus Krone is an actual circus, founded in Munich in 1905. Since 1919, it has also owned the Circus Krone building—a large open-space hall in central Munich, not far from the main train station.

[4] The London Dictate, also known as the London Ultimatum or the London Schedule of Payments, reconfirmed the overall liability of the Central Powers (primarily Germany) at 132 billion marks, based on their defeat and alleged culpability for World War One. It was an absurd and utterly unrealistic figure, designed to give the impression of a severe punishment for the losers, and to hold as a perpetual threat over Germany.

minutes, by typewriter, the text of the poster, and at the same time hired the Circus Krone for the next day, Thursday, 3 February.

In those days, this was a tremendous venture. Not only because of the uncertainty of filling that vast hall, but also because of the risk of the meeting being wrecked.

Our security troops weren't adequate for this vast hall. I was also uncertain about what to do in case the meeting was broken up. At the time, I felt that it would be much harder for us in the Circus building than in a normal hall. But as it turned out, the opposite was the case. In that vast space, it was much easier to control a group of disturbers than in a cramped hall.

One thing was certain: A failure would throw us back for a long time to come. If one meeting was wrecked, our prestige would be seriously injured and our opponents would be encouraged to repeat their success. That would lead to sabotage of our future meeting work, and would have required months of difficult struggle to overcome.

We had only one day in which to display our posters, Thursday. Unfortunately it rained in the morning and there was reason to fear that many people would prefer to remain at home rather than hurry to a meeting through rain and snow, especially when there was likely to be violence and bloodshed.

And indeed on that Thursday morning, I was suddenly struck with fear that the hall might not be filled, (which would have made me look ridiculous in the eyes of the working committee). So I therefore immediately dictated a few leaflets, and had them printed and distributed in the afternoon. Naturally they contained an appeal to attend the meeting.

I hired two trucks, which were decorated as much as possible in red, and each had our new flag hoisted on it and was filled with 15 or 20 party members; orders were given to canvas the streets thoroughly—in short, to conduct propaganda for the mass meeting that evening. It was the first time that trucks had driven through the streets with banners but without Marxists. The bourgeoisie stared open-mouthed at these red-draped cars with fluttering swastika banners, and in the outlying districts, clenched fists were angrily raised at this new evidence of 'provocation of the proletariat.' Only the Marxists had the right to hold meetings and to drive around in trucks.

THE ESSENTIAL MEIN KAMPF

At 7:00 pm, the Circus was not yet full. I was informed by telephone every ten minutes and was becoming uneasy; usually at 7:00 or 7:15 our meeting halls were already half-filled, sometimes even nearly full. But I soon found out why. I had entirely forgotten to take into account the huge dimensions of this new hall: a thousand people in the Hofbräuhaus made it impressively full, but the same number in the Circus Krone was simply swallowed up. You could hardly see them. Shortly afterwards, though, I received more hopeful reports, and at 7:45 I was informed that the hall was three-quarters filled, with huge crowds still lined up at the box offices. I then left for the meeting.

I arrived at the Circus at 8:02. There was still a crowd of people outside, some just curious, and many opponents who preferred to wait outside for developments.

When I entered the great hall, I felt the same joy I had felt a year earlier at the first meeting in the Munich Hofbräuhaus Hall. But it wasn't until I had forced my way through the solid wall of people and reached the platform that I saw the full measure of our success. The hall was before me, like a huge shell, packed with thousands and thousands of people. Even the arena was packed solid. More than 5,600 tickets had been sold and, allowing for the unemployed, poor students, and our own security men, there must have been 6,500 present.

My theme was 'Future or Downfall,' and I was filled with joy at the thought that the future lay there before me.

I began, and spoke for about two and a half hours. After the first half-hour, I felt that the meeting was going to be a big success. Contact had been established with all those thousands of individuals. After the first hour, the speech was already being interrupted by spontaneous outbreaks of applause, but after the second hour, this died down to a solemn stillness that I was to experience so often later on, in this same hall, and which will forever be remembered by all those present. Nothing broke this impressive silence, and only when the last word had been spoken did the applause thunder forth, culminating in the "Deutschland" song, sung with the greatest fervor.

I watched the scene for almost 20 minutes, as the vast hall slowly drained a sea of humanity. Only then did I leave the platform, overjoyed, and made my way home.

— 15 —

Pictures were taken of this first meeting in the Circus Krone in Munich. They speak louder than words about the magnitude of the demonstration. The bourgeois papers ran pictures, but reported the meeting as having been merely a 'nationalist' demonstration, and in their usual modest fashion they omitted all mention of its organizers.

Thus for the first time, we had developed far beyond the bound of an ordinary party. We could no longer be ignored. And to dispel all doubt that the meeting was merely an isolated success, I immediately arranged for another at the Circus for the following week, and again we had the same success. Once more the vast hall was overflowing with masses of people, such that I decided to hold a third meeting in the same style. And for a third time, the giant Circus was packed full of people, bottom to top.

After this introduction to the year 1921, I further increased our activity in Munich. I not only held meetings once a week, but during some weeks even two mass meetings; yes, and in midsummer and autumn, it was sometimes three. We met regularly at the Circus and it gave us great satisfaction to see that every meeting brought us the same success.

The result was an ever-increasing number of supporters and members for our movement.

AN ATTEMPTED DISRUPTION (section 7.11)

Naturally, such success did not leave our opponents inactive. At first their tactics fluctuated between the use of terror and silence in our regard, but they soon recognized that neither could hinder the progress of our movement. So they had recourse to a final act of terror that was intended to put a definite end to our meeting activity.

As a pretext for this action, they used a very mysterious attack on one of the governmental deputies, named Erhard Auer.[5] It was declared that someone had shot at said Erhard Auer one evening. This meant that he was not actually shot, but that an attempt had been made to shoot him. A fabulous presence of mind and heroic courage on the part of Social Democratic leaders not only prevented the insidious attack, but also put the

---

[5] Auer (1874-1945) was a Bavarian politician. He was complicit with Jewish revolutionaries like Ernst Toller and Kurt Eisner, and played a leading role in the hated Weimar government.

would-be assassins to flight. They fled so quickly and so far that subsequently the police couldn't find even the slightest trace of them. This mysterious episode was used by the organ of the Social Democratic Party in Munich to agitate against our movement, and while doing so it delivered its old hints about the tactics that were to come. Their purpose was to see to it that our movement not get out of hand, and that proletarian fists would intervene.

A few days later came the day of the disruption.

It was eventually decided to interrupt one of our meetings planned for the Munich Hofbräuhaus Festsaal, and at which I myself was to speak.

On 4 November 1921, between 6:00 and 7:00 pm, I received the first precise news that the meeting would definitely be broken up, and that to carry out this action, they decided to send in great masses of workers from certain Red factories.

It was due to an unfortunate accident that we didn't receive this news sooner. On that day, we had given up our old business office in the Sternecker Gasse in Munich[6] and moved into other quarters—or rather, we had given up the old offices, and our new quarters weren't yet in working order. The telephone had been cut off by the former tenants and had not yet been reinstalled, and several attempts that day to inform us by telephone of the intended break-up didn't reach us.

Consequently our security troops were very weak at that meeting. Only one squad was present, which consisted only of about 46 men. And our warning apparatus wasn't yet sufficiently organized to be able to bring enough reinforcements within an hour or so. It must also be added that on several previous occasions we had been forewarned, but nothing special happened. The old saying, that announced revolutions rarely come off, had hitherto been proven true in our experience.

Perhaps for this reason as well, we hadn't taken sufficiently strong precautions on that day to counter the brutal determination of our opponents to break up our meeting.

Finally, we didn't believe that the Hofbräuhaus Festsaal in Munich was suitable for an attempted break-up. We were more afraid with the bigger halls, especially the Circus. But on this point, we learned a valuable lesson that day. Later, we studied this whole question according to a scientific

---

[6] Today, known as the Sternecker Strasse. The original DAP office was in a side room of the Sterneckerbräu, a brewery on the corner of Sternecker and Tal. The building still stands, although it now is a residential and commercial unit.

method and arrived at results—both interesting and incredible—and which subsequently were an essential factor in our organization's leadership and in the tactics of our storm troops.

When I arrived in the entrance hall of the Hofbräuhaus at 7:45 pm, there was no doubt of the intentions. The hall was filled, and therefore the police had it closed. Our opponents, who had arrived very early, were in the hall, and our followers were for the most part outside. The small SA guard awaited me at the entrance. I had the doors leading to the main hall closed, and then asked the 45 or 46 men to come forward. I made it clear to the boys that perhaps on that evening, for the first time, they would have to show their unyielding loyalty to the movement, and that not one of us should leave the hall unless carried out dead; I myself would remain in the hall and I didn't believe that one of them would abandon me; and if I saw any one of them acting the coward, I myself would personally tear off his armband and badge. Then I demanded that they should step forward if the slightest attempt were made to disrupt the meeting, and that they must remember that the best defense is always attack.

I was greeted with a triple *Heil*, which sounded more robust and violent than usual.

I then went into the hall and assessed the situation with my own eyes. Our opponents sat closely huddled together, piercing me with their eyes. Innumerable faces glowing with hatred were fixed on me, while others with sneering grimaces shouted at me in no uncertain terms. Today they would 'finish us off,' we must look out for our guts, they would smash our mouths…and other such lovely phrases. They knew that they had superior numbers and acted accordingly.

Yet we were able to open the meeting, and I began to speak. In the Hofbräuhaus Festsaal, I always stood on one of the long sides of the room, and my podium was a beer table. I was actually right in the midst of the people. Perhaps this circumstance was responsible for creating a certain mood that I never found elsewhere.

Before me, and especially to my left, there were only opponents seated or standing. They were mostly robust youths and men from the Maffei factory, from Kustermann's, from the factories of the Isaria Meter Works, etc. Along the left wall, they were thickly massed quite close to my table, and began to collect beer mugs—that is, they were ordering beer and stashing the mugs under the table. Thus, whole batteries were collected, and it would have been a miracle if the meeting ended peacefully.

After about an hour and a half—I was able to speak that long, amidst interruptions—it almost seemed as if I was going to master the situation. The leaders of the disrupters appeared to sense this themselves; they steadily became more uneasy, often left the hall, returned, and spoke to their men with obvious nervousness.

I then committed a small psychological error in replying to an interruption, which I myself realized the moment the words left my mouth, and this gave the sign for the outbreak.

There were a few angry shouts, and suddenly a man jumped on a chair and shouted: "Freedom!" At that signal, the freedom-fighters began their work.

In a few seconds, the entire hall was filled with a yelling and shrieking mob, above which flew—like howitzers—innumerable beer mugs; amid this uproar, one heard the smash of chair legs, the crashing of mugs, groans, and yells, and screams.

It was a crazy spectacle.

I stood my ground and observed my boys thoroughly doing their duty.

I would have liked to have seen a bourgeois meeting like this!

The dance had hardly begun when my storm troops—as they were called from that day forward—attacked. Like wolves they threw themselves on the enemy again and again, in packs of eight or ten, and began to steadily thrash them out of the hall. Even after five minutes, I saw hardly one of them that wasn't streaming with blood. I really came to know those men that day; first of all, my brave Maurice;[7] my current private secretary Hess;[8] and many others who, even though seriously wounded, attacked again and again, as long as their legs held out. The pandemonium

---

[7] Emil Maurice (1879-1972) was a watchmaker by trade, and an early leader of the SA, and eventually of the SS. Interestingly, Maurice was later revealed to have had partial Jewish ancestry; Himmler wanted him expelled from the SS, but Hitler intervened, making an exception for him.

[8] Rudolf Hess (1894-1987) was another leader of the SA, and among Hitler's closest personal confidantes. Eventually he would become Deputy Führer of the NSDAP, one of its highest-ranking members. It was Hess who took dictation for most of *Mein Kampf* from Hitler during their time together in the Landsberg Prison.

— 15 —

continued for 20 minutes, but then the opponents, who numbered 700 or 800, were mostly driven from the hall or thrown out headlong by my men, who numbered not even 50. Only in the left corner, a big crowd still held out against our men and put up a bitter fight. Then two pistol shots suddenly rang out from the hall entrance, toward the platform, and now a wild din of shooting broke out. One's heart almost rejoiced at this spectacle that recalled old war memories.

At that moment it was impossible to identify who had fired the shots; but at any rate I could see that my boys renewed the attack with increased fury, until finally the last disturbers were overcome and driven out of the hall.

About 25 minutes had passed; the hall looked as if a bomb had exploded. Many of my comrades had to be bandaged, and others carried away, but we remained masters of the situation. Hermann Essen, who was chairman this evening, declared: "The meeting will continue. The speaker has the floor." And so I went on with my speech.

When we ourselves closed the meeting, an excited police officer rushed in, waved his hands and declared to the hall: "The meeting is dismissed."

Unintentionally, I had to laugh at this late-comer to the event; real police arrogance. The smaller they are, the greater they must always appear.

That evening we learned a lot, and our opponents never forgot the lesson they received.

As of the autumn of 1923, the *Münchener Post* never again mentioned the fists of the proletariat.

— 16 —
THE REVOLUTION, FEDERALISM, AND BUILDING THE MOVEMENT

THE RESULTING DISORGANIZATION (section 9.4)

Hence the German Revolution, from the very start, was only conditionally popular. This act of Cain wasn't committed by the German people per se, but by an obscure rabble of deserters, hooligans, and so on.

The man at the Front welcomed the end of the bloody struggle, and was happy to return home and see his wife and children once again. But he had no inner connection with the Revolution; he didn't like it, nor did he like its instigators and organizers. During the four-and-a-half years of that bitter struggle, he forgot the party hyenas, and all their wrangling became foreign to him.

The Revolution was really popular only with a small part of the German people: namely, that class of accomplices who had selected the backpack as the hallmark of all honorable citizens in this new State. They didn't like the Revolution for its own sake—as many still erroneously believe today—but because of its consequences.

But it was very difficult to establish any authority on the popularity of these Marxist gangsters. And yet the young Republic needed authority at any cost, unless it was ready to be overthrown after a brief chaos by a retributive force assembled from the last elements among the best of our people.

Those responsible for the Revolution feared nothing more than to lose a foothold amidst the turmoil that they created, and to be suddenly seized by an iron fist—as has happened more than once at such junctures in the life of peoples. The Republic had to be consolidated at any price.

Hence it was almost immediately forced to erect, alongside its wavering pillar of popularity, an organization of force, in order to secure a firmer authority.

In those days of December, January, and February 1918-19, the matadors of the Revolution felt the ground trembling beneath their feet, and they looked around them for men who, through love of their people, would strengthen them—by force of arms. The 'anti-militaristic' Republic needed soldiers. But the first and only pillar of their State authority—namely, their popularity—was grounded only on a society of hooligans, thieves, burglars, deserters, slackers, etc. Therefore it was useless to look within that extreme worst portion of the nation for men willing to sacrifice their lives in the service of a new ideal. The class supporting the revolutionary idea and carrying out the Revolution was neither able nor willing to call on the soldiers to protect it. This class had no wish whatsoever to organize a republican State, but to disorganize what already existed in order to better satisfy their own instincts. Their watchword was not: the organization and construction of the German Republic, but rather: the plundering of it.

Hence the cry for help sent out by the public representatives, in agony, went unheard—indeed, on the contrary, it aroused bitterness and resistance. The revolutionaries looked upon this as a breach of faith and trust. In the building up of an authority no longer based on popularity but on force, they saw the beginning of a hostile move against what the Revolution essentially meant for those elements: against the right to rob, and against unconditional rule by a horde of thieves and plunderers—in short, the worst rabble—who had broken out of prison and left their chains behind.

The public representatives could cry out as much as they liked, but no one stepped forward. Only the counter-cry, 'traitor,' came from those popular supporters.

Then for the first time, large numbers of young Germans appeared who were ready once again to button on the military uniform in the service of 'peace and order,' shouldering the carbine and rifle, and donning the steel helmet to oppose the destroyers of their homeland. As volunteer soldiers, they formed into free corps and, although hating the Revolution, began to defend and thus, in practice, to secure it.

They acted in the best of faith.

The real organizer of the Revolution and its actual wire-puller, the international Jew, had correctly sized up the situation. The German people were not yet ripe to be drawn into the bloody swamp of Bolshevism, as happened in Russia. This was because there was a closer racial union between the German intellectual classes and the manual workers. Also, the broad social strata were permeated with cultured people, such as was the case also in the other Western European countries, but was completely lacking in Russia. There the intelligentsia were mostly of non-Russian nationality, or at least they didn't have Slavic racial characteristics. The thin upper layer of intellectuals that then existed in Russia could have been abolished at any time because there was no intermediate stratum connecting it with the great mass of people. There, the mental and moral level was frightfully low.

In Russia, the moment the agitators were successful in inciting the uneducated hordes of the broad masses—who couldn't read or write— against the thin upper layer of intellectuals who weren't in contact with the masses or permanently linked with them in any way, at that moment the destiny of the country was decided, and the Revolution succeeded. Then the illiterate Russian became the defenseless slave of his Jewish dictators who, for their part, were shrewd enough to name their dictatorship 'the people's dictatorship.' ...

JEWISH INCITEMENT ACTIVITY (section 10.5)

Before the Revolution, the Jew was successful in distracting attention from himself and his war societies by inciting the masses, and especially the Bavarians, against Prussia. After the Revolution, he had to camouflage his new, and ten-times greater, campaign of plunder. And again he succeeded, in this case by provoking the so-called 'national' elements against one another: the conservative Bavarians against the equally conservative-minded Prussians. And again he acted with extreme cunning, inasmuch as he who held the reins of the Reich's destiny provoked such crude and tactless aggressions that they set the blood boiling of those who were affected. Never against the Jew, but always against the German brother. The Bavarian didn't see the Berlin of 4,000,000 industrious and efficient workers, but only the rotten, decadent Berlin of the vilest West Side! And his hatred wasn't directed against this West Side but against the 'Prussian' city.[1]

It really drove one to despair.

The Jew's ability to turn public attention away from himself and toward another direction may be studied again today.

In 1918 there was nothing like an organized anti-Semitism. I still remember the difficulties we encountered the moment we mentioned the word 'Jew.' We were either confronted with dumb-struck looks or else a lively resistance. Our first attempts to point out the real enemy to the public seemed to be hopeless, but then slowly things began to change for the better. As bad as the 'Watch and Resist League' was, at least it had the great merit of reopening the Jewish Question.[2] In any case, in the winter of 1918-19, a kind of anti-Semitism slowly began to take root. Later on, the National Socialist movement presented the Jewish Question in a new light. Taking the question beyond the restricted circles of the upper and lower bourgeoisie, we succeeded in transforming it into the driving impulse of a great popular movement.

But the moment we succeeded in placing this problem before the German people in the light of a great, unified struggle, the Jew reacted. He resorted to his old tactics. With amazing swiftness he hurled the torch of discord into the folkish movement and opened a rift. Bringing up the ultramontane question, and the resulting clash between Catholicism and Protestantism, was the sole possibility, at the time, of distracting public attention and thus warding off a concentrated attack against Jewry.[3] Those who dragged our people into this controversy can never atone for their wrongs. In any case, the Jew had attained his desired end: Catholics and Protestants fighting a merry war with one another, while the mortal enemy of Aryan humanity and all Christendom laughs up his sleeve.

---

[1] The west side of Berlin was known as the Jewish quarter.

[2] The *Schutz- und Trutzbund*, founded in 1919, was a German nationalist group that sought to protect Germany from Jewish influences and Bolshevism more broadly. Among their symbols was the swastika—evidently the inspiration for Hitler.

[3] 'Ultramontanism' refers to the old dispute between Catholics and Protestants regarding the authority and legitimacy of the pope.

— 16 —

DENOMINATIONAL DISCORD (section 10.6)

At one time it was possible to occupy public attention for years with the struggle between federalism and centralism, wearing out its energy while the Jew trafficked in the nation's freedom and sold our Fatherland to international high finance. Now he has succeeded again, this time by raising disputes between the two German religious denominations while the foundations of both are being corroded and undermined by the poison of the international world Jew.

Look at the ravages that our people are suffering daily as a result of Jewish bastardization, and consider that this blood poisoning can only be eliminated from the national body after centuries, if ever. Think further of how the process of racial disintegration is debasing and often even destroying the fundamental Aryan values of our German people, such that our national cultural creativeness is regressing and we run the risk, at least in our large cities, of sinking to the present level of southern Italy. This pestilential contamination of the blood, blindly ignored by hundreds of thousands of our people, is being systematically conducted by the Jew today. These black parasites of our nation systematically corrupt our innocent blond girls and thus destroy something irreplaceable in this world.

Both, yes, both Christian denominations look on with indifference at the desecration and destruction of a noble and unique creature who was given to the world by God's grace. The future of the world, however, doesn't depend on whether Protestants defeat Catholics, or Catholic Protestants; what matters is whether Aryan humanity survives or perishes. And yet the two Christian denominations are not fighting against the destroyer of this kind of man but are trying to destroy each other. The folkish-oriented man has a sacred duty, within his own denomination, to make people stop talking about God's will and instead actually fulfill God's will, and to not let God's work be desecrated.

God's will gave men their form, essence, and abilities. Whoever destroys His work declares war against God's creation, the divine will. Therefore everyone should consider it his first and most solemn duty, within his own denomination, to oppose anyone whose conduct tends, either by word or deed, to go outside his own religious group and quarrel with another. In view of the religious schism that exists in Germany, to attack the essential characteristics of one denomination must necessarily lead to a war of extermination between the two denominations. There's no comparison between our position and that of France or Spain, or even Italy. In those three countries, one can, for instance, propagandize against clericalism or Ultramontanism without thereby incurring the danger of a national rift among the French, Spanish, or Italian people. In Germany, however, that's not the case, for here the Protestants would also take part in such propaganda. And thus the resistance, which elsewhere only Catholics would organize against political encroachment by their own clergy, would become a Protestant attack against Catholicism. What may be tolerated by the faithful in one denomination, even when it seems unjust, will at once be indignantly rejected if the opponent is of another creed.

This is so true that even men who would be ready and willing to correct an abuse within their own religious denomination will drop their own fight, and turn their activities against the outsider, the moment that such a correction is advised or demanded by someone of another faith. They consider it unjustified and inadmissible, and even indecent, for outsiders to meddle in matters that don't affect them. Such attempts are not excused even when they are in the higher right of the national community, because even in our day, religious feelings go deeper than all feeling for political and national expediency. That cannot be changed by denominations opposing each other in bitter conflict, but only if, through a spirit of mutual tolerance, the nation can be assured of a great future that would gradually operate as a conciliating factor.

I have no hesitation in saying that in these men who seek today to embroil the folkish movement in religious quarrels are worse enemies of my people than any international communist. The National Socialist movement's mission is to convert those communists. But anyone who takes the movement away from its mission is reprehensible. Consciously or unconsciously—it doesn't matter—such a person is fighting for Jewish interests. It's in Jewish interests today that the energies of the folkish movement are bled out in religious conflict, because it's beginning to become a danger for the Jews. I deliberately emphasize the phrase 'bled out'; only someone who is entirely ignorant of history could imagine that this movement can solve a problem that has defied the centuries and the greatest statesmen.

— 16 —

Anyhow, the facts speak for themselves. The men who suddenly discovered, in 1924, that the highest mission of the folkish movement was to fight against 'Ultramontanism' didn't smash it, but they did succeed in splitting the movement. I have to guard against any immature mind arising in the folkish movement who thinks he can do what even a Bismarck failed to do. It will be the first duty of the leaders of the National Socialist movement to unconditionally oppose any attempt to drive it into such a conflict, and to immediately expel any propagandists of such an intention.

As a matter of fact, by autumn 1923 we succeeded entirely. The most devoted Protestant could stand side by side with the most devoted Catholic in our ranks without the slightest conflict with his religious convictions. On the contrary, the mighty common struggle that both waged against the destroyer of Aryan humanity taught them natural respect and esteem. And it was just in those years that our movement had to engage in a sharp struggle with the Center, not on religious grounds but for national, racial, and economic-political reasons. The results spoke in our favor, just as today they testify against the know-it-alls.

In recent years, things have gone so far that folkish circles, in the God-forsaken blindness of their denominational strife, didn't recognize the insanity of their conduct. This was so, even given the fact that atheist Marxist newspapers advocated the cause of one religious community or the other, when convenient, so as to create confusion through slogans and remarks that were often immeasurably stupid. They stirred the fire to keep it ablaze.

But in the case of a people like the Germans, whose history has so often shown them capable of fighting to the last drop of blood for mere phantoms, every war-cry is a mortal danger. In this way, our people have often been drawn away from the real problems of their existence. While we were exhausting ourselves in religious wars, others were carving up the world. And while the folkish movement is debating whether the ultramontane danger is greater than the Jewish, or vice versa, the Jew is destroying the racial basis of our existence and thereby destroying our people forever. Regarding that kind of 'folkish' warrior, on behalf of the National Socialist movement and therefore of the German people, I pray with all my heart: "Lord, protect us from such friends, and then we can easily deal with our enemies." ...

THE ESSENTIAL MEIN KAMPF

REORGANIZATION OF THE MOVEMENT (section 11.5)

Up to the middle of 1921, this simple activity sufficed to benefit the movement. But in the summer of that year, certain events happened that suggested that the organization should be aligned with the gradual success of the propaganda.

An attempt by a group of folkish dreamers, supported by the then-party chairman, to take over leadership led to the break up of this little intrigue. By unanimous vote at a general meeting, members gave me leadership of the whole movement. At once, a new statute was passed that invested sole responsibility in the chairman of the movement. It also replaced the committee decision process with a system of division of labor, which has worked excellently since then.

From 1 August 1921 onwards, I undertook this internal party reorganization and was supported by a number of excellent men, whom I will mention later on.

In my attempt to turn the results of propaganda to an organizational advantage and thus to stabilize them, I had to abolish a number of old habits and introduce principles that none of the other parties possessed or would even have recognized.

In the years from 1920 to 1921, the movement was controlled by a committee elected by the members at a general meeting. It had a first and second treasurer, a first and second secretary, and a first and second chairman at its head. Additionally there was a membership secretary, propaganda director, and various committeemen.

Strangely enough, the committee actually embodied that which the movement was fighting against, namely, parliamentarianism. It was obvious that this principle embodied the very system under which we all suffered, and still suffer—from the smallest local groups, through the districts, counties, and provinces, up to the Reich leadership.

It was imperative to change this, if this poor foundation in the internal organization was not to ruin the movement forever, thus making it impossible to fulfill its high mission.

Committee sessions were ruled by a protocol in which decisions were made according to majority vote, presenting in reality a miniature parliament. Here too, there was no such thing as personal responsibility.

Here too reigned the same absurdities and unreasonableness as in our great State representative bodies. Secretaries, treasurers, membership secretaries, propaganda agents, and God knows what else, were named. And then they all deliberated together on every single question and decided it by vote. Accordingly, the propaganda man voted on things that concerned the finance man, and the latter in turn voted on things that concerned only the organization, and the organizer voted on things concerning only the secretary, and so on.

Why appoint a special man for propaganda if treasurers, secretaries, etc., could deliver judgment on questions concerning it? To one with a sound mind, such a thing seems as incomprehensible as it would be if, in a great industrial firm, the board of directors or engineers were to decide on questions that they had nothing to do with.

I refused to submit to that kind of nonsense, and after awhile I avoided the meetings. I did only my propaganda work, and didn't permit any incompetent to poke his head into my activities. Conversely, I didn't interfere in the affairs of others.

RESPONSIBILITY OF THE LEADER (section 11.6)

When the new statute was approved and I was appointed as first chairman, I had the necessary authority and right to end all that nonsense. In place of committee decisions, the principle of absolute responsibility was introduced.

The chairman is responsible for overall control of the movement. He apportions the work among the committee members under him and among others as needed. Each of these gentlemen is solely responsibility for the task assigned to him. He is subordinate only to the chairman, whose duty is to supervise overall coordination, by selecting personnel and giving general directions for this.

This law of fundamental responsibility is gradually being adopted throughout the movement, at least within the party leadership. In the small local groups—and perhaps in the counties and districts—it will take years before this principle can be imposed, because cowards and incompetents are naturally opposed to it; for them, sole responsibility for an act is always unpleasant; after every hard decision, they always feel freer and better when hiding behind the majority of a so-called committee. But it seems to me necessary to take a decisive stand against that view. We must not make any concessions to cowardice in the face of responsibility, even though it takes some time to achieve a conception of a leader's duty and ability. Ultimately this will bring forth leaders who are truly called and chosen for the role.

In any case, a movement that wants to fight against this parliamentary nonsense must be immune from this sort of thing. Only thus will it win the strength for its struggle.

At a time when majority rule dominates all, a movement that's based on the principle of the leader-ideal, and the corresponding responsibility, will one day overcome the present situation and emerge victorious. This is a mathematical certainty.

BUILDING THE MOVEMENT (section 11.7)

This idea made it necessary to internally reorganize our movement. The logical development of this led to a sharp distinction between the business activities of the movement and the general political leadership. The principle of personal responsibility was extended to all party activities, bringing a healthy liberation from political influences and allowing them to operate solely on economic principles.

When I joined the six-man party in the fall of 1921, we had neither headquarters nor clerks, no forms or even a stamp, and no printed material of any sort. The committee at first met in a tavern on the Herrengasse and then in a café on Gasteig. It was an impossible condition. I quickly set to work, going around to several Munich restaurants and taverns with the idea of renting a room for use by the party. In the former Sterneckerbräu on Tal, there was a small room with arched roof that had previously been used as a sort of festive tavern for the Bavarian counselors. It was gloomy and dark, and accordingly as well-suited to its former uses as it was ill-suited to its new purpose. Its only window looked out on an alley that was so narrow that the room remained dim and gloomy even on the brightest summer day. This was our first business office. Rent came to 50 marks per month (an enormous sum for us!), but we couldn't make many demands. We dared not complain even when, before we moved in, they removed the wooden paneling that was intended for the Imperial counselors. The place began to look more like a basement vault than an office.

Still it marked an enormous step forward. Slowly we got electric light, and slower still a telephone; a table and some borrowed chairs were brought in, finally an open bookstand and later a closet; two cupboards belonging to the landlord held our leaflets, posters, etc.

The previous system of running the movement with weekly leadership meetings was unsustainable. Only a paid official of the movement could guarantee ongoing operation.

But that was difficult at the time. The movement still had so few members that it was hard to find among them a suitable person who would make few demands for himself, and yet could meet the innumerable demands of the movement.

After long a search, we found a soldier and old war comrade of mine, Schüssler, to be our first business manager. At first he came to our new office daily between 6:00 and 8:00 pm, later from 5:00 to 8:00, and ultimately every afternoon. Finally it became a full-time job and he worked from morning until late at night. He was an industrious, upright, and thoroughly honest man, faithful and devoted to the movement itself. Schüssler brought with him his own small Adler typewriter. It was the first machine to be used in the service of the movement. Later the party acquired it through installment payments. We needed a small safe in order to protect our papers and membership roles from thieves. It certainly wasn't needed for any large sum of money that we might have had. On the contrary, we were always quite poor, and I often contributed from my own small savings.

A year and a half later, our business office had become too small, so we moved to a new place in the Corneliusstrasse. Again our office was in a tavern, but instead of one room we now had three smaller rooms and one large room with great windows. At the time, it was very nice. We stayed there until November 1923.

In December 1920, we acquired the *Völkischer Beobachter*.[4] This newspaper, which, as its name implies, championed folkish interests, was now to become the organ of the NSDAP. At first it appeared twice weekly, but it became a daily at the start of 1923, and by late August 1923 appeared in the well-known large format.

---

[4] Literally, "The People's Observer."

THE ESSENTIAL MEIN KAMPF

As a complete novice to journalism, I learned many a costly lesson.

The fact that, in contrast to the enormous Jewish press, there was hardly a single significant folkish newspaper, was a matter of concern. As I later learned by experience, the reason for this can be attributed to the incompetent management of the so-called folkish enterprises. These were conducted too much according to the view that conviction should prevail over achievement. A totally wrong standpoint, because conviction of itself is something internal and is best expressed in achievement. The man who does valuable work for his people expresses his valuable convictions, whereas another who merely talks about convictions and does nothing really useful for his people is opposed to real conviction. And his conviction is a burden for the community.

The *Völkischer Beobachter* was a so-called 'folkish' organ, as its name indicates. It had all the advantages, but still more the faults and weaknesses, inherent in all folkish institutions. Though its contents were sincere, its business management was simply impossible. Here too, the underlying idea was that folkish newspapers should be subsidized by folkish contributions, without recognizing that it had to compete with the others and that it was dishonest to expect the subscriptions of good patriots to make up for negligence or errors.

As soon as I recognized these conditions, I promptly tried to eliminate them. Luck was on my side here, insofar as it brought me the man who, since that time, has rendered invaluable services to the movement—not only as business manager of the paper but also the party. In 1914, in the battlefield, I made the acquaintance of Max Amann (then my superior), who is today general business manager of the party.[5] During four years in the war, I had occasion to continually observe the unusual ability, diligence, and rigorous conscientiousness of my future collaborator.

In midsummer 1921, when the movement was in a grave crisis, I turned to my old regimental comrade, whom I met one day by chance, and asked him to become business manager of the movement. I was quite dissatisfied with several of our employees, particularly with one of whom I had had a very bitter experience. After a long hesitation—Amann then

---

[5] Amann (1891-1957) ultimately became head of the NSDAP press office, overseeing all official publications. He survived WW2, was captured, and spent 10 years in a prison camp. It was Amann who suggested to Hitler the title "Mein Kampf."

held a good position—he agreed to my request, but only on the condition that he not be at the mercy of incompetent committees. Rather, he wanted to answer only to one single leader.

It is to the inestimable credit of this first business manager of the movement—a man of comprehensive business knowledge—that he brought order and integrity into the party's business affairs. Since then, these have remained exemplary and unequaled by any other branches of the movement. But, as often happens in life, great ability provokes envy and disfavor. That also had to be expected in this case and borne patiently.

Already by 1922, firm regulations existed for both the commercial and purely organizational development of the movement. There now exists a central filing system covering all enrolled members. Financing of the movement is now to be on a sound basis. Current expenses are covered by current receipts, and special receipts can be used only for special expenditures. Thus, notwithstanding the difficulties of the time, the movement remained practically debt-free, except for small current accounts. Indeed, there was even a steady increase in the funds. Things work as in a private business: Employees hold their jobs by virtue of their achievement and can in no sense take cover behind that famous 'conviction.' The conviction of every National Socialist lies in his willingness to work, and in his diligence and ability at accomplishing the duties assigned to him by the community. He who doesn't fulfill his duty in the job he holds cannot boast of his conviction—against which, in reality, he sins.

Opposing all possible influences, and with the utmost energy, the new business manager firmly supported the view that there were no meaningless positions in the party administration for supporters and members who don't want to work. A movement that fights so sharply against party corruption of our civil service must keep its own apparatus pure of such vices. It happened that some men were taken on the staff of the paper who had formerly been adherents of the Bavarian People's Party, but their work showed that they were excellently qualified for the job. The result of this experiment was generally outstanding. It was owing to this honest and frank recognition of individual efficiency that the movement won the hearts of its employees more swiftly and more profoundly than had ever been the case before. Subsequently they became good National Socialists and remained so—not only in word, but they proved it by the conscientious, steady, and honest work that they performed in the service of the new movement. Naturally, a well-qualified party member was preferred to another, equally-qualified but non-party member. But no one got a position based solely on party membership.

The firmness with which our new business manager applied these principles and gradually enforced them, despite all opposition, later worked to the movement's greatest advantage. To this alone was it possible—during the difficult inflation period, when thousands of businesses failed and thousands of newspapers closed—for the movement's leadership to not only keep the business afloat and meet all its obligations, but also to steadily expand the *Völkischer Beobachter*. It thereby ranked among the great newspapers.

The year 1921 was of further importance because, in my position as party chairman, I gradually succeeded in ending the criticisms and the intrusions of many committee members regarding various party activities. This was important because we couldn't get a capable man to take on a job if incompetents were constantly interfering, pretending that they knew better than anyone else and creating a hopeless mess. Then these know-it-alls modestly retired, seeking another field for their inspiring supervisory activities. Some men seemed to have a pathology for looking for something behind everything; they were, so to say, always pregnant with magnificent plans, ideas, projects, and methods. Naturally, their noble aims and ideals were always the formation of a committee that could pretend to be a controlling organ in order to nose its way into the serious work of others. But it's offensive and un-National Socialist when incompetent people constantly interfere in the work of capable persons. But this doesn't even enter their consciousness. In any case, I felt it my duty in those years to protect all those who were entrusted with regular and responsible work from such elements, to give them cover and to leave them free to do their work.

Such committees—which either did nothing or cooked up impractical decisions—were best made harmless by giving them real work to do. It was then laughable to see how the membership would silently fade away and was suddenly nowhere to be found. It made me think of our great institution of the same kind, the Reichstag. How quickly they would evaporate if they had some real work to do instead of talking, especially if

— 16 —

each of those braggarts were made personally responsible for the work assigned to him.

I always demanded that—just as in private life, so too in the movement—we should keep seeking until we found a capable and honest clerk, administrator, or leader for the various business units. Once installed in his position, he was given absolute authority and full freedom of action towards his subordinates but full responsibility towards his superiors. No one was placed in authority over his subordinates unless he himself knew the work better than they. In the course of two years, I put my views more and more into practice; today, at least concerning the highest leadership, they are taken for granted.

The visible success of this attitude was shown on 9 November 1923: Four years earlier, when I entered the movement, it didn't even have a rubber stamp. On 9 November 1923, the party was dissolved and its property confiscated. The total sum of all the objects of value and the newspaper amounted to more than 170,000 gold marks.

— 17 —
GERMAN POST-WAR ALLIANCE POLICY

PRESENT EUROPEAN POWER RELATIONS: ENGLAND AND GERMANY (section 13.5)

The characteristic of our present foreign policy is that there are no discernible or even intelligible lines of conduct. Whereas before the war, the fourth way was mistakenly followed—and this only in a halfhearted manner—not even the sharpest eye can detect any path that's being followed since the Revolution. Even more than before the war, there's no systematic plan, except the attempts to smash the last possibility of a national revival.

An objective assessment of present-day European power relations leads to the following results:

For the past 300 years, the history of our continent has been fundamentally determined by England's efforts to keep the European states opposed to one another in an equilibrium of forces, thus assuring the necessary protection of its own rear while pursuing the great aims of British world-policy.

The traditional tendency of British diplomacy ever since the reign of Queen Elizabeth[1] has been to systematically employ every possible means to prevent any one European power from dominating over the others and, if necessary, to break it by means of armed intervention. The only parallel to this has been the Prussian army's tradition. England made use of various military means to carry out its purpose, choosing them according to the actual situation or the task to be faced; but the determination and willpower

---

[1] Reigned from 1558 to 1603.

to use them has always been the same. Indeed, the more difficult England's position became in the course of history, the more the leadership of the British Empire considered it necessary to maintain a condition of political paralysis among the various European states, as a result of their mutual rivalries. The political independence of the North American colonies made it even more necessary to use every effort to maintain the defense of Britain's flank in Europe. And so—after the destruction of Spain and the Netherlands as great sea powers—England concentrated all its forces against the increasing strength of France, until, with the downfall of Napoleon, the hegemony danger of this perilous military power was finally broken.

The shift in British policy against Germany took place only very slowly. This was true not only because the German nation did not represent an obvious danger for England as long as it lacked national unification, but also because British public opinion, steered by propaganda toward other goals, was slow to move in a new direction. The calm knowledge of the statesman is transformed into popular sentiment, which is not only more effective but also more durable. When the statesman has attained one of his goals, he can immediately turn his thoughts to new ones. But only by the slow work of propaganda can mass sentiment be shaped into an instrument for the leaders' new view on life.

As early as 1870-71, England had decided on its new stance. At times, minor policy fluctuations were caused by the growing importance of America in the world economy and also by the increasing political power of Russia. Unfortunately, though, Germany didn't take advantage of these events and, therefore, the original tendency of British diplomacy was only reinforced.

England saw Germany as a power of commercial and world-political importance, partly because its enormous industrialization was increasing to such threatening proportions that the two countries were already contending as equals. The 'peaceful economic' conquest of the world—which, in the eyes of our leaders, represented the highest peak of wisdom—was what led English statesmen to adopt a policy of resistance. The fact that this resistance assumed the form of a vast organized aggression was in full conformity with a type of statesmanship that aimed not at the maintenance of a dubious world peace but at the consolidation of British world-domination. England thus allied itself with those countries that had a definite military importance, and this was consistent with its traditional caution in estimating the adversary's power and also in recognizing its own temporary weakness. This cannot be called 'unscrupulous,' because such a comprehensive organization for war purposes must not be judged from the heroic viewpoint but from that of expediency. Diplomacy must see to it, not that a nation goes down heroically, but rather that it survives in practice. Hence every road that leads to this goal is expedient, and the failure to take it must be seen as a criminal neglect of duty.

When the German Revolution occurred, England's fears of a German world hegemony came to a satisfactory end.

Since then, it has not been in English interests to see Germany totally erased from the geographic map of Europe. On the contrary, the astounding collapse that took place in November 1918 confronted British diplomacy with a situation that at first appeared impossible.

For four-and-a-half years, the British Empire fought to break the presumed prevalence of a continental power. A sudden collapse now occurred that removed this power from the picture. That collapse exposed the lack of even a basic instinct of self-preservation, such that European equilibrium was unhinged within 48 hours: Germany destroyed, and France the first European continental power.

The enormous propaganda that was carried on during this war for the purpose of encouraging the British public to hold out, aroused all the primitive instincts and passions of the populace and was bound to eventually hang as a lead weight on the decisions of British statesmen. With the colonial, economic, and commercial destruction of Germany, England's war aims were attained. Anything beyond this was a hindrance to British interests. Only England's enemies could profit by the disappearance of Germany as a continental power in Europe. Nonetheless, from November 1918 through mid-summer 1919, it was no longer possible for England to change its diplomatic attitude because it had expended the emotional energy of the broad masses. It wasn't possible from the viewpoint of existing attitudes of its own people, and it wasn't possible due to the military relation of forces. France took the initiative and could impose upon others. During those months of negotiations and bargaining, the only power that could have altered the course of things—Germany itself—was torn asunder by a civil war, and its so-called statesmen declared themselves ready to accept any dictate.

Now, in the life of peoples, if one nation loses its instinct for self-preservation and ceases to be an 'active' ally, it sinks to the level of an enslaved people and its territory must suffer the fate of a colony.

ENGLAND'S WAR AIM NOT ACHIEVED (section 13.6)

To prevent France from becoming too great a power, England had to participate in a predatory lust.

In fact England did not attain its war aim. Not only was it impossible to prevent the rise of a European power above the continental state system, but it was given increased support.

In 1914, Germany, considered as a military State, was wedged between two countries, one of which had equal power and the other greater. Then there was England's overwhelming sea power. France and Russia alone hindered and opposed the development of German greatness. The Reich's unfavorable military-geographical situation might be looked upon as another coefficient of security against an exaggerated increase of power. From a naval viewpoint, the coastline was unfavorable for a conflict with England, as it was short and cramped. The land frontier, by contrast, was widely extended and open.

France's position is different today: It is the first military power without a serious rival on the continent; it's almost entirely protected along its southern border with Spain and Italy; against Germany, it's safeguarded by the prostrate condition of our Fatherland; and a long stretch of its coastline faces the vital nerve system of the British Empire. Not only could French airplanes and long-range batteries attack the vital centers of England, but submarines could threaten its sea lanes. A submarine campaign based on the long Atlantic coast and on the European and North African coasts of the Mediterranean would have disastrous effects.

Thus the political result of the war to prevent the development of German power was French hegemony on the continent. The military result: the consolidation of France as the first continental power and the recognition of the Union as an equal sea power. The economic result: the surrender of great spheres of British interests to former allies.

POLITICAL GOALS OF FRANCE AND ENGLAND (section 13.7)

Just as England's traditional political goals wanted and required the Balkanization of Europe, France's desired the Balkanization of Germany.

England's wish is, and remains, to prevent any one continental power from attaining a position of world importance—that is, the maintenance of a definite balance of power among the European States; this seems to be a precondition for British world-hegemony.

France's wish is, and remains, to prevent Germany from becoming a unified power. It wants to maintain a system of small German states with balanced power relations and without central leadership, and it wants to possess the left bank of the Rhine as a prerequisite for the establishment and safeguarding of hegemony in Europe.

The final aims of French diplomacy will be in perpetual opposition to the final tendencies of British statesmanship.

ALLIANCE POSSIBILITIES FOR GERMANY (section 13.8)

Taking this as a starting-point, anyone who investigates alliance possibilities for Germany must come to the conclusion that there remains no other option except to approach England. The consequences of England's war policy were, and are, disastrous for Germany, but we cannot close our eyes to the fact that, today, England has no necessary interest in the destruction of Germany. Indeed, on the contrary, England's diplomacy must, from year to year, tend more towards curbing France's unbridled lust after hegemony. Now, an alliance policy cannot be pursued by bearing grudges, but it can be rendered fruitful by taking account of past experiences. Experience should have taught us that alliances formed for negative purposes suffer from intrinsic weakness. The destinies of nations can be welded together only under the prospect of a common success, of common gain and conquest—in short, a mutual extension of power.

The ignorance of our people on foreign politics is clearly demonstrated by current press reports about "friendship towards Germany" by one or the other foreign statesman, whereby this is taken as a special guarantee of a policy that will be beneficial to our people. This is absolutely unbelievable nonsense—mere speculation of unparalleled simplicity by the average German man. No British, American, or Italian statesman ever was 'pro-German.' Every English statesman will naturally be English first of all, every American American, and no Italian statesman would be prepared to adopt a policy that wasn't pro-Italian. Therefore, anyone who expects to form alliances with foreign nations on the basis of a pro-German feeling among their statesmen is either an ass or a deceiver.

The premise for linking together the destinies of nations is never mutual esteem or mutual sympathy, but rather the prospect of advantages for both contracting parties. That is: It's true that an English statesman will always follow a pro-English and not a pro-German policy, but so too is it true that certain definite interests involved in this pro-English policy may coincide on various grounds with German interests. Naturally this can be true only to a certain degree, and may one day be completely reversed; but the art of statesmanship is shown when, at certain periods, allies are found who must take the same road in order to defend their own interests.

The practical application of these principles at the present time depends on the answer given to the following questions: What States at present have no interest in allowing French military and economic power to achieve hegemony, through the total exclusion of a German Central Europe? Indeed, which states see this as a threat to their own future, based on their own requirements for existence, and on their previous political tradition?

Ultimately we must be very clear on this point: France is, and will remain, Germany's implacable mortal enemy. It doesn't matter what governments have ruled or will rule France, whether Bourbon or Jacobin, Napoleonic or Bourgeois-Democratic, Clerical Republican or Red Bolshevik: Their foreign policy will always be directed towards acquiring possession of the Rhine frontier, and to consolidating France's position on this river by dismembering and shattering Germany.

England doesn't want Germany to be a world power, but France wants no power at all called 'Germany': quite an essential difference! Today we are not fighting for our position as a world power but rather only for the existence of our Fatherland, for national unity, and for our children's daily bread. From this viewpoint, only two European states remain as possible allies: England and Italy.

England doesn't want to see a French military fist unchecked by the rest of Europe, one that might adopt a policy that would clash with English interests one day. England never wants to see France possess the immense western European iron and coal deposits that would make it possible for it to gain a threatening economic world position. And England furthermore never wants a France whose continental political position, owing to the dismemberment of the rest of Europe, seems so absolutely assured that it is not only enabled, but compelled to resume a French world-policy on great lines. Zeppelin bombs might be multiplied by the thousand every night; France's military predominance weighs heavily on the heart of Great Britain's world empire.[2]

And Italy cannot and will not want any further strengthening of France's power in Europe. Italy's future will always be conditioned by the development of events in the Mediterranean basin. It wasn't a desire to build up France that drove Italy into the war, but rather to deal a mortal blow to its hated Adriatic rival. Any further strengthening of France on the Continent would hamper the development of Italy's future, and we mustn't deceive ourselves by thinking that national relations will in any way exclude rivalries.

Serious and cool-minded consideration shows that these two states, England and Italy, have natural self-interests that not only are not in opposition to Germany's essential conditions for existence, but are indeed, to a certain extent, identical with them.

IS GERMANY CAPABLE OF ALLIANCE TODAY? (section 13.9)

But when we consider the possibilities of alliances, we must be careful not to overlook three factors. The first concerns ourselves, and the other two the states in question.

Can anyone ally themselves with present-day Germany? Can a power, one that seeks an alliance for the purpose of securing assistance in carrying out offensive aims, form an alliance with a State whose rulers have, for years, presented a spectacle of deplorable incompetence and pacifist cowardice, and where the majority of the populace, in a democratic-

---

[2] It's hard today to envision the extent of the British Empire at the time this was written. It encompassed over 400 million people, about 20% of the global total. It covered roughly a quarter of the Earth's entire land surface area, including such present-day nations as Canada, Australia, India, Pakistan, Egypt, South Africa, Sudan, and Kenya, among many others.

Marxist blindness, betrays the interests of their own people and country in a way that cries to high heaven? Can any power today hope to establish useful relations in the fight for common interests when this State obviously has neither the courage nor the desire to lift a finger even in the defense of its own naked existence? Can such a power—for which an alliance must be much more than a pact to guarantee a state of slow decay, like the disastrous old Triple Alliance[3]—associate itself for better or worse with a State whose most characteristic signs of life consist of a rampant servility in external relations and a scandalous repression of national virtues at home? Or can it be associated with a State that possesses no greatness because its whole behavior shows that it doesn't deserve it? Or can alliances be made with governments that are despised by their own citizens and thus have no possibility for respect abroad?

No—any self-respecting power that expects something more from alliances than commissions for greedy parliamentarians will not ally itself with our present-day Germany; indeed, it cannot. Our present inability to form alliances furnishes the deepest and ultimate principle for the solidarity of the enemy thieves. Because Germany doesn't defend itself in any other way except the flamboyant 'protests' of our parliamentarian elect, there's no reason why the rest of the world should fight in our defense. And God does not follow the principle of granting freedom to a nation of cowards—despite all the whimperings of our patriotic associations. Therefore, even for those states that don't have a direct interest in our total destruction, no other course remains except to participate in France's campaign of plunder, or at least to prevent the exclusive strengthening of France alone.

Second, we must not overlook the difficulty in overcoming the mass propaganda of our former enemies, which have turned popular opinion toward a fixed direction. When a nationality has been represented to the public for years as a horde of 'Huns,' 'robbers,' 'vandals', etc., they cannot suddenly overnight be presented as something else, and the former enemy cannot be recommended as the ally of tomorrow.

---

[3] The Triple Alliance was a pact between Germany, Austria-Hungary, and Italy. It was formed in 1882 and survived until the start of World War One.

DIVERGENCE BETWEEN BRITISH AND JEWISH INTERESTS (section 13.10)

But the third factor deserves greater attention, since it is of essential importance for establishing future alliances in Europe:

From a British state viewpoint, even though there isn't much interest in the further destruction of Germany, such a development is greatly in the interests of the international stock-exchange Jews. The cleavage between the official, or rather traditional, British statesmanship and the controlling Jewish stock-exchange powers is nowhere so clearly manifested as in the various attitudes on the questions of British foreign policy. Contrary to the interests and welfare of the British state, Jewish finance desires not only the absolute economic destruction of Germany but its complete political enslavement. The internationalization of our German economy—that is, the transference of our productive forces to Jewish world finance—can only be completely carried out in a politically Bolshevik state. But the Marxist fighting forces of international Jewish stock-exchange capital cannot finally smash the German national State without friendly help from outside. French armies must therefore first besiege the German state-structure, and then the exhausted Reich would succumb to the Bolshevik fighting troops of international Jewish world finance.

Hence it is that the Jew today is the great agitator for the complete destruction of Germany. Whenever in the world we read of attacks against Germany, Jews are their fabricators. In peacetime and during the War, Jewish stock-exchange and Marxist press systematically stirred up hatred against Germany, until one state after another abandoned its neutrality and placed itself at the service of the world war coalition, renouncing the real interests of people.

JEWISH WORLD INCITEMENT AGAINST GERMANY (section 13.11)

The Jewish way of reasoning thus becomes clear. The Bolshevization of Germany—that is, the rooting out of national folkish German intellectuals to make it possible for the German labor force to bear the yoke of Jewish world finance—is only a prelude to an extension of the

Jewish tendency for world conquest. As so often in history, Germany is the great pivot in this mighty struggle. If our people and our State should become victims of these bloodthirsty and avaricious Jewish tyrants of nations, the whole Earth would fall prey to this polyp; and if Germany were to be freed from its grip, this greatest of dangers to nations would be broken for the whole world.

It is certain that Jewry uses all its agitational efforts not only to maintain national animosity toward Germany but, if possible, to increase it even more; and it's equally certain that only a fraction of these activities are in keeping with the true interests of the poisoned peoples. In general, Jewry carries on its campaign in the various countries by the use of weapons that are calculated to appeal to the mentality of the respective nations and are most likely to produce the greatest success. In our blood-diluted, exceptionally-torn national body, it is the more or less 'cosmopolitan,' pacifist-ideological thoughts that arise; in short, the internationalist tendencies that they use in their struggle for power. In France, they exploit the well-known and accurately-estimated chauvinism, and in England, the commercial and world-political outlook; in short, they always work with the essential qualities that belong to each national mentality. When they have in this way achieved a decisive influence in economic and political spheres, they discard the limitations of their borrowed weapons, and expose, to the same degree, the true inner purposes of their will and their struggle. Their destruction then accelerates, reducing one state after another to a mass of ruins, upon which they will erect the sovereign and eternal Jewish Empire.

In England and Italy, the contrast between the view of the better kind of statesmanship and the policy of the Jewish world stock-exchange is clear—indeed, sometimes strikingly obvious.

Only in France today does there exist, more than ever before, a profound accord between the views of the Jew-controlled stock exchange and the chauvinistic national statecraft. This identity constitutes an immense danger for Germany. For this reason, France is and will remain by far the most terrible enemy. This people, who are becoming more and more niggarized, represent an enduring danger to the existence of the white race in Europe because they are bound up with the Jewish goal of world domination.[4] Contamination through Negro blood on the Rhine, in the very heart of Europe, is in accord with the sadistic and perverse lust for vengeance by this hereditary enemy of our people, just as an ice-cold Jewish calculation uses this to begin a bastardization at the center of the European continent, and to deprive the white race of the basis for a sovereign existence by infection with a lower humanity.

France's activities in Europe today, spurred on by their lust for vengeance and systematically led by the Jews, are a sin against the existence of white humanity. These actions will one day arouse a spirit of vengeance against them by a race that has recognized racial pollution as the original sin of mankind.

For Germany, however, the French danger involves a subordinating of all sentiment, and extending a hand to those who are threatened with the same menace and who are unwilling to suffer or tolerate France's lust for domination.

For the foreseeable future, there will only be two European allies for Germany: England and Italy.

PANDERING TO FRANCE (section 13.12)

If we take the trouble to cast a backwards glance at German foreign policy leadership since the Revolution, we must—in view of the constant and incomprehensible failure of our governments—either lose heart or, in a flaming rage, take up the fight against such a regime. Their actions cannot be attributed to a lack of understanding: What seemed inconceivable to every thinking man was accomplished by these intellectual Cyclopses of our November parties: They courted France's favor. Yes indeed—during all these years, with the touching simplicity of incorrigible visionaries, they pandered to France again and again, they bowed to the 'great nation,' and they believed that they saw a visible change of feeling in every shrewd trick of the French hangman.

Naturally, the actual political wire-pullers never shared in this absurd belief. For them, pandering to France was only an obvious means of thwarting every attempt at a practical alliance policy. They had no illusions

---

[4] France today has by far the highest percentage of black population in Europe: 5.6%, or some 3.8 million people. Next highest is the UK (3.8%, or 2.5 million), followed by Italy (1.8%) and Spain (1.5%). Germany today has around 1% black population. By comparison, the current US black population is about 12.3% (40 million).

about French aims or those of the men behind the scenes. What induced them to act as if they honestly believed that the fate of Germany could possibly be changed, was the sober calculation that otherwise our people might head off in another direction.

Naturally it's hard for us, within our own movement, to propose England as a possible future ally. Our Jewish press has always been adept at concentrating hatred against England in particular, and many of our good German simpletons have willingly fallen into the Jewish trap. They babble about a 'strengthening' of German sea power and protest against the theft of our colonies, and thus they furnish material that the Jewish scoundrel transmits to his English clansmen for purposes of practical propaganda. Our simple-minded political bourgeoisie cannot grasp the idea that today we don't have to fight for 'sea power.' Even before the War, it was absurd to direct German national energies towards this end without first having secured our position in Europe. Such a hope today rises to a stupidity that, in the political field, may be called criminal.

It often becomes maddening to see how the Jewish wire-pullers succeed in concentrating the people's attention on things that are only of secondary importance today. They incited them to demonstrations and protests, while at the same time France was tearing away at our national body, piece by piece, systematically removing the very foundations of our independence....

CONCENTRATION ON ONE ENEMY (section 13.18)

One must recognize the fact that it takes a long time for a people to completely understand the inner purposes of a government, because one cannot explain the ultimate aims of preliminary political work; rather, one either has to count on the blind faith of the masses or on the intuitive instinct of the intellectually-superior ruling class. But since many people lack this political insight, and since political considerations forbid a public explanation, a certain portion of intellectual leaders will always oppose new tendencies that can be viewed as mere experiments, because they aren't easily grasped. Thus the concerned, conservative state elements began to resist.

For this reason, our highest duty is to keep any weapons from falling into the hands of those who would interfere with a mutual understanding among nations. This is especially so in our case, where we have to deal with the impractical and fantastic talk of our social patriots and petty bourgeoisie café politicians. The cry for a new battle fleet, the restoration of our colonies, etc., is simply nonsense and impractical, as any serious thinker would realize. These harmless and sometimes half-crazy spouters in the protest fight are serving the interests of our mortal enemy; their words are exploited in England in a way that cannot be considered as advantageous to Germany. They squander their energies in futile demonstrations against God and the whole world, and they forget the fundamental principle that is a precondition for every success, namely: Whatever you do, do it thoroughly! By howling against five or ten states, we fail to concentrate all the forces of our will and physical strength for a blow to the heart of our bitterest enemy, and we sacrifice the possibility of strengthening ourselves through an alliance.

Here, too, is a mission for the National Socialist movement. It must teach our people to overlook the small things and focus on the great ones; to not become divided over minor issues; and to never forget that the object for which we fight today is the naked existence of our people, and that the sole enemy that we must confront is and remains that power which is robbing us of this existence.

Some things may become hard to bear. But this is by no means an excuse for renouncing reason and for raising senseless outcries against the whole world, instead of concentrating all our forces against the most deadly enemy.

RECKONING WITH THE TRAITORS (section 13.19)

Moreover, the German people have no moral right to complain of the manner in which the rest of the world acts towards them, as long as they themselves have not called to account those criminals who sold and betrayed their own country. We cannot hope to be taken very seriously if we indulge in long-range abuse and protests against England and Italy, and then allow those scoundrels to circulate undisturbed in our own country who were in the pay of the enemy war propaganda, who took away our weapons, broke our moral backbone, and bartered away the Reich for 30 pieces of silver.

The enemy only did what was expected. And we should learn from his conduct and actions.

Anyone who cannot rise to the level of this outlook must realize that, otherwise, nothing would remain than to renounce the idea of any alliance policy in the future. If we cannot form an alliance with England because it has stolen our colonies, or with Italy because it has South Tyrol, or with Poland or Czechoslovakia, then there remains no one else in Europe except France—which, incidentally, robbed us of Alsace-Lorraine.

There can scarcely be any doubt as to whether this serves the German people. But if one thing is in doubt, it's whether such an opinion comes from a mere simpleton or an astute adversary.

When it comes to the activities of leaders, I always believe the latter.

A transformation in the individual psyche of those formerly enemy peoples, whose true interests may well correspond with ours in the future, may be possible if our State's internal strength and our will to self-preservation show that we could be a worthy ally once again. Moreover, our incompetence and criminal conduct shouldn't provide grounds to be used by those who would oppose our alliance with former enemies.

FASCIST ITALY AND JEWRY (section 13.20)

The hardest to answer is the third objection.

Is it conceivable that those who represent the true interests of those alliance-possible nations could uphold their views against the will of the Jewish mortal enemy of free peoples and nation-states?

For example, could the forces of traditional British statesmanship break the disastrous Jewish influence, or not?

This question, as already said, is very difficult to answer. It depends on too many factors to form a conclusive judgment. In any case, one thing is certain: In one state, governmental power is so stabilized, and is so absolutely at the service of the country's interests, that one cannot speak of a real and effective obstruction of political necessities by international Jewish forces.

The fight that fascist Italy is waging against the Jews' three principal weapons—though perhaps in the deepest sense unconsciously (but I don't believe this myself)—furnishes the best proof that the poisonous fangs of this supra-state power are being torn out, albeit indirectly. The prohibition of Freemason secret societies, the suppression of the supra-national press, and the continuous demolition of international Marxism, together with the steady reinforcement of the fascist state-concept—all this will, over the years, enable the Italian government to more and more serve the interests of the Italian people, without regard to the hissing of the Jewish world-hydra.

ENGLAND AND JEWRY (section 13.21)

Things are harder in England. In that country of 'the freest democracy,' the Jew exerts an almost unlimited dictatorship, indirectly, through public opinion.[5] And yet there is a perpetual struggle between advocates of British state interests and the proponents of Jewish world-dictatorship.

---

[5] Jewish influence in Britain has been significant ever since their 'emancipation' there in 1858. Important early figures included Isaac Goldsmid, David Salomons, and Benjamin Disraeli. The Rothschild family established banking enterprises there already in the 1790s, and through their profits in the Napoleonic wars in the early 1800s, gained considerable wealth and influence. By 1880, British writer Laurence Oliphant could write of the Jews' "financial operations on the largest scale" and "the powerful influence which they wield in the press of many countries." He adds, "Owing to the financial, political, and commercial importance to which the Jews have now attained, there is probably no one power in Europe that would prove so valuable an ally...as this wealthy, powerful, cosmopolitan race" (1880: 503). A decade later, Oxford historian Goldwin Smith observed that, "almost without exception, the press throughout Europe is in Jewish hands, and is largely produced from Jewish brains. International finance is captive to Jewish energy and skill. In England, the fall of the Barings [bank] has left the lonely supremacy of the house of Rothschild, unchallenged and unassailable. ... Judaism is now the great financial power in Europe, that is, it is the greatest power of all" (1893: 260-280). Winston Churchill was closely tied to Jewish influence from at least 1904. Martin Gilbert (2007: 9) notes that Churchill's political opponents accused him "of being in the pocket, and even in the pay, of wealthy Jews." Michael Makovsky (2007: 46) writes that Churchill "came to count many of [his father's] wealthy Jewish friends as his own." As Hitler was well aware, Britain sought and obtained the aid of "world Jewry" in fighting World War One. David Lloyd George was particularly eager to engage American Jews' assistance, to draw in the neutral Americans. The end result was a "contract with Jewry": to offer them a Zionist homeland in Palestine if they would help England win the war. This 'contract' was codified in the infamous Balfour Declaration of 1917. For details, see Dalton (2013). In sum, Hitler was certainly correct: Jews did indeed have a virtual dictatorship over Britain by the 1920s. It continues to this day.

THE ESSENTIAL MEIN KAMPF

After the War it became clear for the first time how sharp this contrast is, when British state leaders took one stand on the Japanese problem and the press took another.

Just after the end of the War, the old mutual antipathy between America and Japan began to reappear. Naturally the great European powers couldn't remain indifferent to this new war danger. Despite ties of kinship, there was a certain amount of jealousy in England over the growing importance of the American Union in all spheres of international economics and politics. The former colonial territory, child of a great mother, seemed about to become the new world-master. It's quite understandable that today England should reexamine her old alliances, and that British statesmanship should look nervously to a point in time when it won't be said: "Britain rules the seas!" but rather: "The seas for the American Union!"

The gigantic American state-colossus, with its enormous wealth of virgin soil, is much harder to attack than an encircled German Reich. If the die were to be cast and an ultimate decision reached, England would be doomed if it stood alone. Therefore they eagerly reach for the yellow fist and cling to an alliance that, from a racial viewpoint, is perhaps unpardonable; but from a political viewpoint it represents the sole possibility of reinforcing Britain's world position in the face of the up-surging American continent.

Despite a common struggle on the European battlefields, the English government did not conclude an alliance with their Asiatic partner, and the whole Jewish press jumped on this idea from behind.

How is it possible that, up to 1918, Jewish organs championed the British struggle against the German Reich, and then suddenly became disloyal and went their own way?

The destruction of Germany was not an English interest, but primarily a Jewish one—just as today the destruction of Japan less serves British interests than it does the broader wishes of the leaders of the anticipated Jewish world-empire. While England endeavors to maintain its position in the world, the Jew organizes his attack for its conquest.

He already sees the present European states as pliant tools in his hands, whether indirectly through so-called Western democracy or in the form of direct domination by Russian Bolshevism. But it's not only the Old

World that he holds in his snare; rather, the same fate holds for the New. Jews control the stock-exchange forces of the American Union.[6] Every year they increase their control over the labor force, in a nation of 120 million people; only very few, to their chagrin, still remain fully independent.[7]

They show consummate skill in manipulating public opinion and using it as an instrument in the fight for their own future.

Jewry's greatest heads see the pending fulfillment of the Old Testament prophecy about the great devouring of nations.[8]

Among this great herd of denationalized colonial territories, one independent state could bring about the ruin of the whole structure at the last hour. A Bolshevik world cannot exist unless it encompasses everything.

If only one state preserves its national strength and greatness, the Jewish satrapy world empire, like every other tyranny in the world, would have to succumb to the force of the nationalist idea.

JAPAN AND JEWRY (section 13.22)

Now, due to his thousand years of adaptation, the Jew knows very well that he can undermine European nations by racial bastardization, but that

---

[6] Jewish influence in America at this time went well beyond the stock exchange, and was almost certainly more extensive than Hitler realized. Jewish population was rising rapidly, from 0.5% of the country in 1880 to 2.9% by 1918. The partly-Jewish Teddy Roosevelt became president in 1901, after the Jewish-inspired assassination of President William McKinley. Jewish bankers like Paul and Felix Warburg, Jacob Schiff, and Bernard Baruch exercised considerable influence. Jewish lawyers such as Oscar Straus, Louis Marshall, Henry Morgenthau Sr., Louis Brandeis, and Samuel Untermyer all had substantial clout in finance and government. Such individuals were decisive in persuading Woodrow Wilson and Congress to enter World War One. For more information, see Dalton (2013).

[7] The original first edition of this volume had the words "only a single great man, [Henry] Ford, remains fully independent." Ford was a noted critic of Jewish influence in America, and was long praised by Hitler for standing up to them. For further details on Ford's views, see Dalton (2012).

[8] See for example: *Genesis* (27:29): "Let peoples serve you, and nations bow down to you". *Deuteronomy* (15:6): "You shall rule over many nations," and (28:10) "they shall be afraid of you". *Isaiah* (60:10): "Foreigners shall build up your walls, and their kings shall minister to you…that men may bring you the wealth of nations," and (61:5) "you shall eat the wealth of nations."

he could not subject an Asiatic national state like Japan to the same fate. Today he can mimic the ways of the German and the Englishman, the American and the Frenchman, but he has no means of approach to the yellow Asiatic. Therefore he seeks to break the Japanese national state by using other such formations, so that he may rid himself of a dangerous opponent before he transforms the last state power in his fist into a tyranny over the defenseless.

In his millennial Jewish empire, he dreads a national Japanese state, and therefore wants to destroy it before establishing his own dictatorship.

And so he incites nations against Japan today, as he once did against Germany. Thus while British statesmen are still trying to establish an alliance with Japan, the British-Jewish press is leading a fight against the ally, and prepares for a war of destruction under the proclamation of democracy, and by using the war-cry: "Down with Japanese militarism and imperialism!"

That's how insubordinate the Jew has become in England today.

And for this reason, the struggle against the Jewish world-danger will begin there.

OUR FIGHT AGAINST THE WORLD-ENEMY (section 13.23)

And here again, the National Socialist movement has a tremendous task to fulfill: It must open our peoples' eyes in regard to foreign nations, and it must continually remind them of the true enemy of the present-day world. In place of hatred against Aryans—from whom we may be separated on almost every other ground but with whom the bond of common blood and kindred civilization unite us—we must devote ourselves to arousing a general wrath against the maleficent enemy of mankind, as the real author of all our sufferings.

We must see to it that, at least in our own country, the mortal enemy is recognized, and that the fight against him may become a beacon of light toward brighter days, showing other nations the way of salvation for an embattled Aryan humanity.

Finally, may reason be our guide and will-power our strength. May the sacred duty to act give us determination, and may our faith be our supreme protection.

— 18 —
GERMANY'S POLICY IN EASTERN EUROPE

SIGNIFICANCE OF THE STATE'S AREA (section 14.2)

The only healthy condition is one that assures a people's sustenance on their own soil. Any other situation is unhealthy, even though it may endure for centuries or even thousands of years. Sooner or later, this will lead to the decline or even destruction of the people concerned.

Only a sufficiently large space on this Earth can assure a peoples' free existence.

The necessary extent of territorial expansion for settlement must not be estimated by present requirements nor even by the magnitude of its agricultural productivity in relation to the population.

In the first volume, under the heading "Germany's Alliance Policy before the War," I have already explained that a state's land area is of importance, not only as the source of the nation's food, but also militarily and politically.[1] Once a people is assured of its sustenance by the amount of soil, it must consider how to defend it. This depends on a state's power-political strength, which in turn depends on the military-geographical possibilities.

Thus the German nation can assure its own future only as a world power. For nearly 2,000 years, the defense of our national interests was a matter of world history, as can be seen from our more or less successful activities in the field of foreign politics. We ourselves have been witnesses to this: The gigantic struggle of nations from 1914 to 1918 was only the

---

[1] An apparent reference to volume one, chapter 4; see in particular sections 4.2 and 4.3 above.

struggle of the German people for their existence on this globe, but we designated this type of event as a World War.

Germany entered this struggle as a presumed world power. I say 'presumed' because, in reality, it was no such thing. In 1914, if there had been a different relation between our area and population, Germany really would have been a world power and, aside from other factors, the war would have ended in our favor.

It's neither my task nor my intention here to discuss what would have happened 'if' in case the 'but' did not exist. But I feel it absolutely necessary to show the present conditions in their bare and unadorned reality, pointing out the weakness inherent in them, so that, at least in the ranks of the National Socialist movement, they should receive the necessary insight.

Germany today is no world power. Even if our present military weakness could be overcome, we still would have no claim to this title. What importance does a State have on this planet in which the relation of population to area is so miserable as in the present German Reich? In an era in which the world is being gradually divided among states—many of whom almost embrace whole continents—one cannot speak of a world power in the case of a structure whose political Motherland is confined to the laughable area of barely 500,000 square kilometers.[2]

FRENCH AND GERMAN COLONIAL POLICY (section 14.3)

From a purely territorial point of view, the area of the German Reich is vanishingly small compared with the other so-called world powers. England mustn't be cited as a proof to the contrary, for the English Motherland is in reality the great capital of the British world empire, which owns almost a fourth of the Earth's surface. Furthermore we must consider the American Union as foremost among the colossal states, also Russia and China. Some of these spatial areas are more than ten times greater than the present German Reich.

And France itself must also be ranked among these states. Not only is it adding to its army's strength in a constantly increasing measure by recruiting colored people from its gigantic empire, but also racially its

---

[2] For reference, the area of present-day Germany is around 357,000 square kilometers. If we include Austria, the total comes to 441,000 sq km.

niggarization is progressing, such that one can now actually speak of the creation of an African state on European soil. France's present-day colonial policy cannot be compared with that of Germany in the past. If France continues to develop in the present manner for the next 300 years, all traces of French blood will finally be submerged in the growing Euro-African mulatto state. This would be a formidable, self-contained settlement area from the Rhine to the Congo, filled with an inferior race that gradually emerged through a process of continuous bastardization.

This distinguishes French colonial policy from the old German one.

The former German colonial policy, like everything, was carried out half-way. It neither increased the settlement area of the German race, nor did it attempt—as criminal as it would have been—to strengthen the Reich through the use of black blood. The Askari in German East Africa represented a small and hesitant step along this road. But in reality they served only for the defense of the colonies themselves. The idea of importing black troops into a European battlefield—entirely aside from its practical impossibility in a world war—was never entertained as a proposal to be realized under better circumstances; whereas, on the contrary, the French always looked upon this as fundamental to their colonial activities.

Thus the world today has not only a number of states that are much greater than our German nation in population, but they also have a land area that is, above all, the basis of their political power. Never has the relation between area and population in the German Reich been as unfavorable relative to other world states as at the beginning of our history 2,000 years ago, and again today. Formerly we were a young people, storming into a world of crumbling great states, whose last giant, Rome, we helped to bring down. Today we find ourselves in a world of great power-states, in which our own Reich is constantly sinking into insignificance.

THE HISTORICAL MISSION OF NATIONAL SOCIALISM (section 14.4)

We must always face this bitter truth clearly and calmly. We must study the population and area of the German Reich in relation to other states, and compare them down through the centuries. I know that everyone will then come to the same sad conclusion that I did at the start: Germany is no longer a world power, regardless of whether its military strength is strong or weak.

THE ESSENTIAL MEIN KAMPF

There's no comparison between us and the other great states on Earth, thanks to the wholly catastrophic leadership of our people in foreign policy, to our lack of—I should almost say—a testamentary goal in foreign policy, and to the loss of every sound impulse and instinct for self-preservation.

If the National Socialist movement wants to be recognized by history as having a great mission for our people, it will have to painfully recognize the real truth of our situation in the world. It must courageously fight against the aimlessness and incompetence that has hitherto guided our German nation in foreign policy. Then, without respect for 'tradition' or preconceptions, it must find the courage to organize our national forces and set them on a path that will lead them away from the present restricted living space and toward new land and soil. Thus will the movement save us from the danger of perishing from this Earth or of serving others as a slave nation.

The National Socialist movement must seek to abolish the present disproportion between our population and land area, considering the latter as the source of our sustenance and as a basis of political power. And thus it must abolish the contrast between past history and the hopelessness of our present impotence. In doing so, it must bear in mind the fact that we are members of the highest humanity on this Earth, that we have a correspondingly high duty, and that we will fulfill this duty only if we inspire the German people with a racial sensitivity, so that they will not only breed good dogs, horses, and cats, but also care for their own blood....

RESUMPTION OF EASTERN POLICY (section 14.8)

Therefore we National Socialists have purposely drawn a line through our pre-war conduct of foreign policy. We resume where we left off, six centuries ago. We put an end to the perpetual Germanic march towards the south and west of Europe, and turn our eyes towards the land of the East. We finally shut off the colonial- and trade-policy of pre-war times, and pass over to the land-policy of the future.

But when we speak of new land and soil in Europe today, we must principally think of Russia and its subject border states.

Destiny itself seems to wish to point the way for us here. In delivering Russia over to Bolshevism, it robbed the Russian people of that intelligentsia that had once created and secured the Russian state. The

— 18 —

organization of the Russian state-structure was not a result of Russian Slavic political ability, but rather was a marvelous example of the state-building capacity of the Germanic element amidst an inferior race.

Many powerful empires were created on the Earth in this way. More than once, lesser peoples with Germanic organizers and leaders became formidable states, and endured as long as the racial nucleus of the state-creating race survived. For centuries, Russia owed its sustenance to the Germanic nucleus of its ruling upper class.

Today this class has been almost completely rooted out and extinguished. The Jew has taken its place. As impossible as it is for the Russian himself to shake off the Jewish yoke, so too is it impossible for the Jew to keep this mighty empire forever. He himself is no organizing element, but rather a ferment of decomposition.[3] This colossal Eastern Empire is ripe for dissolution. And the end of Jewish rule in Russia will also be the end of Russia as a state. We are chosen by Fate to be witnesses of a catastrophe that will afford the strongest confirmation of the folkish race-theory.

Our task, and the mission of the National Socialist movement, is to develop the political insight in our people that will enable them to realize that their future aim is not the fulfillment of some new and wildly adventurous March of Alexander, but rather as the industrious labor of the German plow, for which the sword will provide the soil. ...

GERMAN ALLIANCE WITH RUSSIA? (section 14.12)

Today we must adopt the same position towards Russia. Present-day Russia, deprived of its Germanic ruling class, is not a possible ally in the struggle for German freedom, even setting aside the inner intentions of its new rulers. From a purely military viewpoint, a Russo-German coalition waging war against Western Europe, and probably against the whole world, would be catastrophic. The struggle would be played out on German, not Russian, soil, and without the slightest support from Russia. The means of power of the present German Reich are so miserable and so inadequate for a war that it would be impossible to defend our borders against Western Europe,

---

[3] "Ferment of decomposition" is a paraphrase of the prominent German historian Theodor Mommsen (1817-1903). In his monumental work *The History of Rome* (1856), he wrote: "Also in the ancient world, Judaism was an effective ferment of cosmopolitanism and of national decomposition" (1856/1871: 643).

England included. And Germany's industrial area would lie undefended to the concentrated attack of our adversaries. Additionally, the Polish state lies between Germany and Russia, and it's completely in French hands. In case of a German-Russian war against Western Europe, Russia would have to defeat Poland before their first soldier could arrive on the German Front.

But it's not so much a question of soldiers as of technical equipment. In this regard, the World War situation would be repeated, but in a more terrible manner. German industry then was drained to help our glorious allies, and from the technical side, Germany had to conduct the war almost alone. Likewise here, Russia, as a technical factor, would count for nothing. We would have practically nothing to oppose to the general motorization of the world, which in the next war will appear in an overwhelming and decisive form. In this most-important field, Germany has not only shamefully lagged behind, but with the little it has it would have to reinforce Russia, which at present doesn't possess a single factory capable of producing a functioning motor vehicle. Thus any such war would assume the character of a sheer massacre. German youth would have to shed even more blood than before, because, as always, the honor of fighting would fall on us alone, and the result would be an inevitable defeat.

But even allowing that a miracle occurred and that this war did not end in the total destruction of Germany, the final result would be that the German people would be bled white, and, surrounded by great military states, its real situation would remain unchanged.

It's useless to object here that, in case of a Russian alliance, we shouldn't immediately think of war, or that, if we did, we could thoroughly prepare for it. No. An alliance whose goal isn't a view to war is senseless and worthless. Alliances are formed only for struggle. And even if, at the moment, the prospect for war is a distant one, the alliance still must focus on a view to military involvement. And don't think that any power would ever interpret an alliance in any other way. A German-Russian coalition would either remain on paper, and thus would have no meaning for us, or the letter of the treaty would be visibly put into practice—and the rest of the world would be warned. How naïve to think that, in such a case, England and France would wait a decade for the German-Russian alliance to complete its technical preparations. No; the storm would break over Germany with lightning-speed.

— 18 —

Therefore the fact of forming an alliance with Russia would be a plan for the next war. The result would be the end of Germany.

Furthermore, consider the following:

(1) Those in power in Russia today have no thought of forming an honorable alliance, let alone observing one.

One must never forget that the present rulers of Russia are bloodstained criminals, that they are the dregs of humanity which, favored by circumstances in a tragic hour, overran a great state, extinguished and rooted out millions of the leading intelligentsia out of sheer blood-lust, and that now, for nearly ten years, they have ruled with the most savage tyranny of all time. One must also never forget that these rulers belong to a people in whom the most bestial cruelty is allied with an inconceivably artful lying, and which is, today more than ever, conscious of a mission to impose its bloody oppression on the rest of the world. One must never forget that the international Jew, who is today the absolute master of Russia, regards Germany not as an ally but as a state condemned to the same fate. One does not form alliances with someone whose only aim is the destruction of its partner. Above all, one doesn't form alliances with subjects for whom no treaty is sacred, because they don't live on this world as agents of honor and sincerity but rather as the representatives of lies, deception, thievery, plunder, and robbery. The man who thinks that he can bind himself by treaty with parasites is like a tree that believes it can form a profitable agreement with mistletoe.[4]

(2) The danger to which Russia succumbed is ever-present for Germany.

Only a bourgeois simpleton could imagine that Bolshevism has been

---

[4] As Hitler was well aware, it was the Jewish-dominated Bolsheviks that had conducted the Russian Revolution in 1917, overthrowing and eventually murdering Czar Nicholas and his family. The Bolsheviks were led by the quarter-Jewish Vladimir Lenin, full Jew Leon Trotsky, and a large number of ruthless Jewish accomplices, including the likes of Zinoviev, Sverdlov, Kamenev, Radek, Krassin, Litvinov, and Kaganovich. The *Times of London* reported that "not less than 75 percent [of Bolshevik leaders] are Jews… The Jews provide the executive officers" (29 Mar 1919, p. 10). Churchill concurred: "The majority of the leading figures are Jews," adding that, in Soviet institutions, "the predominance of Jews is even more astonishing" (1920/2002: 25). Lenin died in 1924, and thus, at the time of this writing, in 1926-27, the Soviet government was being run by Trotsky and (non-Jewish) Joseph Stalin. For more details, see Dalton (2013). (Mistletoe, incidentally, is a parasitic vine that can strangle its host tree.)

banished. With his superficial thinking, he doesn't suspect that we are dealing here with an instinctive process—that is, the striving of the Jewish people for world domination, a process that's as natural as the Anglo-Saxon impulse to dominate the Earth. And just as the Anglo-Saxon chooses his own way of reaching those ends and fights for them with his own weapons, likewise the Jew. He goes his own way—the way of sneaking in among nations and boring from within; and he fights with his own weapons—lies and slander, poison and corruption, intensifying his struggle to the point of bloodily rooting out his hated opponents. In Russian Bolshevism we see an attempt undertaken by Jewry in the 20th century to secure world domination—just as, in other epochs, they worked towards the same goal but with different, though related, means.

Their efforts are fundamentally grounded in the nature of their being. As little as any other nation would voluntarily renounce its own impulse towards expanding its nature and power, but would only do so when compelled by external circumstances or senile impotence, so little too will the Jew abandon his path toward world dictatorship by voluntary renunciation or self-suppression. He too will either be thrown back on his path by external forces, or will end his quest for world domination by dying out. But the impotence of nations, their death through senility, only comes with loss of blood purity. And this is something that the Jew has preserved better than anyone else on Earth. Therefore he advances along his destined road until he is opposed by a superior force, which, in a mighty struggle, casts the heaven-stormer back to Lucifer.

Germany is today the next great war-aim for Bolshevism. All the force of a fresh missionary idea is needed to raise up our nation once again, to rescue it from the coils of this international snake, and to stop the inner contamination of our blood. Thus the forces of our nation, once liberated, may be employed to preserve our nationality and prevent the repetition of the recent catastrophe, even in the most distant future. If this would be our goal, it would be insanity to ally ourselves with a power whose master is the mortal enemy of our future. How can we release our people from this poisonous grip if we turn ourselves over to it? How can we teach the German worker that Bolshevism is an accursed crime against humanity if we ally ourselves with this hellish monstrosity and thus recognize its legitimacy? By what right can we condemn the members of the broad masses who sympathize with a certain worldview, if our State leaders choose the representatives of that worldview as their allies?

The fight against Jewish world-Bolshevization demands a clear stance towards Soviet Russia. One cannot cast out the Devil with Beelzebub.

If folkish circles today grow enthusiastic about the idea of a Russian alliance, then let them look around Germany and become aware of who is supporting them. Or do these folkish people believe that a policy recommended and acclaimed by the international Marxist press can be beneficial to the German people? Since when has the Jew acted as shield-bearer for the militant nationalist?

GERMANY AND RUSSIA BEFORE THE WAR (section 14.13)

There's one main reproach that could be made against the old German Reich, with regard to its alliance policy: that it spoiled its relations with everyone by leaning this way and that, and by its pathological weakness in trying to preserve world peace at any price. But it cannot be said that it failed to maintain good relations with Russia.

I frankly admit that, in pre-war times, I thought it would have been better if Germany had abandoned its senseless colonial policy and its naval policy, and had allied with England against Russia—thereby replacing its weak world policy with a determined European policy of territorial acquisition on the Continent. I can't forget the constant insolent threats that Pan-Slavist Russia made against Germany.

I haven't forgotten the continual, impudent threats issued by the then pan-Slavic Russia against Germany. I haven't forgotten the constant practice military mobilizations that served only to antagonize Germany. I cannot forget the tone of Russian public opinion which, in pre-war days, excelled in hateful outbursts against our nation and Reich. Nor can I forget the big Russian press, which was always more favorable to France than us.

But despite everything, there was still a second way possible before the war. We could have relied upon Russia and turned against England.

Circumstances are different today. If, before the war, we could have thrown all sentiment to the winds and marched aside Russia, this is no longer possible today. The hand of the world-clock has moved forward since then. The hour is striking loudly, in which our peoples' destiny must be decided one way or another. The present consolidation of the great states of the world is the last warning signal for us to look to ourselves and bring our people back from their dream-world to hard reality, and to point the way to a future that alone will lead the old Reich to a new blossoming.

If, in view of this great and most important task, the National Socialist movement sets aside all illusions and takes reason as its sole guide, the catastrophe of 1918 may turn out to be an infinite blessing for the future of our nation. From that collapse, it may formulate an entirely new orientation for its foreign policy conduct. Furthermore, and internally reinforced through its new worldview, the nation may reach a final stabilization of its policy. Ultimately it will gain what England has, what even Russia had, and what France again and again utilized to base correct decisions for its own interests, namely: a political testament.

In its dealings with the outside world, the political testament of the German nation should, and must always be, the following:

> Never permit two continental powers to arise in Europe! Any attempt to organize a second military power on the German border by the creation of a state capable of military strength, will be viewed as an attack against Germany. Such a situation confers not only the right but the duty to use every means, including armed force, to prevent it from happening—and to crush such a state, if it has already arisen.
>
> See to it that our nation's strength is grounded not on colonial foundations but on the soil of our European homeland! Never consider the Reich secure unless, for centuries to come, it can give every descendant of our people his own piece of land and soil! Never forget that the most sacred right in the world is man's right to the Earth that he tills himself; and that the holiest of all sacrifices is the blood that one sheds for the Earth!

THE GERMAN-ENGLISH-ITALIAN ALLIANCE (section 14.14)

I don't want to conclude these thoughts without referring once again to the sole possibility for alliances that exists for us in Europe at the moment. In the previous chapter, I examined the German alliance problem, and cited England and Italy as the only two European states that would be desirable and advantageous allies.[5] Here I want to again emphasize the military importance of such an alliance.

The military consequences of forming this alliance would be the direct opposite of the consequences of a Russian alliance. Most important of all is the fact that an approach to England and Italy would in no way involve a danger of war. The only power that could oppose such an arrangement, France, would be in no position to do so. But the alliance would give Germany the possibility of peacefully preparing for a reckoning with France, which would be required within the framework of such a coalition. The full significance of such an alliance lies in the fact that, upon conclusion, Germany would no longer be exposed to a sudden, hostile invasion. Rather, the opposing alliance would automatically break down. The Entente, which brought such misfortune to us, would dissolve, and France—the mortal enemy of our people—would be isolated. And even if at first this success would only have a moral effect, it would suffice to give Germany unimaginable freedom of action. The upper hand would lie with the new European Anglo-German-Italian alliance, and no longer with France.

A further result would be that, at one stroke, Germany would be freed from its unfavorable strategic position. The beneficial effects of this new state organization would be, on the one hand, that our flank would be strongly protected and, on the other, the complete assurance of food and raw materials.

But almost more important would be the fact that this new league would include states with technical qualities that mutually complement each other. For the first time, Germany would have allies who would not be like leeches on our economy but who can and would contribute their part to complete our technical arms.

And we mustn't overlook a final fact, namely, that in both cases we'd be working with allies who cannot be compared with Turkey or present-day Russia. The greatest world power on this Earth and a young nationalist state would offer different conditions for a European struggle than the putrid state carcasses that Germany allied itself with in the last war.

---

[5] See section 13.8.

THE ESSENTIAL MEIN KAMPF

CONDITIONS FOR EASTERN POLICY (section 14.15)

Assuredly, as I emphasized in the previous chapter, the difficulties opposing such an alliance are great. But was the formation of the Entente any less difficult? What King Edward VII achieved, partly against natural interests, we must and will achieve, if the recognition of the necessity of such a development so inspires us that we act with skill and, with astute self-control, act accordingly. And this will be possible the moment when, incited to action by misery, we adopt a single conscious goal instead of the aimless foreign policy of past decades.

The future goal of our foreign policy must be neither West- nor East-oriented, but rather must be an Eastern policy in the sense of securing the necessary soil for our German people. For this we need force, but the mortal enemy of our nation, France, now strangles us and robs us of our strength; hence we must stop at no sacrifice in our effort to destroy French striving towards hegemony in Europe. Our natural ally today is every power who feels that French domination on the Continent is unacceptable. No attempt to approach those powers should appear too difficult for us, and no sacrifice too great, if the final outcome makes it possible for us to defeat our grimmest enemy. Then, if we can cauterize and close the biggest wounds, the minor ones will be cured by the beneficent effects of time.

— 19 —
THE RIGHT TO EMERGENCY DEFENSE

With the lay-down of arms in November 1918, a policy was adopted that, in all likelihood, was bound to gradually lead to our complete subjugation. Historical examples show that nations that voluntarily lay down their arms subsequently prefer to submit to the greatest humiliations and extortions rather than try to change their fate by a renewed appeal to force.

This is humanly explicable. A shrewd victor will always enforce his demands on the conquered only in stages, wherever possible. Then he can be sure that a people who have lost all character—which is always the case with every nation that voluntarily submits—won't find any one or more of these oppressive acts to be sufficient grounds for taking up arms again. The more numerous the extortions thus passively accepted, the less will resistance appear justified by the people—and especially so, if they have already patiently and silently accepted greater misfortune.

The fall of Carthage is a most terrible instance of the slow, self-earned execution of a people.[1]

COWARDLY SUBMISSION BRINGS NO MERCY (section 15.1)

Clausewitz expressed this idea admirably in his *Three Confessions* and gave it an eternal form when he said: "The shame of cowardly submission can never be effaced; the drop of poison which thus enters the blood of a

---

[1] Carthage was an ancient Phoenician city-state founded in the 800s BC in the area of present-day Tunisia. For centuries it was one of the most powerful cities in the world, eventually coming into conflict with the Roman Empire. Rome defeated Carthage in 146 BC in the Third Punic War, utterly destroying the city.

nation will be transmitted to posterity, and will undermine and paralyze the strength of later generations." But on the other hand, he added: "Even the loss of its liberty after a bloody and honorable struggle assures the rebirth of the nation, and is the kernel of life from which one day a new tree can establish firm roots."[2]

Naturally, a nation that has lost all honor and character won't feel the force of such a doctrine. But any nation that takes it to heart will never sink very low; and only those who forget it or don't wish to know it will collapse. Hence those who embody a characterless submission cannot be expected to suddenly begin to reflect, using reason and all human experience, and act differently than before. On the contrary, they will repudiate such a doctrine, until the people either become permanently habituated to the yoke of slavery, or the better forces push forward and forcibly take power from the hands of the notorious corrupters. In the first case, they will be pleased because the conquerors often entrust them with supervising the slaves—and these utterly characterless beings then rule over their own people more cruelly than any foreign beast installed by the enemy himself.

Developments in Germany since 1918 prove that the hope of winning the victor's favor by voluntary submission has the most disastrous influence on the political views and conduct of the broad masses. I say the broad masses explicitly, because I cannot persuade myself that the things that were done or neglected by our peoples' leaders can be attributed to a similar disastrous insanity. Seeing that the direction of our post-war historical destiny was now openly controlled by the Jews, it's impossible to admit that defective knowledge was the sole cause of our misfortune. Rather, we must conclude that our people were intentionally driven to ruin. From this point of view, we find that the apparent foolishness of our nation's leadership in foreign policy was really a shrewd, ice-cold logic, carried out in service of the Jewish idea of, and struggle for, world domination.

---

[2] Karl von Clausewitz (1780-1831) was a general and preeminent military strategist. His *Three Confessions* appeared in 1812, and his most famous book, *On War*, was published posthumously in 1832.

— 19 —

SEVEN YEARS TO 1813 – SEVEN YEARS TO LOCARNO (section 15.2)

From 1806 to 1813, Prussia came back from a state of total collapse to acquire new life-energy and determination for struggle. But an equal time-span today has not only passed unused, but, on the contrary, has led to an ever-greater weakening of our State.

Seven years after November 1918, the Locarno Treaty was signed![3]

Thus the development was as indicated above: Once the shameful armistice was signed, our people were unable to raise sufficient courage and energy to suddenly halt the oppressive measures of our opponents, which were thus constantly renewed. The enemy was too shrewd to put forth all his demands at once. He confined his extortions to those which, in his opinion—and that of our German leadership—were momentarily bearable, such that they didn't risk an explosion of popular feeling. But the more such individual impositions were endorsed and tolerated, the less justified they seemed. Especially so, due to the lack of a single individual imposition or humiliation to do what had not previously been done: to offer resistance. This is the 'drop of poison' that Clausewitz speaks of: Once this lack of character is manifested, the condition becomes steadily aggravated, weighing like an evil burden on all future decisions. It becomes a lead weight that the nation cannot shake off, and which ultimately drives it down to the condition of a slave race.

Thus in Germany, edicts for disarmament, enslavement, and political and economic plundering followed one after the other. Finally they created a mood that caused many to look upon the Dawes Plan as a blessing, and the Locarno Treaty as a success. From a higher standpoint, we may speak of one sole blessing amidst so much misery, namely that, although men can be fooled, Heaven cannot be bribed. It withheld its blessing: Since then, misery and worry have been the constant companions of our people,

---

[3] The Locarno Treaty was a series of seven compacts signed in October 1925 in Locarno, Switzerland. Its purpose was to formalize post-WWI borders and to promote reconciliation, but Hitler and the German nationalists saw it as a further surrender of vital German interests. The primary German signatory was Foreign Minister Gustav Stresemann, who was viewed by nationalists as a key member of the traitorous Weimar regime; notably for Hitler, Stresemann's wife, Käte Kleefeld, was Jewish. Hitler would ultimately repudiate the Treaty on 7 March 1936, and militarily re-occupy the Rhineland.

and our one loyal ally has been distress. Destiny made no exceptions in this case, but rather gave us what we deserved. Since we forgot how to value honor, at least it taught us to value freedom as bread. Now our people have learned to cry for bread, but one day they may pray for freedom.

As bitter and apparent as was our national collapse in the years after 1918, anyone who dared to prophesy what later happened was violently persecuted. As incompetent as the leaders of our people were, they were equally conceited, especially regarding taking care of unwelcome—because unpleasant—prophets. We then witnessed (as we do today!) the spectacle of our greatest parliamentary blockheads, truly common saddlers, and glove-makers—not merely by trade, for that would mean little—suddenly raised to the rank of statesmen, and sermonizing from that pedestal to ordinary mortals below.

It didn't, and doesn't, matter that such a 'statesman,' having displayed his talents for six months or so, is revealed as a mere windbag, becoming the object of public ridicule and contempt, nor that he has provided unmistakable proof of his complete incompetence! No, that doesn't matter at all; on the contrary: The less real service provided by the parliamentary statesmen of this Republic, the more savagely they persecute all who expect accomplishments, and who dare to point out their failures, and to predict more failure in the future. If we finally succeed in nailing down one of these parliamentarians, so that this political artist can no longer deny the collapse of his whole activity, he will then find thousands of grounds for excuse, but will never admit that he himself is the chief cause of all evil....

WHAT SHOULD HAVE BEEN DONE AFTER THE RUHR OCCUPATION? (section 15.5)

Nevertheless, the French invasion of the Ruhr opened up great possibilities for the future—not only in Germany's foreign policy but also internally. A considerable section of our people who, thanks to the persistent influence of our lying press, saw France as the champion of progress and liberalism, were suddenly cured of this illusion. In 1914 the dream of international solidarity suddenly vanished from the heads of our German workers, and they were brought back into the world of eternal struggle, where one creature feeds on the other and where the death of the weaker implies the life of the stronger. The same happened in the spring of 1923.[4]

When the French put their threats into effect and penetrated, at first hesitatingly and cautiously, into the lower German coal district, the great and decisive hour of destiny had struck for Germany. If at that moment our people had changed not only their attitude but also their conduct, the German Ruhr district could have become a Napoleonic Moscow for France. Indeed, there were only two possibilities: either let the action stand and do nothing, or turn the gaze of the German people toward that region of sweltering forges and flaming furnaces, and set their wills afire with determination to end this persistent disgrace, confronting a momentary terror rather than submitting to an endless one.

Reich Chancellor Cuno can claim the 'immortal merit' of having discovered a third way, and our bourgeois parties merit the still 'more glorious' honor of having admired it and collaborated with him.

Here I'll deal with the second way as briefly as possible: By occupying the Ruhr, France committed a glaring violation of the Versailles Treaty. This action brought it into conflict with several of the signatory powers, especially England and Italy. France could no longer hope that those states would back it up in its selfish campaign of robbery. It would have to rely on itself to bring this adventure—and that's what it was at first—to a satisfactory conclusion. For a German national government, there was only one option, namely, that which honor prescribed. Certainly at the beginning we could not have opposed France with an active force of arms; but it should have been clearly recognized that any negotiations that weren't backed by force would be ridiculous and fruitless. Without the possibility of active resistance, it was absurd to take up the standpoint "We shall not enter into any negotiations." But it was still more absurd to finally enter into negotiations after all, without having organized the necessary power.

Not that it was possible for us to prevent the occupation of the Ruhr militarily. Only a madman could have recommended such a decision. But under the impression produced by this French action, and while it was being carried out, measures could have, and should have, been undertaken without any regard to the Versailles Treaty—which France itself had shredded—to provide those military resources that would serve to back up

---

[4] France moved forces into the Ruhr region on 11 January 1923.

later negotiations. It was quite clear from the beginning that the fate of this district occupied by the French would one day be decided at some conference table. But it must have been equally clear that even the best negotiators would have little success as long as the ground on which they stood, and the chair on which they sat, weren't under the armed protection of their own people. A weakling cannot contend against athletes, and a defenseless negotiator must always yield when a Brennus throws his sword onto the scales of the enemy's side—unless he has his own to throw.[5] Or was it not truly distressing to observe the comedy of negotiations that, ever since 1918, regularly preceded each dictate?

We presented a sorry spectacle to the whole world when we were invited, for the sake of derision, to attend conference tables simply to be presented with decisions and programs prepared long before, and which we were permitted to discuss, but from the start had to be considered as unalterable. It's true that in scarcely a single instance did our negotiators prove to be of more than mediocre abilities. And for the most part, they justified only too well the insolent observation made by Lloyd George when he sarcastically remarked, in the presence of former Reich Minister Simons, "that the Germans aren't able to choose intelligent men as their leaders and representatives."[6] But in view of the enemy's determined will-power and the lamentable defenselessness of our own people, even geniuses couldn't have achieved much.

In the spring of 1923, however, anyone who might have wanted to make France's Ruhr occupation an occasion for reconstructing our military means of power would first have had to restore the nation's spiritual weapons, to strengthen its will-power, and to destroy the corrupters of this most valuable national strength.

---

[5] Brennus was a 4th-century BC leader of the Gauls who led a successful attack on Rome in 387 BC. As the Romans were on the brink of defeat, they offered a large amount of gold in exchange for freedom. A dispute about the process of weighing the gold caused Brennus to throw his sword onto the scales, in his own favor, exclaiming "Woe to the conquered!"

[6] Walter Simons (1861-1937) was Foreign Minister in the Weimar government from 1920 to 1921.

— 19 —

FAILURE TO RECKON WITH MARXISM (section 15.6)

Just as in 1918, when we had to pay with our blood for the failure to crush the Marxist snake once and for all in 1914 and 1915, so we now have to suffer retribution for the fact that, in the spring of 1923, we didn't seize the opportunity to finally halt the handiwork of the Marxist traitors and murderers of our people.

Any idea of resisting French aggression was pure nonsense, as long as the fight hadn't been taken up against those forces that, five years earlier, broke the German resistance on the battlefields from within. Only bourgeois minds could have arrived at the unbelievable opinion that Marxism might perhaps have changed, and that the lowly leadership-creatures of 1918—who callously trampled on two million dead as stepping-stones by which to climb into various government positions—would now, in the year 1923, suddenly become ready to pay tribute to the national conscience. It was an unbelievable and truly insane thought—the hope that these traitors would suddenly turn into fighters for German freedom! They never had any such intention! Just as a hyena won't leave its carrion, so a Marxist won't give up treason.

One needn't bother with that stupidest of arguments: that so many workers gave their blood for Germany. German workers, yes indeed, but they were no longer international Marxists. If the German working class in 1914 had consisted of real Marxists, the war would have ended within three weeks. Germany would have collapsed before the first soldier had set foot beyond the border. No—the fact that the German people were still fighting proved that the Marxist delusion hadn't yet been able to penetrate deeply. But in the course of the war, German workers and soldiers gradually fell back into the hands of the Marxist leaders, and in the same proportion were lost to the Fatherland. If, at the beginning of the war, or even during the war, 12- or 15,000 of these Hebraic corrupters of the people were held under poison gas—as happened to hundreds of thousands of our best German workers in the field—then the sacrifice of millions at the Front would not have been in vain.[7] On the contrary: If 12,000 of these scoundrels had been eliminated in

---

[7] As surprising as it may be, this appears to be the only time, in print or speech, that Hitler explicitly called for the death of Jews. And by poison gas, no less (recalling the gas attacks of WWI). Notably, it's not all of the Jews, or even most of them, that he suggests be killed; just one or two percent of the then-existing

time, it would have saved the lives of perhaps a million decent men—men who would have been of great value for the future. But it was in accordance with bourgeois 'statesmanship' to subject millions to a bloody end on the battlefield, all without batting an eye, while they looked upon 10- or 12,000 traitors, profiteers, usurers, and swindlers as precious national treasures, and thus openly proclaiming their inviolability. One never knows which is greater in this bourgeois world: imbecility, weakness, and cowardice, or a thoroughly sleazy attitude. It's a class that's certainly doomed to go under, but unfortunately it drags the whole nation down with it into the abyss.

The situation in 1923 was the same as in 1918. No matter what form of resistance was decided upon, the first prerequisite was always the elimination of the Marxist poison from our national body. And in my opinion, the first task then of a truly national government was to seek and find those forces that were determined to wage a war of destruction against Marxism, and to give these forces a free hand; it was their duty not to bow down before the idiocy of 'peace and order' at a moment when the enemy was dealing the Fatherland a most destructive blow, and when high treason lurked behind every street corner at home. No—a truly national government should have welcomed *dis*order and *un*rest, if this turmoil would have afforded a principled reckoning with the Marxist mortal enemies of our people. If this were not done, then it was pure madness to think of resisting, no matter what form.

Of course, such a reckoning of real world-historical importance couldn't be conducted by some secret council or a shriveled-up cabinet minister; rather, it would have to be in accordance with the eternal laws of life on this Earth, which are and will remain those of a struggle for life. It must always be remembered that a hardy and healthy nation has often emerged from the bloodiest civil war, while an artificially-constructed peace has, more than once, produced a rottenness that reeked to the skies. A nation's fate cannot be changed with kid gloves. And so in the year 1923, brutal action was required to seize the vipers that fattened themselves on the body of the nation. If so, then the precondition for an active resistance would have been met.

---

population in Germany. That would have sufficed to strike fear in the militant Jews, to demonstrate German resolve, and likely to preempt any Jewish thoughts of revolt—as ultimately happened in 1918. All of Hitler's other threatening terminology toward the Jews, including *vernichten* ('destroy') and *ausrotten* ('root out'), were expressed in non-lethal or non-genocidal contexts. For further details, see Dalton (2015: 100-104).

— 19 —

At that time I often talked myself hoarse in trying to make clear, at least to the so-called national circles, what was then at stake, and that by repeating the errors of 1914 and the following years, we would come to the same end as in 1918. I frequently implored them to let Fate have a free hand and to make it possible for our movement to settle with the Marxists; but I preached to deaf ears. They all knew better, including the army chief, until finally they faced the vilest capitulation of all time.

I then realized in my innermost consciousness that the German bourgeoisie had come to the end of its mission and had no further calling. I then also saw how all the bourgeois parties had been fighting Marxism merely from a spirit of competition without sincerely wishing to destroy it; for a long time they had been accustomed to assist in the destruction of the Fatherland, and their one great care was to partake in the funeral banquet. For this alone did they 'fight.'

At that time—I openly admit—I conceived a profound admiration for the great man south of the Alps, whose ardent love for his people inspired him not to bargain with Italy's internal enemies but rather to use all ways and means to destroy them. What places Mussolini in the ranks of the world's great men is his decision not to share Italy with the Marxists, but to destroy internationalism and save the Fatherland.

What miserable dwarves our sham German statesmen appear by comparison, and how nauseating it is to witness the conceit of these nonentities in criticizing a man who is a thousand times greater than them; and how painful it is to think that this takes place in a land that could point to a Bismarck as its leader barely half a century ago!

The bourgeoisie attitude in 1923, and the sparing of Marxism, decided from the outset the fate of any active resistance in the Ruhr. With that deadly enemy in our own ranks, it would have been sheer lunacy to fight against France. The most that could then have been done was to stage a sham fight in order to partly satisfy the German nationalistic element, or in reality to deceive the 'boiling soul of the people.' Had they really believed in what they did, they would have recognized that national strength lies, first of all, not in its weapons but in its will, and that before conquering the external enemy, the internal enemy must be destroyed; otherwise, victory would have to be achieved on the very first day! The shadow of a single defeat is sufficient to break the resistance of a nation that hasn't been freed from its internal enemies, thus making the opponent the final victor.

One could have predicted all this by early 1923. Let no one ask about the questionability of a military success against France! If the result of German action regarding the French invasion of the Ruhr had only been the destruction of Marxism at home, success would have been on our side. A Germany liberated from the deadly enemies of its existence would possess forces that the whole world could not have stopped. On the day that Marxism is broken in Germany, its chains will be smashed forever. Never in our history have we been conquered by the strength of our foes, but always by our own failings, and by the enemies in our own camp.

Since the German government was unable to take such heroic action at that time, it could only have chosen the first way: namely, to do nothing at all and let things take their own course. ...

NOVEMBER 1923 (section 15.9)

Up to midsummer, several officers—who certainly weren't the worst—really hadn't believed in such a shameful development. They all had hoped that, if not openly, then at least secretly, precautions would be taken to make this insolent French invasion a turning-point in German history. Even in our ranks, many at least put their faith in the Reichswehr. This conviction was so ardent that it decisively influenced the conduct and especially the training of innumerable youth.

But when the disgraceful collapse set in and the humiliating capitulation followed, indignation against such a betrayal of our unfortunate nation burst into a blaze at the sacrifice of billions of marks and thousands of young Germans—who were foolish enough to believe the promises of the Reich leaders. A bright and clear conviction suddenly arose in billions of heads that only a radical elimination of the entire ruling system could save Germany.

There never was a better time for such a solution. On the one hand, naked treason against the Fatherland was shamelessly revealed, and on the other, a people were economically driven to slow starvation. Since the State itself had trampled all concepts of faith and loyalty, made a mockery of citizens' rights, rendered the sacrifice of millions of its truest sons worthless, and robbed other millions of their last penny, it could no longer

— 19 —

expect anything but hatred from its subjects. And this hatred against those who had ruined the people and Fatherland was bound to find an outlet. At this point I can only point to the closing sentence of my last speech in the great trial of spring 1924:

"The judges of this State may calmly condemn us for our conduct at that time, but History—as goddess of higher truth and better justice—will smile as she tears up this verdict, acquitting us all of guilt and blame."

But History will then also summon before her own tribunal those who, vested with power today, have trampled on law and justice, condemning our people to misery and ruin, and who, amidst their Fatherland's misfortune, valued their own ego more than the life of the whole.

I won't here relate the course of events that led to, and brought about, 8 November 1923. I won't do so because I cannot see any use for the future, and also because no good could come of reopening old wounds that have scarcely healed. Moreover, it would be pointless to talk about the guilt of men who perhaps in the depths of their hearts have an equal love for their people, but who merely didn't follow, or failed to understand, the common road.

In view of the great common misfortune of our Fatherland, I must abstain from offending and perhaps alienating those who must, at some future date, form one great united front of truly loyal Germans, against the common front of the enemies of our people. I know that a time will come when even those who treated us as enemies will venerate the men who traveled the bitter path of death for the sake of the German people. Here at the end of this second volume, let me again bring to mind the memory of those 16 fallen heroes[8] to whom I dedicated the first volume, in order to remind our supporters and champions of those who, in the clearest consciousness, sacrificed their lives for us all. We do so in order to encourage the weak and wavering among us to fulfill their duty—a duty that those heroes fulfilled with absolute faith, even to its final consequences. And among them, and as one of the best of all, I wish to mention a man who devoted his life to reawakening his—our—people, through his writing, his ideas, and finally his deeds: Dietrich Eckart.[9]

---

[8] See the Dedication in the present work.

[9] Eckart (1868-1923) was one of the three traditional founders—along with Gottfried Feder and Anton Drexler—of the German Workers' Party (DAP), the precursor to the NSDAP. Eckart died of a heart attack in 1923 at age 55.

— 20 —
CONCLUSION

On 9 November 1923, four and a half years after its founding, the National Socialist German Workers' Party was dissolved and forbidden throughout the whole of the Reich. Today, in November 1926, it again stands free before us, stronger and internally more solid than ever before.

All persecutions of the movement and its individual leaders, all vilifications and slander, have been unable to harm it. Thanks to the correctness of its ideas, the purity of its will, and the spirit of self-sacrifice that animates its members, it has emerged from all oppression stronger than before.

If, in the world of our present parliamentary corruption, our movement always remains aware of the deepest essence of its struggle, feels itself to embody the value of race and personality, and acts accordingly—then it will, with almost mathematical certainty, someday emerge victorious from its struggle. In the same way, Germany must necessarily win its rightful place on this Earth if it is led and organized by the same principles.

A State that, in an age of racial poisoning, devotes itself to preserving its best racial elements must one day become ruler of the Earth.

Our movement's adherents must never forget this, whenever they may have misgivings, lest the greatness of the sacrifices seem unjustified by the possible success.

APPENDIX

THE 25-POINT PROGRAM OF THE NSDAP

1. We demand the union of all Germans in a Greater Germany, on the basis of the principle of self-determination of all peoples.
2. We demand that the German people have rights equal to those of other nations, and that the Peace Treaties of Versailles and St. Germaine be abrogated.
3. We demand land and territory (colonies) for the maintenance of our people and the settlement of our surplus population.
4. Only those who are our fellow countrymen can become citizens. Only those who have German blood, regardless of creed, can be our countrymen. Therefore no Jew can be a countryman.
5. Those who are not citizens must live in Germany as foreigners and must be subject to the law of aliens.
6. The right to choose the government and determine the laws of the state shall belong only to citizens. We therefore demand that no public office, of whatever nature, whether in the central government, the province, or the municipality, shall be held by anyone who is not a citizen. We wage war against the corrupt parliamentary administration whereby men are appointed to posts by favor of the party without regard to character and ability.
7. We demand that the state shall above all undertake to ensure that every citizen shall have the possibility of living decently and earning a livelihood. If it is not possible to feed the whole population, then aliens (non-citizens) must be expelled from the Reich.

8. Any further immigration of non-Germans must be prevented. We demand that all non-Germans who have entered Germany since 2 August 1914 shall be compelled to leave the Reich immediately.
9. All citizens must possess equal rights and duties.
10. The first duty of every citizen must be to work, mentally or physically. No individual shall do any work that offends against the interest of the community to the benefit of all.
Therefore we demand:
11. That all unearned income, and all interest-slavery, be abolished!
12. Since every war imposes on the people fearful sacrifices in blood and treasure, all personal profit arising from the war must be regarded as treason to the people. We therefore demand the total confiscation of all war profits.
13. We demand the nationalization of all trusts.
14. We demand profit-sharing in large industries.
15. We demand a generous increase in old-age pensions.
16. We demand the creation and maintenance of a sound middle-class, the immediate communalization of large stores which will be rented cheaply to small businessmen, and that the strongest consideration be given to ensure that small businessmen shall deliver the supplies needed by the state, the provinces, and the municipalities.
17. We demand agrarian reform in accordance with our national requirements, and the enactment of a law to expropriate the owners without compensation of any land needed for the common good. We demand the abolition of basis rents, and the prohibition of all land speculation.
18. We demand that ruthless war be waged against those who work to the detriment of the common welfare. Traitors, usurers, profiteers, etc., are to be punished with death, regardless of creed or race.
19. We demand that Roman law, that serves a materialist ordering of the world, be replaced by German common law.
20. In order to make it possible for every capable and industrious German to obtain higher education, and thus the opportunity to reach into positions of leadership, the state must assume the responsibility of thoroughly organizing the entire public cultural system. The curricula of all educational establishments shall be adapted to practical life. The

APPENDIX

conception of the state idea (civics) must be taught in the schools from the very beginning. We demand that exceptionally talented children of poor parents, whatever their station or occupation, be educated at the state's expense.

21. The state has the duty to help raise the standard of national health by providing maternity welfare centers, by prohibiting juvenile labor, by increasing physical fitness through the introduction of compulsory games and gymnastics, and by the greatest possible encouragement of associations concerned with the physical education of the young.
22. We demand the abolition of the regular army and the creation of a national folk army.
23. We demand that there be a legal battle against those who propagate deliberate political lies and disseminate them through the press. In order to make possible the creation of a German press, we demand:
(a) All editors and their assistants on newspapers published in the German language shall be German citizens.
(b) Non-German newspapers shall only be published with the express permission of the state. They must not be published in the German language.
(c) All financial interests that in any way affect German newspapers shall be forbidden to non-Germans by law, and we demand that the punishment for transgressing this law be the immediate suppression of the newspaper and the expulsion of the non-Germans from the Reich.
(d) Newspapers transgressing against the common welfare shall be suppressed. We demand a legal battle against those tendencies in art and literature that have a disruptive influence upon the life of our people; any organizations that offend against the foregoing demands shall be dissolved.
24. We demand freedom for all religious faiths in the state, insofar as they do not endanger its existence or offend the moral and ethical sense of the Germanic race. The party as such represents the point of view of a positive Christianity without binding itself to any one particular confession. It fights against the Jewish materialist spirit within and without, and is convinced that a lasting recovery of our people can only come about from the principle: Common Good before Individual Good.

25. In order to carry out this program we demand the creation of a strong central authority in the state, and the unconditional authority by the political central parliament of the whole state and all its organizations. Also: The formation of professional committees and of committees representing the several estates of the Reich, to ensure that the laws promulgated by the central authority shall be carried out by the federal states.

BIBLIOGRAPHY

Churchill, W. 1920/2002. "Zionism versus Bolshevism." In *51 Documents: Zionist Collaboration with the Nazis* (L. Brenner, ed.). Barricade Books.

Dalton, T. 2010. "Nietzsche and the origins of Christianity." Online: <http://www.theoccidentalobserver.net>

Dalton, T. 2011. "Eternal strangers: Anti-Jewish musings throughout history" (Part I). *The Occidental Quarterly* 11(2). Online: <http://www.toqonline.com/archive>

Dalton, T. 2011b. "Eternal strangers: Anti-Jewish musings throughout history" (Part II). *The Occidental Quarterly* 11(3). Online: <http://www.toqonline.com/archive>

Dalton, T. 2011c. "A most subterranean conspiracy: Nietzsche and the Judeo-Christian worldview." In *Nietzsche: Thoughts and Perspectives* (T. Southgate, ed.). Black Front Press.

Dalton, T. 2012. "Anglo-American perspectives on anti-Semitism" (Part II). *The Occidental Quarterly* 12(4).

Dalton, T. 2013. "The Jewish hand in the world wars" (Part I). *Inconvenient History* 5(2). Online: <http://www.inconvenienthistory.com/archive>

Dalton, T. 2014. "The Jewish hand in the world wars" (Part II). *Inconvenient History* 6(2). Online: <http://www.inconvenienthistory.com/archive>

Dalton, T. 2015. *Debating the Holocaust* (2nd ed). Castle Hill.

Dalton, T. 2016. *The Holocaust: An Introduction*. Castle Hill.

Darkmoon, L. 2014. "Pornography as a secret weapon." Online: <http://www.darkmoon.me>

Davis, M. 2012. *Jews and Booze*. New York University Press.

Gertzman, J. 1999. *Bookleggers and Smuthounds*. University of Pennsylvania Press.

Gordon, S. 1984. *Hitler, Germans, and the 'Jewish Question.'* Princeton University Press.
Hitler, A. 2018. *Mein Kampf* (2 volumes; T. Dalton, ed.).. Clemens and Blair.
Houkes, J. 2004. *An Annotated Bibliography on the History of Usury*. Edwin Mellen.
Joyce, A. 2015. "Jews and moneylending." Online: <http://www.occidentalobserver.net>
Kershaw, I. 1998. *Hitler 1889-1936: Hubris*. W. W. Norton.
Maderthaner, W. and Silverman, L. 2009. "'Wiener Kreise': Jewishness, politics, and culture in interwar Vienna." In *Interwar Vienna* (Holmes and Silverman, eds.). Camden House.
Maser, W. 1974. *Hitler's Letters and Notes*. Harper and Row.
Mommsen, T. 1856/1871. *The History of Rome*, vol. 4 (W. Dickson, trans.). Scribner.
Mumford, L. 1966. "Technics and the nature of man." *Technology and Culture* 7: 303-317.
Nation of Islam. 1991. *The Secret Relationship between Blacks and Jews*. The Final Call.
Poliakov, L. 1965. *The History of Anti-Semitism* (3 volumes). Vanguard Press.
Rudolf, G. 2011. *Lectures on the Holocaust* (2nd ed). Barnes Review.
Schopenhauer, A. 1851/2010. *Parerga and Paralipomena* (vol. 2; E.F.J. Payne, trans.). Oxford University Press.
Taeusch, C. 1942. "The concept of 'usury'." *Journal of the History of Ideas* 3(3): 291-318.
Twain, M. 1898. "Stirring times in Austria." *Harper's New Monthly Magazine* (March).
Twain, M. 1899. "Concerning the Jews." *Harper's New Monthly Magazine* (September).

Useful Websites
www.hitlerpages.com
www.hitler.org
www.research.calvin.edu/german-propaganda-archive

INDEX

Acropolis 175
Adler, Victor 61n2, 72
alcoholism 257
Alsace-Lorraine 312
Alte Rosenbad 156
Amann, Max 294
America 107, 314
  Jewish power in 314-315
anti-Semitism 273, 286
  not religious-based 93-95
architecture, modern decay 175-176
aristocracy 76, 83
art 174
Aryans 111, 179-198, 229, 287, 316
  as founders of culture 114, 182-193, 247-249
  as nomads 195-196
  as self-sacrificing, idealistic 188-191
Askari 319
Auer, Erhard 277
Austerlitz, Friedrich 72

Balkan War (1912-13) 118
Barry, Charles 77
Barth, Emil 142
Bavarian Medical College 151
Bavarian Peoples' Party 237, 295
Bayreuth 51
Beelitz (Germany) 135
Belgium *see* Flanders, and specific cities

Benedikt, Moritz 64n5
Berlin 136
Berlin Palace 176
Bernstein, Eduard 145n8
Bible 205, 315
"Big Lie" 161
Bismarck, Otto von 42, 128-129, 164
black race *see* Negroes
blood *see* race
Boer War 118
Bolshevism 217n26, 285, 307, 314-315, 320, 323-325
Bolshevist Revolution *see* Russian Revolution
Braunau (Austria) 39
Brennus 334
Brest-Litovsk Treaty 233, 264, 267-268
Britain *see* England

Cadorna, Luigi 140
capital, international finance 150-152, 165
Caporetto, Battle of 137n3
Carthage 329
Central America 179
Chamberlain, Houston Stewart 111n7
Christian Socialism 66, 93-95, 270
Christianity 198, 254, 261
Christians, and Jews 203, 207
Churchill, Winston 313n4, 323n4
Circus Krone 273-281

Clausewitz, Karl von 329-331
Columbus Egg 177
Comines (Belgium) 144
contraceptives 253
cultural decay 173-176
culture, as function of race 181-195
Cuno, Wilhelm 333

Dadaism 62
Dalton, Thomas 145n8, 162n2, 194n5, 198n11, 201n16, 261n2, 313n4, 315n5, 315n6, 323n4, 336n7
Darkmoon, Lasha 69n12
"*Das Kapital*" 152
Davis, M. 69n12
Dawes Plan 331
democracy, critique of 77-93, 104, 243-244
Demosthenes 235
"*Deutschland über Alles*" 47, 120, 122, 142
Deutschen Reich 233
"*De Wacht am Rhein*" 121
Dinaric 250
Drexler, Anton 155-156, 339n9

Eberlbräu Keller 233
Ebert, Friedrich 142
Eckart, Dietrich 339
Edward VII, King 328
Eisner, Kurt 145n8, 149, 152
Elizabeth, Queen 299
Ellenbogen, Wilhelm 72
England 107-109, 113, 299-316, 326-327
  Jewish power in 313-315
Esperanto 198
Essen, Hermann 281
eugenics 101, 173, 253-256, 320

Feder, Gottfried 150-154, 339n9
Ferdinand, Franz 50, 118

Fichte, Johann 111n6
Flanders 122, 134, 142-144, 147
"folkish" 234, 253-258
Ford, Henry 315n6
France 131, 302-310, 327-328
  Jewish power in 307-309
  occupation of the Ruhr 332-334, 337-338
  racial contamination by Negroes 318-319
Franco-Prussian War *see* War of 1870
Frederick the Great 203
Freemasons 206, 212, 265
Friedlander, Max 64n5

German Campaign of 1813 *see* Wars of Liberation
German National People's Party 237
German 'political testament' 326
German Revolution *see* November Revolution
German Workers' Party (DAP) 153-159, 339n9
Gertzman, J. 69n12
Gilbert, Martin 313n4
Gobineau, Arthur de 111n7
Goethe, Wolfgang von 81, 195, 203

Haase, Hugo 145n8
Habsburg, House of 48, 50, 95-96
Hansen, Theophil 77
Harrer, Karl 156, 232-233
Hecateus 69n11
Hecuba 265
Hermies (France) 134
Herodotus 147n9
Herzl, Theodor 64n5
Hess, Rudolf 280
Hilferding, Rudolf 145n8
Hitler, Adolf
  as architecture student 55-57
  as art student 44-45

INDEX

conversion to anti-Semitism 66-75
critique of democracy 77-93
DAP member #7 159
decision to enter politics 148
father, death of 52
mother, death of 52, 146
on the Big Lie 161
wounded in WWI, first time 134-135
wounded in WWI, second time 144-145
Hofbräuhaus (am Platzl) 99, 238, 243, 263, 278-281
Hofbräuhaus Keller (=Hofbräukeller am Weiner Platz) 232
Hohenzollern, House of 146
Homer 57n1, 265n4
Houkes, J. 201n14

Independent Social Democratic Party 145n8
internal colonization 102-105
Isonzo Front 131
Italy 137, 304, 308-309, 326-327
  and defeat of Jewish power 312-313, 337

Japan 118, 183, 315-316
Jesus 104, 198
Jews 57, 104, 117, 224, 247
  anti-Semitism and 93-95, 273
  as artful liars 74, 161, 323
  as blood-suckers 136, 201-202, 205
  as 'chosen people' 69-70, 72, 136, 191
  as 'court Jews' 202-205
  as democratic wire-puller 92
  as despised throughout history 69n11, 162n2
  as dialectical liars 73-74
  as disease 171
  as eternal fungus 95
  as 'ferment of decomposition' 321
  as 'great master of the lie' 162, 196, 210, 229
  as leaders of Social Democracy 71-73
  as liars 161-162, 196-198, 215, 265, 323-324
  as mass murderers 217
  as moral pestilence 69
  as parasites 111-114, 195-196, 217, 287, 323
  as pernicious bacillus 196
  as personification of devil 215
  as poisoners of the masses 69-70, 125, 136, 165, 265
  as polyp 308
  as racial poisoners 207, 216, 287, 289, 308-309
  as 'state within the state' 111, 201
  as symbol of all evil 215
  as threat to human race 76, 230
  as wire-pullers 270, 285, 310
  as world-hydra 313
  as world-swindlers 216
  attempts to control nature 180-181
  compulsion to lie 196
  contempt of manual laborers 209-211
  control of trade unions 212-215
  democracy and 208, 216
  expulsions of 64n4, 196
  Freemasonry and 206, 265
  gassing of 335
  global finance and 136, 204, 307-310
  gradual integration into society 200-217
  in America 314-315
  in England 313-315
  in France 308-309
  in Italy 312-313, 337
  in Munich 136-137
  in November Revolution 126, 136-137, 145, 148-149

in Russia 217, 285, 320-321, 323
in the press, propaganda 70, 72, 165, 194, 206-207, 212-215, 229, 310
in universities 125
in Vienna 63-70
in Weimar Republic 330
Japan and 315-316
Jewish State and 193-194
Judaism as fake religion 196-198
lack of belief in afterlife 197
lack of culture 193-195
lack of idealism 193-197
marrying into royalty, nobility 166, 203
Marxism and 75-76, 211-216 (see also Marxism)
materialism 198
moral and cultural corruption by 71, 217
Palestine/Israel and 215-216
Protocols of Zion and 199-200
racial purity 198, 204, 207
religious conflict and 286-289
stench of 68
tenacious will-to-live 191-192
usury and 201, 336
world domination and 244, 259, 307-309, 314-316, 323-324, 330
Jogiches, Leo 145n8
Joyce, Andrew 69n12
Judaism 207
as fake religion 196-198

Kindl-Keller 274

Lambach (Austria) 41
land, importance of 102-108, 317-321, 326
Landauer, Gustav 145n8
Landesberg, Otto 145n8
Lenin, Vladimir 323n4
Liebknecht, Karl 142, 145n8

Linz (Austria) 40, 49, 63
Lloyd George, David 313n4, 334
Locarno Treaty 331
London 139
London Dictate 274
Ludendorff, Erich 161
Ludwig I, King 175
Ludwig III, King 121
Lueger, Karl 66
Luxemburg, Rosa 142n7, 145n8

Maderthaner, W. 73n13
Makovsky, Michael 313n4
Marne river 131
marriage 170-173
Marx, Karl 151-152, 247
Marxism 57, 62, 76, 260, 270-271, 335-338
  democracy and 80, 243-244
  German attitudes toward 124-125, 128-129, 153, 219, 227
  Jews and 75-76, 211-216
materialism, as a vice 164
Maurice, Emil 280
Mohamad, Mahathir 259n1
Mommsen, Theodor 321n3
Muehsam, Erich 145n8
Mumford, Lewis 187n4
Munich 118, 231-232, 263
  culture of 99-100, 174-175
  Hitler in 149-152
  Jews in 136-137
  November Revolution and 145
Mussolini, Benito 337
mustard gas 144-145

Napoleon Bonaparte 300
Nation of Islam 69n12
National Socialist flag 271-273, 275
National Socialist German Workers' Party (NSDAP) 151, 234, 238
  platform 237-239, Appendix

INDEX

nationalism, German 222-229
navy, German 144-145
Negroes 216, 254, 308, 319
Nicholas II, Czar 139, 323n4
Niederwald Statue 121
Nietzsche, Friedrich 210n24
nomadic way of life 195-196
Nordau, Max 64n5
North America 179
November Revolution (1918) 131-148, 239, 283-285, 301

Odeon 99
Oktoberfest 99
Oliphant, Laurence 313n4
opera 51, 55, 57
Ostmark 46, 107

Palestine/Israel 215-216, 313n4
Palm, Johannes 39
Pantheon 175
Paris 131, 139
parliamentarianism 77-81, 84-93
Parvus, Alexander 145n8
Pasewalk 144
Passau (Germany) 40
Pericles 83
Philostratus 201n16
Pinakothek 99
plague 162
Plato 256n3
Pötsch, Leopold 49
Poland 322
population control 100-103
press, Viennese 64-66
propaganda 131-133, 227-228, 290-291
prostitution 170-174
"Protocols of the Elders of Zion" 199-200
Prussia, contrived hatred of 285-286
Punic Wars 329n1

race
  and culture 95-96
  importance of 167-174, 177-220, 224, 247-258, 320, 341
racial poisoning 50, 248, 252, 256, 318-319, 341
Radek, Karl 145n8
Revolution, German (1918) *see* November Revolution
Rhine river 121
Rome 175
Roosevelt, Theodore 315n5
Rothschild family 313n4
Ruhr, French occupation of 332-334, 337-338
Russia 139-140, 320-326
Russian Revolution 137, 285
Russo-Japanese War (1904-5) 118

Scheidemann, Philipp 142
Schiller, Friedrich 112, 186
Schlageter, Leo 40
Schmiedt, Ernst 149
Schopenhauer, Arthur 162, 196, 229
Serbia 119-120
Severing, Carl 40
Siegfried (mythology) 239
Sieghart, Rudolf 64n5
Simons, Walter 334
Slovenia 131n1, 137n3
Smith, Goldwin 313n4
Social Democracy 61-62, 78-79, 227, 270, 277-278
soil *see* land
Somme, Battle of 134, 143
South America 179
South Tyrol 140, 265
Stalin, Joseph 323n4
Star of David 220
Sternecker Brewery 154, 156, 278n6, 292
Stresemann, Gustav 331n3

THE ESSENTIAL MEIN KAMPF

Stürgh, Karl von 73n13
swastika 272-273, 275
syphilis 165-173, 253

Tacitus 162n2
Talmud 197
Tannenberg, Battle of 139
Thirty Years' War 249
Toller, Ernst 145n8
Traunstein 149
Triple Alliance 306
Trotsky, Leon 323n4
tuberculosis 162
Twain, Mark 79n3

ultramontanism 286-289
unions (trade) 222
United Kingdom *see* England
United States of America *see* America

Versailles Treaty 233, 263-264, 267-268, 333
Völkischer Beobachter 293-296

Wagner, Richard 51
War of 1870 42
Wars of Liberation 117, 174
Wervick (Belgium) 144
Wilhelm I, Kaiser 121n6
Wilhelm II, Kaiser 65, 126, 132, 148, 164
William Tell 51
Wilson, Woodrow 181, 315n5
Wittelsbach, House of 100, 145
World War One 117-148, 317-318

Ypres 143-144

Zionism 68, 215, 313n4

www.ingramcontent.com/pod-product-compliance
Lightning Source LLC
Chambersburg PA
CBHW020351080526
44584CB00014B/977